KENNEDY'S BLUES

KENNEDY'S BLUES

AFRICAN-AMERICAN BLUES AND GOSPEL SONGS ON JFK

GUIDO VAN RIJN

UNIVERSITY PRESS OF MISSISSIPPI / JACKSON

AMERICAN MADE MUSIC SERIES
Advisory Board

David Evans, General Editor
Barry Jean Ancelet
Edward A. Berlin
Joyce J. Bolden
Rob Bowman
Susan C. Cook
Curtis Ellison
William Ferris
Michael Harris

John Edward Hasse
Kip Lornell
Frank McArthur
Bill Malone
Eddie S. Meadows
Manuel H. Peña
David Sanjek
Wayne D. Shirley
Robert Walser

www.upress.state.ms.us

The University Press of Mississippi is a member of
the Association of American University Presses.

Copyright © 2007 by University Press of Mississippi
All rights reserved
Manufactured in the United States of America

Frontis: Detail of "With NAACP leaders," 12 July 1961. Photograph by
Robert Knudsen, courtesy the John F. Kennedy Presidential
Library and Museum, Boston. (KN-18353)

∞

Library of Congress Cataloging-in-Publication Data

Rijn, Guido van, 1950–
  Kennedy's blues : African-American blues and gospel songs on JFK / Guido van
Rijn. — 1st ed.
    p. cm. — (American made music series)
  Includes bibliographical references (p.   ) and index.
  ISBN-13: 978-1-57806-957-6 (cloth : alk. paper)
  ISBN-10: 1-57806-957-2 (cloth : alk. paper) 1. Blues (Music)—History and
criticism. 2. Gospel music—History and criticism. 3. African Americans—
Music—Political aspects. 4. Kennedy, John F. (John Fitzgerald), 1917–1963—
Songs and music—History and criticism. I. Title.
  ML3521.R54 2007
  782.421643'1599—dc22   2007002377

British Library Cataloging-in-Publication Data available

FOR MY MOTHER

CONTENTS

Foreword   [ix]
Acknowledgments   [xix]
Introduction   [xxi]

1. JOHN F. KENNEDY, THE MAN AND THE MYTH   [3]

2. JFK SAYS I'VE GOT TO GO   [19]

3. TWISTIN' OUT IN SPACE   [47]

4. THE WELFARE TURNS ITS BACK ON YOU   [59]

5. MARCH ON, DR. MARTIN LUTHER KING   [69]

6. THE DAY THE WORLD STOOD STILL   [109]

CONCLUSION   [167]

Notes   [175]
Bibliography   [193]
Song Index   [201]
Artist Index   [205]
General Index   [209]

FOREWORD

When Guido van Rijn published his award-winning book *Roosevelt's Blues* in 1997, American historians, blues and gospel scholars, and fans of the music immediately hailed it as a major achievement. As Paul Oliver wrote in his appreciative foreword, the strength of van Rijn's book lay not only in the fact that he had unearthed a previously unimagined variety of blues and gospel recordings relating to Franklin Delano Roosevelt, the Great Depression, and World War II, but that he had "undertaken so rigorously and sympathetically the formidable task of transcribing and analyzing the content of large numbers of those records and placing them so precisely in their historical, social and political contexts." Thanks to van Rijn, a once partially hidden transcript of popular black attitudes toward the Depression, the war, and the president who presided over this momentous period in U.S. history was restored to the historical record.

In 2004, *The Truman and Eisenhower Blues* extended van Rijn's research into the post–World War II period. While neither Truman nor Eisenhower could command the almost universal admiration and respect accorded to FDR, the blues and gospel recordings of the era revealed black attitudes toward the most pressing issues of the day: the problems associated with America's reconversion to a peacetime economy; the awesome promise of atomic power and the dreadful specter of atomic annihilation; the perils of the Cold War—and a hot war in Korea; and the emergence of a mass movement for civil rights in the American South. In

Kennedy's Blues, the third volume in his groundbreaking series, van Rijn again brings to light a marvelous cache of blues and gospel recordings, ranging from the relatively well-known to the long lost and forgotten.

In the process of locating, transcribing, and contextualizing these remarkable songs, van Rijn helps us to better understand the diverse ways in which the black community responded to the personality and policies of John F. Kennedy during his thousand days as president. For blues and gospel fans, as for historians of black America and of the modern United States more generally, there is much here that is new and thought-provoking. There are songs about the Cold War, about the space race, about the economy—and, of course, about the civil rights movement that was reaching its zenith in the South during Kennedy's time in office.

Bernice Johnson Reagon, founder of the SNCC Freedom Singers and later of Sweet Honey in the Rock, once referred to the Freedom Singers as "a singing newspaper." To borrow and extend Reagon's analogy, *Kennedy's Blues* can be said to feature a series of musical "editorials" on the state of black America and its collective investment in the promise of the Kennedy administration during the early 1960s. These songs offer tremendous insights into the consciousness of a roused black community, buoyed by a new sense of self-respect and determined to confront racial discrimination in every aspect of American life. Yet, amid the celebrations of black pride and the calls to mass action, the songs and sermons also remind us that the struggle for racial justice was frequently frustrating and often bloody, with unequivocal victories rare, tokenism rampant, and disillusionment always around the corner. Louisiana Red's stirring "Ride On Red, Ride On," for example, turns out to be both a homage to the 1961 Freedom Rides that sought to desegregate interstate transportation in the South and a call for blacks to flee the unrelenting racism of the region. Songs like "The Ballad of Medgar Evers," the SNCC Freedom Singers' moving paean to the murdered Mississippi NAACP field secretary, and even B.B. King's somewhat crass but engaging love song "I'm Gonna Sit In Till You Give In," demonstrate both the overwhelming importance of civil rights issues during this period and the multifarious ways, explicit and implicit, that the Movement shaped African-American consciousness and musical culture.

John F. Kennedy's assassination on 22 November 1963 ensured that the meaning and significance of his abbreviated life and presidency would become the subject of fierce debate. In death, Kennedy's memory has become the site of a relentless cycle of adulation and condemnation, of mythmaking and idol smashing, and occasionally of some balanced journalism and perceptive scholarship. Indeed, one of the most fascinating aspects of *Kennedy's Blues* is the way in which the musical responses to Kennedy's death can be seen as early contributions to this process of constructing the President's posthumous image. As van Rijn demonstrates, the outpouring of genuine black grief, committed to vinyl by blues and gospel artists from John Lee Hooker to Mahalia Jackson and from Otis Spann to the Dixie Nightingales, indicates the extent to which Kennedy had become closely associated with black aspirations for freedom, justice, and equality. The irony is that these sincere musical eulogies for the slain president helped fix into popular memory an image of Kennedy as a tireless and resolutely committed advocate of black civil rights that is at best simplistic, at worst plain wrong.

Some historical context here is useful. In 1960, Kennedy's election victory—secured in no small measure thanks to the votes of African Americans in the North—had been greeted with considerable enthusiasm in the black community. As a candidate, Kennedy had promised to end racial discrimination in housing by executive order and made several important expressions of sympathy toward the travails of the black community, notably when he called Rev. Martin Luther King Jr.'s wife Coretta to express his concern about her husband's latest incarceration in Georgia. Such gestures inspired hope that Kennedy would pursue racial justice in the United States more actively than had his predecessors.

By the spring of 1963, however, some of that early optimism had evaporated. When Kennedy consistently failed to use executive power to end housing discrimination "with the stroke of a pen" as he had promised, an exasperated Congress of Racial Equality sent hundreds of pens to the White House in protest. In an article in the *Nation* magazine, tellingly entitled "Fumbling on the New Frontier," Dr. King captured the growing frustration that many blacks felt toward Kennedy, accusing his administration of "aggressively driving toward the limited goal of token integration." Others were equally disappointed with Kennedy's civil rights record, citing the administration's reluctance to take the lead in promoting comprehensive civil rights legislation as evidence of a lack of genuine commitment to the cause. Moreover, there was a sense that legitimate black demands were being subordinated to Kennedy's personal political needs. For example, black leaders were horrified when Kennedy endorsed the appointment of racist Mississippi judge William Harold Cox to a district judgeship in order to placate the southern wing of the Democratic Party and thus make the president's political life easier.

Kennedy's brother, Attorney General Robert Kennedy, had further infuriated civil rights activists by sending a congratulatory telegram to Albany police chief Laurie Pritchett after that officer's relatively restrained policing of protests had helped to undermine the campaign for desegregation in that Georgia city. Even the administration's advocacy of voter registration through the creation of a tax-exempt Voter Education Project appeared self-serving. While increasing the African-American vote was a crucial goal for most civil rights organizations, some felt that Kennedy had supported the VEP merely to prepare a large loyal black vote for his 1964 reelection campaign. It was certainly no secret that, after the Freedom Rides, Robert Kennedy had called for a "cooling-off" period for the southern civil rights movement, or that the Kennedy brothers viewed voter registration work as a means to get black protesters off the streets, where vicious white violence against largely nonviolent black demonstrators was creating a law-enforcement and international publicity nightmare for the administration.

Some of the songs and sermons from the first two years of the Kennedy administration similarly indicate that the president's reputation among the black masses was much more ambivalent than the content of the material cut after his death might suggest. Several recordings, including Muddy Waters's "Tough Times," captured dissatisfaction with the Kennedy administration's economic and welfare policies, which failed to meet the needs of the American poor, among whom African Americans were disproportionately represented. Many recordings applauded the president's commitment to fighting communism abroad and, in particular, his firm handling of the Cuban Missile Crisis, but others expressed concerns about the president's preoccupation with foreign affairs while he failed to address the domestic problems of racial discrimination and poverty. Some songs, such as Lightnin' Hopkins's "War is Starting Again," lamented the military draft necessary to sustain an increasingly interventionist foreign policy, most notably in Vietnam. The draft fell heavily on black Americans who, having only recently fought for freedom and democracy in World War II and Korea, were still waiting to enjoy those things at home. Such concerns also inspired Rev. Ben Gay's "As the Eagle Stirreth Her Nest"—a blistering sermon recorded at the height of the Albany civil rights campaign, in which Gay questioned the Kennedy administration's claims to moral and democratic leadership on the international stage when it could not even guarantee equality and justice for its own citizens of color.

Even amid this kind of criticism, however, there were clear signs of a kind of qualified and equivocal admiration for Kennedy that had little to do with his rather modest accomplishments in the civil rights field. Even in his lukewarm assessment of the administration's record in the *Nation,* Martin Luther King had admitted that there was "a certain élan in the attention they give to civil rights," conceding that "This administration has reached out more creatively than its predecessors to blaze some new trails." In other words, despite the fact that his actions were often limited and his priorities were frequently disappointing to many in the black community, the promise of meaningful racial reform that Kennedy initially brought to the White House had never entirely vanished. There was always something of a black enchantment with Kennedy, reflecting a charismatic appeal that stemmed in part from his relative youth and—despite the various debilitating illnesses and infirmities that blighted his life—the apparent vitality he and his circle of family, friends, and advisers brought to the corridors of power. In this context, a song like Lula Reed's irresistible "Do the President Twist" may have been a brazen effort to cash in on the latest dance craze, but it also reflected a heartfelt sense of familiarity and intimacy with the president and his family. In such songs, Kennedy was treated with more genuine personal affection than any other president, except perhaps for the sainted FDR.

Even more important in shaping the posthumous black reverence for Kennedy, however, was the fact that in the final months of his life he began to address black grievances in a more decisive and systematic manner. This shift was primarily a response to the sustained pressure of the mass black movement in the South, which mounted more civil rights demonstrations in 1963 than in any other year. The cumulative effect of several years of dignified nonviolent protests, many of them greeted by brutal white violence in front of legions of print, radio, and television journalists, had convinced the majority of Americans of the need for civil rights reform. Whereas it had once appeared politically unwise for Kennedy to support civil rights legislation, by the summer of 1963 the movement had made it politically suicidal for him not to take a bolder stance in support of basic black rights.

The president's perspective on civil rights was also influenced by his brother's growing understanding of the racial situation in America. As the nation's leading law enforcement officer, Bobby Kennedy had eventually come to recognize the impossibility of dealing with each civil rights protest and confrontation in the South on a case-by-case basis. He had also begun to accept the moral imperative for presidential and federal action in support of black rights. On 11 June 1963, the same day that segregationist icon and Alabama Governor George Wallace defied federal authority by standing in the schoolhouse door of the University of Alabama to deny the court-ordered admission of two black students, President Kennedy went on national television. In his speech, Kennedy committed his administration to the passage of a comprehensive civil rights bill and acknowledged that extending equal rights and protections to all American citizens was, indeed, a moral as well as a political issue. This initiative profoundly moved and inspired many sections of the black community and shaped evaluations and memories of the president after his death.

Kennedy's murder meant that he never had a chance to fulfill—or, for that matter, to entirely default on—any of the promises that he made before or during his time in office, including his commitment to his proposed civil rights bill. As the memorial songs van Rijn has uncovered affirm, it suddenly mattered little that Kennedy had taken so long to throw his administration's weight behind civil rights legislation, that the civil rights bill he endorsed was actually rather weak, or that in August 1963 his administration had transformed the March for Jobs and Freedom in Washington, DC, from a radical protest scheduled to include serious condemnations of Kennedy's record on race relations and economic opportunity into a gathering that Malcolm X mocked as "The Farce on Washington"—essentially a choreographed, if emotionally uplifting, celebration of the achievements of the civil rights movement to date and of Kennedy's new civil rights bill in particular. Ironically, when President

Lyndon Johnson pushed through a much tougher act than Kennedy had ever envisioned, he did so in part by packaging it as a fitting memorial to his murdered predecessor. In so doing, Johnson inadvertently reinforced the notion that Kennedy had always been a staunch and indefatigable ally of the black cause, eager for the kind of thoroughgoing civil rights legislation that was enshrined in the 1964 Civil Rights Act.

In the wide and enduring wake of Kennedy's tragic death, few of these subtleties surfaced in the black community. Virtually all of the reservations about the nature and extent of Kennedy's commitment to black aspirations and civil rights disappeared. Most African Americans chose to embrace Kennedy, in Son House's poignantly cracked but still defiant words in "President Kennedy," as "the best friend we had." The dozens and dozens of recordings that chronicled black America's grief about its loss and sympathy for Kennedy's bereaved family were thus important in defining the way in which the president would be remembered and honored in the black community and in the larger American culture. The sheer number and emotional potency of these recordings help to explain why Kennedy has been widely perceived as a civil rights hero: a man whose image was deemed worthy of a place on the wall of many a black home alongside pictures of the other slain giants of 1960s American political life, Martin Luther King Jr. and Bobby Kennedy. There were other factors involved, to be sure, but these songs constitute an underappreciated part of the cultural apparatus whereby the dead president's place in American memory became firmly established.

If Guido van Rijn's exhaustive coverage and commentary on the Kennedy "death songs" adds a new dimension to our understanding of the process by which social memories of the Kennedy presidency were created, this is merely one of the many signal contributions of his book. We also catch glimpses of an industry in transition, with many of the old—and largely arbitrary, commercially driven, or plainly racist—divisions between musical categories collapsing. Some of the "blues" artists, whose politically oriented material is discussed here (Hank Ballard, Ray Charles, Bo Diddley, Little Willie John, Wilbert Harrison, and Robert Parker, for example), straddled the boundaries between blues, rhythm and blues, rock and roll, and nascent soul music. While some—invariably white—critics bemoaned the adulteration of some kind of mythical "pure" blues forms during this period, many of the blues singers of the early 1960s were only too happy to dabble in a little rock and roll or proto-soul. As ever, an often inscrutable mixture of commercial considerations and artistic impulses shaped the stylistic decisions of individual artists.

Part of that decision-making process was doubtless the knowledge that during the early 1960s the likes of James Brown, Sam Cooke, and the early Motown and Stax acts were the most commercially successful artists in the black community. These singers had at least as much claim to be voicing the "real" African-American experience as did their blues and gospel counterparts. Moreover, at a time of integrationist aspirations and efforts, these kinds of artists were often also straddling racial boundaries, appealing to young whites as well as to African Americans to an extent unimagined in previous generations. Many blues singers also hankered after the greater rewards of more mainstream success. Certainly, after decades of being forced to record for and play to a largely segregated black market, the musicians themselves recognized the potentially radical nature of the shifts in American musical styles and tastes that had begun in the mid- to late 1950s and continued into the 1960s. In "Down South," a searing indictment of discrimination in Dixie, Memphis Slim rightly noted that some of the most virulent white hostility to the initial emergence of rock and roll music had come from die-hard southern segregationists who recognized how music played by black and white artists, drawing on black and white stylistic influences, for the entertainment of black and white audiences challenged the basic configuration of racial segregation.

The recordings that van Rijn investigates also reflect a greater willingness on the part of record labels to issue songs that dealt with quite contentious political and racial subjects. Before the 1960s, the recording, radio, and television industries, with their prevailing assumptions about morality, communism, race, gender, and class and about the essentially segregated nature of the American cultural marketplace, ensured that relatively few overtly political black recordings were cut. And of those that were, more than twenty percent remained unreleased. By contrast, van Rijn indicates that, in the heightened political atmosphere of the early 1960s, not only was more political material being cut but that around 95 percent of those songs were actually released. Of course, blues artists continued to spend far more time singing about the trials and tribulations of love and sex than about civil rights campaigns or Cold War diplomacy, just as gospel singers continued to deal more often with matters of personal and collective salvation than with the space race. Nevertheless, the songs in *Kennedy's Blues* capture a moment of peculiarly intense political engagement on the part of many performers working in the blues and gospel fields. These were the blues and gospel songs of artists who joined the civil rights movement's demands for, in the words of "The Jail House King" by Bob Starr, "freedom in this land."

—BRIAN WARD
UNIVERSITY OF MANCHESTER, GREAT BRITAIN

ACKNOWLEDGMENTS

My lifelong involvement with the blues began in 1962 in the first form of Pius X Lyceum in Amsterdam, when my music teacher, Nico Hermans, played a record of "Pinetop's Boogie Woogie" to the class. A few years later Arend Jan Heerma van Voss led me to the Dutch magazine *Jazz Wereld* (1965–73) and later to the British journal *Blues Unlimited* (1963–87).

In 1970, the late Martin van Olderen (1931–2002) and I founded the Dutch Blues and Boogie Organization, and together we organized the first concerts by American blues artists. My thinking on blues in those early years was greatly influenced by Leo Bruin, Herman Engelbart, the late Rob Hoeke (1939–1999), and Wim Verbei. In 1978 I started the Agram Blues reissue label, and have since produced nineteen albums. My friends Hans Vergeer and Cor van Sliedregt have been closely associated with this project. I am indebted to the editors of specialist periodicals such as *78 Quarterly*, *Blues Unlimited*, *Blues & Rhythm*, *Juke Blues*, and *Living Blues* for publishing articles that I have written.

The late Max Vreede (1927–1991) became a respected friend, and many evenings spent discovering the treasure trove in his collection of 78 r.p.m. records did much to deepen my understanding of the blues.

When an opportunity to embark upon a thesis arose, I took as my subject blues and gospel songs about American presidents. I decided to concentrate on President Franklin Roosevelt and to make a deeper analysis of songs specifically relating to him and his presidency. The progress of the Roosevelt manuscript was supervised by Alfons Lammers, Professor of American History at Leiden University, and David Evans, Professor of Music at the University of Memphis. The Ph.D. ceremony took place at Leiden University on 19 October 1995, with Chris Smith and Jan Spoelder as my "paranimfs." The commercial edition of *Roosevelt's Blues* was published by the University Press of Mississippi in 1997.

In 2004 the sequel *The Truman and Eisenhower Blues* was published by Continuum in London and New York. *Kennedy's Blues* is the third volume in the series.

As with the first two volumes, the influence of both Chris Smith and David Evans is felt throughout the present work, both in the analysis of the songs and in the accuracy of their transcription.

A number of other people contributed ideas, support, and information, and I extend my thanks to Johnnie Allen, Ray Astbury, Chris Bentley, Alasdair Blaazer, John Broven, Leo Bruin, Tony Burke, Sandranette Chenet-Hairston, John Cowley, Bob Eagle, Simon Evans, Byron Foulger, Peter Goldsmith, Daniel Gugolz, Cedric Hayes, Jaap Hindriks, Charles Horner, Robert Javors, Bernard Jolivette, Tom Kelly, Klaus Kilian, Dan Kochakian, Mike Kredinac, Alfons Lammers, Robert Laughton, Brian Lee, Kip Lornell, Robert Marovich, Jay Martin, Dave Moore, Opal Louis Nations, John Newman, Tom Neylon, Kevin Nutt, Paul Oliver, Jim O'Neal, Johnny Parth, George Paulus, Victor Pearlin, Doug Price, Morton Reff, Rev. Lawrence Roberts, Gerard Robs, Mike Rowe, Tony Russell, Howard Rye, Robert Sacré, Gianfranco Scala, Richard Shurman, Neil Slaven, Jan Spoelder, Robert Springer, Matthew Starr, Bob Stone, Jeff Titon, Steve Tracy, Karl Tsigdinos, Billy Vera, Wim Verbei, Hans Vergeer, Rosie Wallace, Brian Ward, Tony Watson, Hans Westerduijn, George White, and Rien Wisse.

Much research was conducted in libraries and/or by librarians at my request, and I would especially like to thank the British Newspaper Library in Colindale, North London; the Kennedy Institute of Freie Universität in Berlin; the Library of Vrije Universiteit, Amsterdam; Todd Harvey of the American Folklife Center of the Library of Congress; Leiden University Library; the Koninklijke Bibliotheek, The Hague; Rob Kroes of the Amerika Instituut of the Universiteit van Amsterdam, and Hans Krabbendam and Gonny Pasaribu of the Roosevelt Study Center, Middelburg.

Finally, I must thank my wife, Nelleke, and my children, Paul and Emily, for their continued and unstinting support.

INTRODUCTION

Despite the growing literature on the black experience during the twentieth century, there are still many important and underappreciated elements of African-American history and culture that can be usefully illuminated by close analysis of black musical forms. This is no simple task, however; only by dogged perseverance and openness to the diverse signals and shades of meaning embedded in black music can a more comprehensive view of the black experience in the United States be formed. Yet the call of this music demands a sensitive response; historians of blues and gospel must learn how "to signify," to borrow the expression from the black idiom that Henry Louis Gates Jr. uses to characterize the process of establishing complex, mutually dependent intertextual relationships in black culture.[1] In other words, in order to understand and interpret blues and gospel songs accurately, the musicologist needs to take into account their connections, not just to other songs in the black repertoire, but also to a whole range of black and white cultural creations and historical circumstances that help determine their meanings and significances. This book pursues that goal by examining those blues and gospel songs from the period November 1960 to 1964 that dealt explicitly with the great social and economic concerns of the Kennedy era.

For outsiders, the blues is often merely entertainment, but for the African-American working class in particular, the music is also a social ritual that "reinforces a sense of order in life and preserves the shared wisdom of the group."[2] Literary theory may help to crack the encodings of black music, but the ways in which it has reflected the social life of a people have often been obscured by what Gates calls a "lack of sophisticated scholarly attention" to its historical context.[3] Since the early 1920s thousands of blues and gospel songs have been recorded, but these important resources have seldom been used by historians in any systematic manner. As Lawrence Levine has observed, "By largely ignoring this tradition, much of which has been preserved, historians have rendered an articulate people historically inarticulate, and have allowed the record of their consciousness to go unexplored."[4] This book represents an attempt to revisit the lost consciousness and restore the silenced voices of many African Americans by examining the blues and gospel songs of the Kennedy years.

Blues lyrics usually deal with experiences common to the singer and his or her audience. Although the lyrics are frequently imaginative, they are usually based on personal experience and thus invoke or even imitate a tangible reality. Many songs allow the artists and their audiences to escape temporarily from hardship by a celebration of "the joys and frustrations of love," as David Evans has argued in an analysis of blues lyricism. In particular, the blues is rich in sexual imagery. Evans explains the emphasis on the man–woman relationship in two ways: "It is the area most subject to daily change and fluctuation in people's lives, and it is closely related to the dancing and partying context in which blues are most often performed." Ultimately, most blues revolves around success or failure in a loving relationship or the anticipation or loss of romance and sex. Meanwhile, most gospel music revolves around either the sweet anticipation of a just and humane Promised Land at some point in the future or the invocation of the Lord's help to survive the hardships of the present.

By contrast with these themes, overt political commentary in recorded blues and gospel songs was relatively rare until the late 1960s. This may have been because of the fear of retribution for any artist or label seen to be challenging the racial status quo in song, but it was also a function of the way in which the politics of the blues worked. The blues do not usually address the issue of racial discrimination; rather, racism is considered implicitly, in terms of its consequences. However, as Evans observes, the singers may unconsciously have channeled "the problem of discrimination into less controversial areas."[5] Nevertheless, a small percentage of blues and gospel recordings did contain overt political commentary.

In my first book, *Roosevelt's Blues: African-American Blues and Gospel Songs on FDR* (1997), the goal was to shed some light on why FDR became so popular among African Americans in the 1930s and 40s by analyzing those blues and gospel recordings of his era that did contain explicit social and political comment. Hidden in the grooves of the old 78 r.p.m. recordings, the black voices of the period could still be heard. A painstaking transcription of the lyrics revealed the emotional coordinates as well as the more pragmatic rationale for black attachment to Roosevelt in ways that few other sources could match. The frequency with which he is mentioned clearly indicates his impact on black lives and consciousness. Only four of the seven presidents from the period 1901–45 are mentioned by name in recorded blues and gospel lyrics, and those mainly in isolated examples. Theodore Roosevelt, Woodrow Wilson, and Herbert Hoover hardly received any attention from the blues and gospel singers. William Howard Taft, Warren Harding, and Calvin Coolidge were ignored altogether. In contrast, after 1933 no fewer than forty-four songs were directly devoted to Franklin Delano Roosevelt, the vast majority of which were highly favorable in content.

In *The Truman and Eisenhower Blues: African-American Blues and Gospel Songs, 1945–1960* (2004), I turned my attention to the period between 1945 and 1960, during which relations between East and West deteriorated. By combining the two presidencies in one book, it was possible to discuss in one continuous narrative the events of the Korean War. Separate sections of the book were devoted to Truman and Eisenhower's varying responses to economic and civil rights issues and the ways in which they were perceived by the African-American community. The development and use of the atomic bomb yielded enough material for a further chapter on that issue alone; and the space race under Eisenhower formed a major part of a later chapter.

When FDR died in 1945, World War II was still in progress and African Americans were still working for a "double V": victory over fascism abroad and victory over discrimination at home. Black servicemen and women had again proved their fighting spirit, democratic idealism, and basic patriotism when the nation called, and the hope was that after the war, both the armed forces and civilian society would accept black Americans on a basis of equality. As the blues and gospel songs analyzed in *The Truman and Eisenhower Blues* so vividly revealed, during the fifteen years that followed the end of the war, those dreams and aspirations were only partially fulfilled. The songs reflected a very different, generally more sharply critical black response to the Truman and Eisenhower administrations than was the case during the Roosevelt presidency. At the same time, however, alongside the obvious black frustration with continued racism and discrimination, one could also detect a rising tide of militancy, determination, and urgency in some of the songs, reflecting the new black consciousness that would find political expression in the civil rights movement of the late 1950s and 1960s.

Kennedy's Blues differs from these earlier volumes in that it is devoted to a mere "1000 days" in the White House, from 20 January 1961 to 22 November 1963. Whereas *Roosevelt's Blues* and *The Truman and Eisenhower Blues* each dealt with four terms in office, *Kennedy's Blues* analyzes less than one. The very fact that a single, albeit rather slim volume could be devoted to the blues and gospel songs dealing with one truncated presidency is evidence of Kennedy's effect on the African-American population. Never having been transcribed and analyzed in a systematic way, these songs about John F. Kennedy provide a hitherto untapped source of oral history on the perception of one of the most intriguing American presidents.

After eight years of Republican rule, the young Democratic president received a warm welcome from African Americans. The charismatic Kennedy family fascinated the American people. At times it seemed as if the United States was no longer a republic but instead a sparkling monarchy. However, when the Cold War necessitated yet another military draft, initial enthusiasm subsided. The plight of African Americans necessitated drastic civil rights measures, but for many the president acted too slowly on the issue and impatience set in. Dr. Martin Luther King Jr. forced the civil rights issue to crises in Albany and Birmingham. The assassination of Medgar Evers sped up African-American discontent, and the 1963 March on Washington was organized to put pressure on Congress to support Kennedy's groundbreaking civil rights bill. The many songs devoted to the assassination and the president's legacy are evidence of JFK's posthumous near-canonization among African Americans. Despite his unfinished accomplishments in the civil rights field, John Fitzgerald Kennedy became a mythical hero.

In the early 1960s the blues was in decline as black popular music and was only beginning to make some inroads in the white folk and pop scene. Younger African Americans increasingly perceived the blues as an old-fashioned art form that reminded them of slavery days; upwardly aspiring African Americans began to look down on the blues with its working-class origins. As a result some of the country blues in this study may have been designed for different audiences. Some of the artists recorded in the field had already retired from music and were no longer performing primarily for the black community. Gospel music was also undergoing a transition at this stage: quartets were losing popularity and soloists and choirs were becoming dominant. At the same time, spiritual and gospel lyrics were being adapted to the civil rights struggle by activists.

The songs analyzed in this book illuminate black consciousness at a crucial, transitional moment in the black experience, just as a new era of mass activism and protest began. The artists who made the recordings are mostly traditional blues and gospel artists, although some of the songs, especially those on the space race, show an occasional inclination toward pop music. Recorded sermons are scrutinized, as they provide much insight into African-American perception of the Kennedy years. This was also a period of increased prominence of comedians in black entertainment and the emergence of black comedians in mainstream entertainment. For the first time black comedians spoke out on politics, and some of the recorded comedy about the Kennedy presidency is analyzed. The sixties saw the rise of soul music, through a merging of rhythm and blues and gospel music. Much attention already has been paid to black consciousness and soul music, so it is not dealt with in this study.[6]

TECHNICAL NOTES

Until RCA Victor introduced the "unbreakable" 7-inch, 45 r.p.m. record in 1949, most recordings were issued on cylinders and brittle 10-inch, 78 r.p.m. records. The 1950s were a transitional period during which both formats were used. By the 1960s 78s were no longer being manufactured. Consequently the songs, sermons, and comedy discussed in *Kennedy's Blues* were either issued on 45s or on the increasingly popular 33 r.p.m. long-play albums.

Accurate discographical information about postwar records is comparatively difficult to obtain, because the prosperity of the immediate postwar years gave rise to a host of small independent companies whose bookkeeping systems were often poorly maintained. Although record labels sometimes provide useful details, many of the personnel who participated in the recording process are deceased or have never been traced. As a result we are often at a loss for information about precise recording dates, and sometimes even locations.

The texts of songs, sermons, and comedy sketches are quoted in the most complete form possible, except that where the singer repeats the first line, as commonly happens in blues formats, the repeated line has been omitted.

The utmost attention has been given to accurate transcription, but the songs should ideally be heard for the full emotional impact of their messages to be appreciated. Accordingly, a CD (Agram Blues ABCD 2019) containing twenty-eight examples is available with the book. Wherever possible, I have given full discographical details in the notes in order that the songs quoted in the book, but not included on the CD, may be sought out for listening purposes.

KENNEDY'S BLUES

1

JOHN F. KENNEDY, THE MAN AND THE MYTH

When a reporter for the *Michigan Chronicle* asked Aretha Franklin's father, the Rev. C. L. Franklin (1915–1984), for his reaction to the president's assassination, he replied that it was "a tragic blow," as tragic as the one that "felled President Abraham Lincoln a century before." He insisted that the "sniper did not pull his trigger alone"; George Wallace, Ross Barnett "and all the forces of hate and evil" were "as surely in Dallas with the sniper as they were in Jackson when Medgar Evers was felled."[1]

Rev. Franklin preached his sermon "Why Have the Mighty Fallen (Tribute to the Kennedys)" in 1968, possibly around 22 November, the fifth anniversary of the president's death. After a rather idealized biography, Franklin asked why the mighty Kennedy had fallen. He compared the President to Saul, Gandhi, Lincoln, and Socrates, all of whom "gave their lives for an idea." The question cannot be answered, Franklin concluded: it is a mystery and the Lord will make it plain.

PART ONE

Tonight, we are gonna try to preach this sermon that we've been announcing that we're gonna preach, but I've got one of the worst colds I've ever had. Eh, I had the doctor this afternoon, after I left church, and at four o'clock my fever was 101. But I have a sense of responsibility and

I decided, in spite of how I felt, inasmuch as I felt that if I didn't at least show, you would be disappointed. So I'm here, and I'm asking your prayers as I make an effort to preach to you tonight.

In the second book of the Kings, the nineteenth verse of the first chapter, we read the following: "The beauty of Israel is slain upon thy high places: how are the mighty fallen!" How are the mighty fallen! How has the mighty fallen! To give this a more comprehensive rendition, or translation, it could very well read: "Why has the mighty fallen?" For this is exactly what, eh, David, eh, is saying in his eulogy of Saul, King Saul and his son Jonathan.

And so we have chosen on this Sunday night to give a tribute to one whom we felt to have been a great American. A great president. A great spirit. Or a great president, a great spirit, or a great soul: the late President John F. Kennedy. Eh, you know, there are people who are world citizens, mm, not just citizens of a community or a state, or even of a nation, but world citizens. And we look upon President Kennedy's life, his administration as a president. As we contemplate his memory, we think of him as a world citizen.

He was born in Brookline, Massachusetts, May 29th, 1917. He was the second of nine children. The president's great-grandparents emigrated to the United States from Ireland in 1858. His grandfather, Patrick J. Kennedy, or maybe I should say his grandfathers Patrick J. Kennedy and John F. Fitzgerald, were natives of Ireland. His grandfather Fitzgerald served several times as mayor of Boston and was a member of the United States House of Representatives. Grandfather Kennedy was a powerful ward boss and served in both houses of the Massachusetts legislature.

The president's father Joseph Kennedy was a brilliant mathematician and became the youngest man, eh, to be president of a bank in the history of this country at twenty-five years old. His mother Rose Kennedy was a devoted religious woman who took her children on walks every day. And every day she would take them into her church and spend some time in the church, every day. Her explanation was that she wanted her children to make God and religion a daily part of their lives. Joe Kennedy placed one million dollars in a trust fund for each of his nine children. His reason was to release them from financial worries and for them to devote their lives to public good. And of course it seems to me that all of them followed that plan. (I don't believe you're praying with me!) As the children grew their parents stressed the important, the importance of the competitive spirit. Father Joe's favorite motto was: "Second place is a loser." That is to say, don't satisfy yourselves with second place. I believe, frequently I used to talk about: "Shoot at the moon," eh, shoot, or aim for the moon. And if you fall among the stars, you'll still be on high ground.

With a, a background for the Kennedy children such as I have been describing to you, we can see why the Kennedy children excelled in sports, in education, in politics, et cetera. John F. Kennedy attended public school in Brookline, Massachusetts. Later he entered a private school in Riverdale, New York, and then to Wallingford, Connecticut. In 1935 to 36 he studied at the London School of Ec– Economics. Then he followed his brother, his oldest brother Joe, Joe Jr., to Harvard. Eh, it was at Harvard that he suffered his first back injury in a game of football. Joe Kennedy Sr. was named ambassador to Great Britain in 1937. John and Joe Jr. went with him, or went with their father, and became international reporters for him and they traveled in many parts of the world while they lived with him in London. Following his graduation from Harvard, he wrote a bestseller entitled Why England Slept.[2]

Because of his old back injury, he had some difficulty getting into the service. He finally, however, got into the Navy, and became the commander of a torpedo boat in the South Pacific in the vicinity of the Solomon Islands. It was here where he was attacked and rammed by a Japanese destroyer and his boat was broken in two. And those who were with him, who went into the water with him, one was so greatly injured, that he put, eh, a life jacket on him and put the strap of the life jacket between his teeth and towed him to safety for five hours. (I don't believe you're praying with me!) For this he was awarded the Navy and Marine medals.

Eh, nearly one year later his brother Joe, his brother Joe's plane exploded over the English coast. After his brother died, John Kennedy compiled a collection of tributes to his brother and entitled them: "As We Remember Joe."[3] The death of his brother Joe deeply affected John Kennedy *in terms of sorrow and destiny. Thus instead of Joe, he embarked upon a political career and abandoned the profession of a newspaperman, as he had previously planned, as Joe had been decided to be the one who would engage in politics.*

In 1946 he campaigned for and won a seat in the United States House of Representatives from the eleventh Massachusian, Massachusetts congressional district. In 1952 he decided to run for the United States Senate from Massachusetts. And again he won against the popular Henry Cabot Lodge. He missed a vice presidential nomination in 1956 and it is said that when he started his campaign for 1960 often he used to tell his audiences: "I am glad you didn't vote for me in 1956, because I would have lost."

PART TWO

He missed the vice presidency, but in the process he learned many helpful things for his campaign for the presidency in 1960. Somebody has rightly said that God frequently closes doors that we are trying to go in, so as to guide us to a bigger door that he has already opened for us (I don't believe you hear me! Listen, if you please!)

After almost three years of productive and creative service the thirty-fifth president of the United States was assassinated by a sniper, or snipers, on November 22nd, 1963. I would like to dedicate just a verse of a poem from Edwin Markham that was written in the la– in the wake of President Lincoln's assassination. Here is what he said: "He went down in whirlwind and storm, like a lovely cedar, green with boughs, a great shout was heard upon the hills, and he left a lonesome place against the sky."[4] *I believe this is applicable to the life of John F. Kennedy, eh, for he was a hero. He was a sports or an athletic hero. He was a political hero. And of course, because of the many things that he did in his lifetime (and we wish we had time to enumerate them), I would only mention what I heard one of the senators say in one of the Democratic national conventions, referring to him. He said: "When Kennedy, when Cuba was trying to arm itself to the teeth with missiles, they ran upon John F. Kennedy standing twelve feet tall in the Atlantic." (You don't hear me!)*

And so they regarded, they regarded, eh, Saul, the nation of Israel regarded Saul and Jonathan, something in the manner that we regard the late John F. Kennedy (Let me see if I can tell you the story, and I'll soon be through! Listen, if you please!)[5] David had been engaged in a battle, in a battle with the Amalekites and he had come to Ziklag, eh, to recuperate. And when he was there two or three days, a young Amalekite soldier came running in and, eh, approached David, and, eh, David asked how was the battle going from that section from which he had come. He declared it wasn't going too well, for he said: "Many of the soldiers have fallen and even Saul and Jonathan are dead." And then, eh, David said now: "On what authority do you give out this kind of information?" He said: "Well, I came upon Saul on the battlefield, and, eh, the enemy was close behind him and he saw no way of escape and he fell on his spear and tried to commit suicide, but, eh, when I reached him and the enemy soldiers were pressing down on him," he said to me: "Come here, my boy, take my sword and stand upon me and put me to death." And of course, the boy said to David: "I took his bracelet and his crown to indicate that I know what I'm talking about. These are Saul's, as you can see. He's dead." And when he told David that, David began to rent or tear off his clothes and began to put dirt upon his head and drape his head in mourning.

And, eh, the others, the soldiers that were around him, they began to join him in weeping. And, eh, when David, eh, had mourned until evening time, well, he said: "Now, bring that young man to me. And, eh, let me talk with him again. And, eh, I wanna find out from that boy, mmm, why wasn't he afraid to lay his hand on God's anointed? Mmm, oh, Lord. Wasn't he fearful to take the life of someone that God had destined to be a King? Oh, Lord. A common soldier, Great God, that's possibly not more than a private, mmm, has taken the life, eh, of the nation's sovereign King. Oh, Lord. (You're not praying with me!) Oh, yeah. And then I heard, eh, David said to one of his men: "Fall upon him and take his life, mmm, for he has admitted, eh, in his own testimony, eh, that he killed God's anointed, eh. Oh, Lord." And then David, eh, began to utilize, eulogize, the King Solomon, or King Saul and his son. Oh, Lord. I heard him say: "Why, mmm, have the mighty fallen? Oh, Lord. There are so many who deserve to be gone, there are so many that make no contribution at all, mmm, who live on continuously. And here are two men, that were the nation's heroes, and they are gone. Oh, Lord."

When I think about men like John F. Kennedy, mmm, when I think about men, like Gandhi, when I think about men, like Abraham Lincoln, when I think about other notable men, like Socrates, who gave their lives, because they believed in an idea. Oh, Lord. I join David in saying: "Why has the mighty fallen?" Oh, Lord. But I'm gonna close, but I tell you this, mmm, oh, well, I've made up in my mind, oh, well. Oh, well, it's clear to me, mmm, yes, it is, that life is full of mystery, life has many unanswered questions. Oh, Lord. Oh, one of these days, I'll understand. Oh, Lord. Oh! One of these days you'll understand it better, by and by, by and by, when the morning comes.[6] When all the saints of God are gathered home, we'll understand it. Yeah, yeah, yeah. But one of these days, I'm gonna keep on toiling, I'm gonna keep on praying, I'm gonna keep on believing. Yes, I am. Yes! Oh, oh, oh, one of these days.

We will understand it better, by and by. Many of the riddles of life, many of the unanswered questions we'll understand, we'll understand. For the Lord will make it plain.

The doors of the church are open for the reception of members by letter of Christian experience or candidates for baptism. If you are here and have no church, I ask you to be prayerful and quiet, while we sing together our trust in the Lord:

> *I will trust in the Lord, (3x) until I die.*
> *I will trust in the Lord, (3x) until I die.*
> *I'm gonna stay on the battlefield, (3x) until I die.*
> *I'm gonna stay on the battlefield, (3x) until I die.*

Quiet. To you who can't decide, to you who would straddle the fence 'fore God, to you who would denounce your commitment to him and stay away from his bighearted service, let me give you one more chance:

> *I will trust in the Lord, (3x) until I die.*
> *I will walk with the Lord, (3x) until I die.*
> *God bless!*[7]

A 2004 *CNN/USA Today*/Gallup poll of presidential job approval ratings shows President Kennedy heading the eleven postwar presidents with a total term average of seventy per cent.[8] More than forty years after his assassination, JFK is still a cult hero to many.

John F. Kennedy had been fascinated by King Arthur from his early days onward, as his mother Rose Fitzgerald Kennedy later wrote: "I remembered him in his boyhood reading and rereading his copy of *King Arthur and the Round Table*."[9]

In his Kennedy biography historian Arthur M. Schlesinger Jr. explained:

> *He was the only one in the family who liked to read; loneliness and sickness made him read all the more. He spent hours in his room at Riverdale or Hyannis Port absorbed in history and biography—King Arthur, Scottish Chiefs, The White Company, Cooper, and later Churchill's Marlborough when he was in his teens. History was full of heroes for him, and he reveled in the stately cadences of historical prose. His memory of what he read was photographic. Situations, scenes and quotations stuck in his mind for the rest of his life.*[10]

The myth of King Arthur stuck in Kennedy's mind and his own life began to show a number of parallels with Arthur's. When Kennedy himself was murdered three years later the myth arose almost instantly.

One week after the assassination of her husband on 22 November 1963, Jacqueline Kennedy confided to Theodore H. White:

> *At night, before we'd go to sleep, Jack liked to play some records; and the song he loved most came at the very end of this record. The lines he loved to hear were:*
>
> > *Don't let it be forgot, that once there was a spot,*
> > *For one brief shining moment that was known as Camelot.*
>
> > *There'll be great presidents again—and the Johnsons are wonderful, they've been wonderful to me—but there'll never be another Camelot again.*[11]

The record Kennedy liked to play contained a recording of the 1960 Alan Jay Lerner and Frederick Loewe musical *Camelot*, a Broadway adaptation of Terence Hanbury White's successful 1958 King Arthur portrayal *The Once and Future King*.

In his article "Lancer: Myth-Making and the Kennedy Camelot," W. Nicholas Knight analyzed the way the myth had arisen. Jacqueline Kennedy told Theodore H. White of her idealistic, romantic, and chivalric dream. "As she watched her personal Camelot vanish, she was creating the public one for history," Knight wrote. As a modern Merlin, White created the Camelot myth around his fellow Harvard student, whom he considered a hero. Knight showed how Theodore H. White had left out some of Jacqueline's words in the *Life* article quoted above that started the myth. He revealed that Jacqueline had called her dream "an obsession." "This compulsion is evidence of psychological need, of myth-making in the process," Knight explained. He summarized the dream thus: "That a good idea can ennoble; that we can all participate in a good cause and gentle our condition; that we can fail and be redeemed, that we can do our best under the worst circumstances, that to seek a better world is not a lost cause; that by banding together we can love each other as we are in order to help each to fulfill his potential and destiny."[12]

Subsequently, the comparison between John F. Kennedy and King Arthur was often drawn by biographers and political analysts as well. Analogies were drawn between Lee Harvey Oswald and Mordred (the incestuous son of Arthur and his sister Morgana who killed King Arthur), between Jackie Kennedy and Guinevere (Arthur's wife), between Theodore White and Merlin (the Druid magician), and between William Manchester and Malory (the author of *Le Morte D'Arthur*, first published in 1485).

Kennedy's style of leadership, which Schlesinger would later label "imperial presidency," inspired the use of the word "Camelot" to describe the charismatic president's "reign." Thomas Brown saw deep latent meanings in Kennedy's Camelot:

> The image is especially interesting because the United States was conceived in the revolt of a simple, virtuous "Country" against the decadence and grandeur of the English "Court."[13] Camelot, then, may

be taken as a metaphor of how the New Frontiersmen conceived of themselves: as a cultured, cosmopolitan elite who would lead the United States away from its provincial past and prepare it for the tasks of empire.[14]

In articles on the Kennedy presidency the comparison with King Arthur's court was often made: "We Want Camelot Again,"[15] "It Was Never Camelot,"[16] "A Shadow over Camelot,"[17] "Kennedy in Camelot: The Arthurian Legend in America,"[18] "Camelot Censored?"[19] Was this comparison far-fetched? Does the life of John Fitzgerald Kennedy really present many similarities with King Arthur's?

In his *The Hero: A Study in Tradition, Myth and Drama*, Lord Raglan proposed that the archetypal life of the mythical hero forms a ritualistic pattern that can be divided into the following twenty-two phases:

1. The hero's mother is a royal virgin;
2. His father is a king, and
3. Often a near relative of his mother, but
4. The circumstances of his conception are unusual, and
5. He is also reputed to be the son of a god.
6. At birth an attempt is made, usually by his father or his maternal grandfather, to kill him, but
7. He is spirited away, and
8. Reared by foster parents in a far country.
9. We are told nothing of his childhood, but
10. On reaching manhood he returns or goes to his future kingdom.
11. After a victory over the king and/or a giant, dragon, or wild beast,
12. He marries a princess, often the daughter of his predecessor, and
13. Becomes king.
14. For a time he reigns uneventfully, and
15. Prescribes laws, but
16. Later he loses favor with the gods and/or his subjects, and
17. Is driven from the throne and city, after which
18. He meets with a mysterious death,
19. Often at the top of a hill.
20. His children, if any, do not succeed him.

21. His body is not buried, but nevertheless
22. He has one or more holy sepulchers.[20]

These characteristics are more or less common to a great many mythical heroes. Lord Raglan not only lists the characteristics the mythical heroes often have in common, he also checks the stories about a number of them against his pattern. King Arthur scores no fewer than nineteen points on the scale of twenty-two.[21]

The same method can be applied to the life of John Fitzgerald Kennedy. The following paragraphs all start with the appropriate reference to the Raglan paradigm:

2. "His father is a king."

Joseph Patrick Kennedy (1888–1969), John Kennedy's father, was called to a royal court, when on 9 December 1937 he was appointed ambassador of the United States at the Court of St. James's in London. The post was considered to be the most prestigious in the diplomatic service. "Joe became a Boston hero, with *The Post* and *The American* running series on his career, including a genealogy headlined 'Kennedy Family Has Royal Blood Antedating the King's.'"[22]

7. "He is spirited away."

Nature made several attempts to kill him in his youth. When John was three years old he contracted scarlet fever. After a long battle improvement finally set in. He was born with a very weak back that was to cause him much pain all his life. In a bicycle race with his elder brother Joe, which ended in a collision, Joe escaped unhurt, whereas John had twenty-eight stitches. John suffered from a mysterious illness, a "blood condition" which the doctors could not diagnose. Leukemia, jaundice, and hepatitis were often mentioned. Later it was discovered that he suffered from Addison's disease.

As a result of all these dangerous diseases the child John Fitzgerald Kennedy was spirited away from everyday life, spending a substantial part of his youth in bed reading about heroes.

8. "He is reared by foster-parents in a far country."

In 1926 the Kennedys left Boston for New York, where they hoped to get even more opportunities. When the father was appointed ambassador in 1937, the family moved to England. After Britain declared war the family was sent back to the United States. Jack was the last one to fly home at the end of September 1939.

10. "On reaching manhood he returns or goes to his future kingdom."

The intended heir to the Kennedy "throne" had been Joe Jr., the eldest brother. "Young Joe" overshadowed his younger brother in everything. When Joe Jr. was killed in an aircraft accident on 13 August 1944, John Fitzgerald Kennedy had to take the place of his brother. By entering the world of politics he inherited his father's kingdom.

11. "The hero gains a victory over the king and/or a giant, dragon, or wild beast."

As a lieutenant in the U.S. Navy John had to fight the Japanese, widely characterized as subhuman animals at the time. His boat, PT 109, was split in two by a Japanese destroyer on 1 August 1943. After the attack he acted so bravely that the *New York Times* of 20 August carried the headline: KENNEDY'S SON IS HERO IN PACIFIC AS DESTROYER SPLITS HIS PT BOAT. The event marked a turning point in the newborn hero's life that completed his initiation, or as Collier and Horowitz saw it: "Making that naked swim into the Blackett Strait was a kind of baptismal rite, and there was a new tone of self-confidence in his letters home."[23] When asked about the event many years later President Kennedy reacted with his inimitable wit. On a trip to the West Coast, he was asked by a little boy: "Mr. President, how did you become a war hero?" "It was absolutely involuntary. They sank my boat."[24] Laconic wit is very often typical of heroes. In 1952, Kennedy ran for the Senate with the slogan "Kennedy will do more for Massachusetts." In a resounding victory, he defeated Republican incumbent Henry Cabot Lodge Jr. by a margin of about 70,000 votes.

12. "He marries a princess, often the daughter of his predecessor."

The hero, who was considered by many the most eligible bachelor in America, married his beautiful princess in 1953. Jacqueline Bouvier (1929–1994), daughter of the wealthy John V. Bouvier III, had a sister who was a real princess: Lee Bouvier, who had married Prince Stanislaus Radziwill, a descendant of the kings of Poland.

13. "He becomes king."

After fighting and defeating a contender (Richard Milhous Nixon), Kennedy took over as a ruler. John Fitzgerald Kennedy became president of the United States in January 1961.

14. "For a time he reigns uneventfully."

After having been elected by a tiny popular majority, the first year of Kennedy's presidency was not a success. He was still finding his way. Kennedy finally proved his leadership when he ordered a blockade of Cuba in October 1962, in response to the Soviet placing of missiles on the island.

15. "He prescribes laws."

Kennedy initiated many bills, but it was left for Lyndon Johnson to push the Civil Rights Act through Congress in a much tougher form than JFK had initially championed.

16. "Later he loses favor with the gods and/or his subjects."

Earlier in his presidency, the 17 April 1961 Bay of Pigs fiasco contributed to the image of a weak, inexperienced president. The invasion of Cuba was doomed to fail miserably. After Kennedy had also been unable to halt the building of the Berlin Wall that same year, Soviet President Khrushchev began to look down on him. As a result the Russians felt safe enough to install missiles on Cuba. Then Kennedy finally proved his leadership. In a complicated balance of interest he took sensible measures and was so determined that the Russians withdrew. Kennedy thereby regained the favor of his subjects.

18. "He meets with a mysterious death."

The assassination of President Kennedy in Dallas, Texas, on 22 November 1963 became one of the greatest controversies of the twentieth century. The suspected killer, Lee Harvey Oswald, was killed by Jack Ruby before he could be properly interrogated. Evidence allegedly disappeared or was tampered with. Despite police investigation and the subsequent findings of the Warren Commission, there is still intense speculation regarding the assassination. How many shots had been fired? Who had fired them? What organization, if any, was behind the assassination? The most popular theory is that both John and Robert Kennedy were murdered by the Mafia, as David E. Scheim argues in his book *Contract on America*. The mystery will probably remain unsolved, although most credible scholars believe that Oswald, acting alone, killed JFK.

19. "Often at the top of a hill."

Amidst great mourning (the first worldwide television funeral), Kennedy was buried on the sacred hillside of Arlington National Cemetery. Senator Hubert Humphrey, who had stood behind Jacqueline Kennedy, afterwards observed: "It seems to me as if he stands as a constant sentinel over the nation's capital. The president's grave is like an outpost for observation of the capital city."[25]

20. "His children, if any, do not succeed him."

John and Jackie Kennedy had three children. Caroline Bouvier (b. 1957), John Fitzgerald Jr. "John-John" (1960–1999) and Patrick Bouvier, who died in 1963, the year of his own birth and his father's death. Neither of the children who survived to adulthood revealed any wish to enter politics. However, his brothers, Robert Francis (1925–1968) and Edward Moore (b. 1932) Kennedy put in a lot of effort to regain Camelot. Robert was campaigning for the Democratic presidential nomination in 1968 when an admirer wrote: "Please reconvene the round table. We want Camelot again."[26] However, like his elder brother, he too was cut off in his prime by an assassin's bullet. In 1969 Edward Kennedy's bid for the presidency was undermined by his misconduct at Chappaquiddick, where he left the scene of a fatal accident.

21. "His body is not buried."

There has always been a great mystery surrounding Kennedy's autopsy. None of the physicians thoroughly examined the body. Dr. Mac Perry's tracheotomy destroyed all evidence of an exit wound. The physicians in Parkland Hospital did not even turn the body over, or they would have discovered the smaller hole in the back of the neck. A fragment of Kennedy's skull was found in Elm Street and suspicion about a coverup abounded. Rumor even had it that Kennedy had not died at all, but led a life of mystery, sequestered from the world.[27] Thomas Brown commented: "Despite the patent absurdity of the story about Kennedy, it has had remarkable persistence in popular folklore, perhaps because of its undercurrents of wishful thinking."[28] Those who think that the body buried in Arlington is not Kennedy's argue that the official photographs of the autopsy show no damage to the back of the head.

22. "Nevertheless he has one or more holy sepulchers."

John F. Kennedy has many shrines (a cultural center, airport, library, highway, and a space launching site). President Johnson renamed Cape Canaveral for the fallen president, although the original name was restored by the local authorities in 1973. One month after the assassination *Time* published an article on this phenomenon entitled "Land of Kennedy: Renaming of Plazas, Bridges, Parks, etc."[29] The Kennedy half dollar coin has been issued since 1964 with Kennedy on the obverse and the Liberty Bell on the reverse. At John F. Kennedy's gravesite in Arlington National Cemetery an eternal flame was lit.

Kennedy scores fifteen points on Raglan's list of twenty-two, all of which he shares with King Arthur. In our survey of blues and gospel lyrics about the president and his politics we shall see that the mass of African Americans certainly perceived JFK as a hero.

Although the comparison between the President Kennedy of our own times and the legendary King Arthur might at first sight seem rather far-fetched, there are in fact many similarities which support the view of Kennedy intimates that he was indeed a modern King Arthur. At the President's inauguration the American poet Robert Frost recited his composition "The Gift Outright," one passage of which in particular characterizes the promise of the new administration:

> It makes the prophet in us all presage
> The glory of a next Augustan age
> Of a power leading from its strength and pride,
> Of young ambition eager to be tried,
> Firm in our free beliefs without dismay,
> In any game the nations want to play.
> A golden age of poetry and power
> Of which this noonday's the beginning hour.[30]

Like King Arthur, Kennedy became a cult hero. He was killed before disillusionment had set in, for as Joseph Campbell wrote in his classic *The Hero with a Thousand Faces*: "The hero of yesterday becomes the tyrant of tomorrow, unless he crucifies himself today."[31]

Perhaps Camelot never existed, but Kennedy's reign held a promise. He had style, heroic style. Historian William Chafe came to the following conclusion:

> *It is still difficult to place the Kennedy presidency in perspective. There was something larger than life about the man, his presidency, his death, and his impact on the American people. Part of this he created himself through his extraordinary style and image. With as much artifice as conviction, the Kennedys helped to generate the myth of Camelot—the beautiful and stylish wife, the active and attractive leader, the high culture, the court entourage of brilliant and dedicated servants—a time that belonged, by design, with the legends of chivalric courts.*[32]

His ideas were a source of inspiration. Kennedy became the mirror we project our own ideas in. The forces of evil can be conquered, or in the words of Victorian poet Alfred, Lord Tennyson, who painted Camelot best in his *Idylls of the King*:

> *For, an ye heard a music, like enow*
> *They are building still, seeing the city is built,*
> *To music, therefore never built at all,*
> *And therefore built forever.*[33]

2

JFK SAYS I'VE GOT TO GO

As the 1960 Democratic convention approached, Kennedy's campaign for the nomination had failed to gather much support among African Americans. A poll of some two hundred prominent Democrat supporters selected by *Jet* magazine showed that he was running a poor third to his main rivals, Adlai Stevenson and Hubert Humphrey. It was felt that Kennedy's poor voting record on civil rights issues[1] and his apparent reluctance to make overtures to prominent activists, even the distinguished African-American labor leader A. Philip Randolph, were weakening his candidacy. In the end Kennedy's youth and war record impressed delegates, and his popularity and campaign spending carried the day. Kennedy chose Lyndon Johnson as vice presidential candidate to balance the ticket and secure southern votes.

A recent interview with the entertainer and activist Harry Belafonte has pinpointed one of the decisive moments in the 1960 campaign. When the Republicans succeeded in enlisting the support of the celebrated sportsman Jackie Robinson, Belafonte was asked whether he would publicly endorse the Democrats. Demanding to know what Kennedy had ever done for blacks, he refused, although Belafonte did suggest that it might be advisable for the candidate to contact Rev. Martin Luther King Jr.

"A Leader Like Roosevelt," *Chicago Defender*, 1 October 1960.

Subsequently, when King received a prison sentence for a minor traffic violation, Belafonte urged both Kennedy and Nixon to intervene. It was at this point that Kennedy made his celebrated telephone call to Mrs. King, offering moral support to the family of the civil rights leader, a deed that made a profound impression on the African-American community, especially when contrasted with Nixon's silence.[2]

The November 1960 edition of *Ebony* magazine carried an article by journalist Carl Rowan, pointing out the growing importance of African-American voters. In 1948 their preference for the Democratic Party had been a major factor in Harry Truman's unexpected defeat of Thomas E. Dewey, but by 1960 a million more were enjoying the use of the franchise. Most of the new voters had left the Deep South for the cities of the North and the West Coast. In Chicago alone the number of Negro potential voters had grown from 265,000 to 460,000 between 1950 and 1960. "I'd be a fool not to consider the Negro vote crucial," Kennedy commented.[3]

The three major networks, CBS, NBC, and ABC, broadcast a series of four televised debates between the two Presidential candidates on 26 September and 7, 13, and 21 October. A national audience of over 100 million was expected. Confident that his well-honed debating skills would expose the immaturity and inexperience of his opponent, Nixon embraced the opportunity. It was an unfortunate decision. In contrast to the youthful vigor of Kennedy, Nixon came across as shifty, looked haggard and perspired freely. Gallup Polls indicated that Kennedy had made a much more favorable impression, particularly with key ethnic minorities and women. Interestingly, Nixon did better among those who had heard the debates on radio.

Immediately after the first debate, the *Chicago Defender* carried out a series of random interviews with local African Americans. One of the interviewees was Morgan Lloyd, a policeman from 727 E. 60th Street: "I like it very much. I think that Nixon seemed tired and lifeless, which gave Kennedy the edge in the first debating session. I think that this will bring people a little closer to the candidate and perhaps swing votes in every direction. Most of the issues taken up by the candidates interested me a great deal."[4]

The Democratic Party advertised heavily in the October issues of the *Chicago Defender.* "Vote Kennedy-Johnson on the Democratic Ticket," the 1 October issue read, quoting Eleanor Roosevelt as saying: "Senator Kennedy will fight to get prompt action on civil rights."[5] In the following week's edition, Kennedy was again placed firmly in the Roosevelt tradition. "His voting record proves his concern for human prob-lems. And the Democratic platform to which he is pledged has the strongest civil rights plank in history."[6] In a special four-page advertisement the main issues were summed up: jobs, education, security, housing, voting, and citizenship. Kennedy was called a "Champion of Human Rights" and it claimed that "Like Roosevelt Kennedy Cares." "After eight years of aloof, do-little Republicanism in the White House it is time again to move democracy forward." The whole section was decked out by photos of the senator with important African-American clergymen, politicians, journalists, and the "champion of entertainers" Nat King Cole. In the final week of October the front

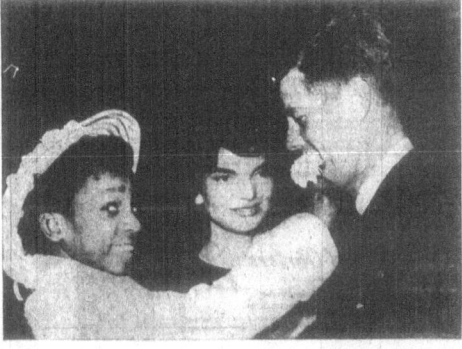

"The Hope of Tomorrow and Today," *Chicago Defender*, 8 October 1960.

"A Leader Like Roosevelt," *Chicago Defender*, 29 October 1960.

page editorial was headlined: "Kennedy Is Our Choice." The paper was satisfied about Kennedy's record on all the main issues outlined above, but none was as important as the "burning issue of Civil Rights."[7] A few pages further there was another large ad about the candidate who "Is Not Afraid to Speak Out." Kennedy and Nixon's voting records were compared: Kennedy was for higher minimum wages, low-rent housing, slum clearance, more social security, a nationwide FEPC (Fair Employment Practices Committee), and on all these issues Nixon had voted against reform.[8]

The final weekly issue of the *Chicago Defender* before the election carried the advertisement: "Mahalia Jackson Believes in Kennedy: Senator Kennedy's the one ... who can put a little more sun and a little more hope in people's lives. The Democrats always try to help people get along by giving them a fair chance to earn their bread and have a home for their children and some hope for the future. I'm going to vote for Senator John Kennedy because he'll be a good president for you and for Mahalia Jackson. You vote for him, too."[9] The Democratic National Committee placed an eight-page advertisement in the same edition, quoting Senator Lyndon B. Johnson's vow that the next administration would make "more progress in the field of civil rights in 4 years than we made in the last 104." Kennedy promised to provide "Leadership for the Sixties"; readers were reminded of his heroic conduct in war. A series of photographs depicted his wife and daughter, President and Mrs. Roosevelt, Harry Belafonte, and African-American politicians Adam Clayton Powell and Rep. William L. Dawson. The candidate's positions on human rights and race relation were set out in detail once again.

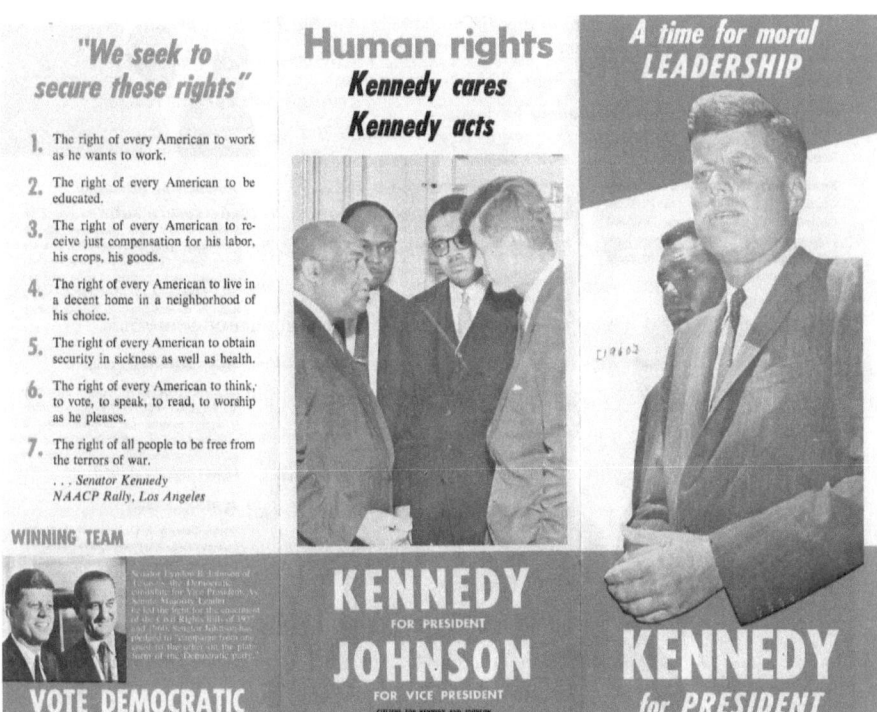

"A Time for Moral Leadership," 1960.

The presidential election took place on 8 November, with Kennedy receiving 49.72 percent of the popular vote as against 49.55 percent for his opponent Richard Nixon. It was subsequently calculated that over 70 percent of the African-American vote went to Kennedy.[10]

On his 1961 LP "In Living Black + White," comedian Dick Gregory (b. 1932) commented on the elections. Gregory pokes fun at the voter tests that segregationists demanded from African Americans, the conduct of the elections on Chicago's South Side, and the new president's religion. The shows were recorded at the Playboy Club in Chicago and presented Gregory to a racially mixed audience after years of experience in the smaller black clubs. As Mel Watkins explained in his study of African-American comedy, Gregory became the first black comedy superstar since Bert Williams and Stepin Fetchit by discarding the clownish appearance, dialect speech, and inside jokes that whites associated with black humor.[11]

I like to see a lot of nice things happen. Not too long ago they put my president in office, Mr. Kennedy, and I wanted to see a change in the White House. We had a Baptist in and Truman gave us eight years of piano playing. Ike gave us eight years of golf. I want four years of bingo![12]

You see, back in my home town they make us take a test to vote: nuclear physics in Russian. And if you pass the test, they tell you: "Boy, you can't vote. To read in Russian you must be Communist."

We won that election for Kennedy right out there on South Side. I hear how they're voting six and seven times. And we don't mean to cheat, or nothing like that. We try to make up for them times we couldn't vote. You read it in the paper, didn't you? Neighborhood out there on Cottage Grove? Eighty-seven people registered, a hundred and two voted and two live in the neighborhood. Yeah, we people, we did all right out there. We won this whole state for 'em. But Republicans doing the same thing, but they don't use us, . . . Chinese!

It didn't make me no difference who won. I'm really for Abraham Lincoln myself. If it hadn't been for Abe I probably still would have been on open market today.

Ah, I have to say I was worried after the elections. I told my wife, I said: "Honey we don't have to worry about nothing. On the 19th of December when the Electoral College vote, we'll know who's in. On 19th of December I was so nervous and excited I flew out to Washington, DC, and walked up to the White House. The guard say: "Hey, hey, fellow, where you're going?" I said: "I wanna see the Electoral College vote so I know who's the next president." He said: "You can't watch them vote, they vote in secret. You have to read the newspapers." I said: "I wanna know now!" He said: "You can't." I tricked him. I found out who was. I laid on the White House lawn, watched the smoke come out the stack. And you, Southern Baptists, just suffer on that one. I can hear Kennedy praying now: "Hail, Mary, full of grace, at last the Protestants in second place." And we are, we are![13]

President Kennedy was not a music lover himself, although he liked poetry very much. As August Heckscher, his special consultant on the arts, observed: "So it was a shading, really, from music, which I think he found painful, into poetry, which for various reasons he found both challenging and quite fascinating."[14] However, for publicity reasons the president liked to surround himself with the stars of the entertainment world, and these included many African-American artists. Mahalia Jackson, Billy Eckstine, and Nat King Cole campaigned for him during the hotly contested 1960 presidential race. There were five inauguration balls on 20 January 1961. Count Basie (1904–1984), whose wife Kate had been very active in the Kennedy campaign, played the one in the Armory district.[15] Ella Fitzgerald (1917–1996) flew in from Australia for the inaugural and Sidney Poitier dropped his acting chores in the movie *Paris Blues* for the occasion. Other artists who performed at the inaugural were Nat King Cole (1919–1965) and Harry Belafonte (b. 1927).

After eight years of Eisenhower, blues singer Memphis Slim (= Peter Chatman, 1915–1988) was relieved to see that the Democrats were finally back in power again. His "The Big Race" from November 1960 employs the well-known animal symbolism of the Republican elephant and the Democratic donkey. Slim declares that he had always voted Democrat in the past, and that on this occasion Kennedy's intervention in the field of civil rights was the decisive factor.

Well, we finally won the big race,
Where the elephant, for eight years, has been taking the pace.
So we finally won the big race!

You know, up stepped a donkey, whom I've always betted on,
To take over the victory, and bring everything back home.

But you know, we had a good jockey, a jockey who was willing to
fight,
And take the inside track, and come on out front with that civil rights.

Yes, we've been running a long, long time,
But oh, happy days, man, you know, when we can go to any track,
And sit in any grandstand and be served,
And be accepted cheerfully, which we so rightly deserve!

Tell 'em a little about it, fellows!

> *So right now, I think I'll take a big pause,*
> *A pause that refreshes, and enjoy a great victory, that I think is good for the cause.*
>
> *Yes, we won the big race!*
>
> *But, you know one of these days,*
> *There'll be no big race,*
> *And we can walk the streets in pride.*
> *Even the elephant and the donkey will walk side by side.*
>
> *Yes, let's go home.*[16]

As the president-elect prepared to take office on 20 January 1961, a new crisis in foreign affairs began to take shape. After the Korean War ended there had been signs of a rapprochement between the United States and the Soviet Union. In May 1960, however, a U-2 reconnaissance airplane was brought down near Sverdlovsk in the Soviet Union and its pilot, Gary Powers, captured. The Soviet premier, Nikita Khrushchev, could not resist the opportunity to make capital of the Americans' embarrassment. President Eisenhower refused to apologize for the incident. A highly anticipated Cold War summit was cancelled and Powers was jailed.

The newly elected President Kennedy was very much impressed by Captain Richard Bissell, who had designed the U-2. To counteract growing Soviet influence in Africa and Asia, Kennedy, like his predecessor, followed the advice of those who advocated the use of infiltration, guerrilla warfare and the encouragement of nationalist factions.[17] Bissell had managed to convince Kennedy of the necessity of a counterrevolution in Cuba, where the communist leader Fidel Castro had constituted an embarrassment in the American sphere of influence since the Cuban Revolution of 1959. The Bay of Pigs invasion on 17 April 1961, when a CIA-supported counterrevolutionary Cuban exile force stormed the beaches of Cuba, failed miserably. In his 1981 analysis of what he called *The Kennedy Imprisonment*, Garry Wills wrote the following succinct criticism of the fiasco:

> *The distinctive note of the Bay of Pigs invasion was that it was a military operation run without the military's control, an invasion force created specially by the CIA itself, a combination of every weapon in*

Bissell's private arsenal—assassination of a leader, propaganda war, guerrilla uprising, and coup from outside. Its success depended on a coordination of all these things in the mind of the master train-scheduler. Later, the plan would look so crazy that people could not credit its acceptance in the first place. But it made sense to a James Bond fan.[18]

New Orleans blues piano player and former boxer "Champion" Jack Dupree (1909–1992) was one of the relatively few blues artists who regularly commented on political developments in a detailed manner. Dupree's "President Kennedy Blues" from October 1961 is optimistic about the prospects offered by a young and (in Dupree's view) peacemaking president. Dupree hopes for peace between the United States and the Soviet Union resulting in cooperation in the race to the moon. Dupree claimed that he had been a prisoner of war in the Pacific (probably in 1942 and 1943), which makes his perspective all the more understandable.

> Well, when President Kennedy got elected, the news went around the world,
> He is the youngest man, to try to satisfy the world.
>
> He said: "I'm gonna find Khrushchev, I wants to see what he's putting down,
> We gonna try to get together, see can't we settle down."
>
> He sent Mr. Khrushchev a letter, said: "Meet me in Geneva town,
> Then we can get together, talk peace, talk peace, to settle down."
>
> Mr. Khrushchev agreed, but he said: "Have to be in Vienna town,
> Then we can get right on down to business, we'll talk peace for the whole world round."
>
> "Then we won't have no war, we'll talk satellites and hitting the moon,
> And everybody will be happy, and all the boys will go back home."[19]

Shortly after entering the White House in January 1961, Kennedy asked for a report on the situation in Berlin, although it was not until April that former Secretary of State Dean Acheson presented his findings. Pointing out that 1961 would be critical, Acheson recommended that the United States should use all its powers to maintain freedom for the people of West Berlin, the continued presence of western troops and free access to the city from the Federal Republic of Germany. At the Vienna Conference of 3 and 4 June Khrushchev demanded a peace treaty between the United States and the Soviet Union that would permanently ensure a divided Germany in which the whole of Berlin would become part of the German Democratic Republic.

Kennedy was adamant that the United States would not allow the Communists to seize control of Berlin. In a televised speech on 25 July he pledged that he would not yield to Soviet pressure. Khrushchev reacted on 13 August by announcing the building of a wall to prevent the inhabitants of East Berlin from fleeing to the West.[20] It was clear that the worsening situation required a rapid buildup of combat troops in central Europe. Draft calls were tripled and enlistments were extended. Two hundred fifty thousand men in the Reserves and the National Guard were called up, including fifty-four Air Force and Naval air squadrons.[21]

Dick Gregory commented ironically that he was not afraid to be drafted under the new president:

Dick Gregory for President, 1968.

And I feel so sorry for Kennedy. The poor man has really caught hell since he's been in. Everything has happened to him. As a matter of fact he moved in the office behind. Do you realize this is the first president we ever elected in the history of this country that moved into a smaller house?

We have it made, we don't have to worry about no war. Not in the next four years, anyway. We're very lucky. First time in the history of this country during a world tension we have a president in office that's young enough to get drafted himself.[22]

Several blues songs referring to the draft were recorded in the Kennedy era, including one by Wilbert Harrison (1929–1994). "Drafted," his 1961 recording for Bobby Robinson's Fury label, shows affection for

the new President by using the JFK abbreviation. As in many songs like this, the major theme is concern about the loved one to be left behind. The rhythm imitates the marching of soldiers, and bugle calls add to the martial atmosphere. Harrison was a thirty-two-year-old veteran when he recorded the song, having served with the Marines for three years between 1946 and 1948.[23]

> *Hut, two, three, four, (3x)*
>
> *Goodbye, my darling,*
> *I have been drafted,*
> *JFK says I've got to go,*
> *My dear, it hurts me so,*
> *How much you'll never know,*
> *And I really hate to go.*
>
> *Going by train, or by plane,*
> *I got to meet that recruiting sergeant,*
> *On land or on sea,*
> *No matter where I may be,*
> *My darling, please, please, wait for me.*
>
> sp: *Yes, yes, yes, yes! Ah, but you know, yeah! Muster!*
> *Hut, hut, hut, hut, hut, yes, yes, yes!*

Might be in the Army, or the Marines,
I'm drafted and that's no dream,
Might be in the Navy, or the Air Force,
Whichever one, I have got no choice,
I'm in the service now,
I guess I'll make it somehow,
Dear, don't forget our lovers' vow.[24]

The threat of war inspired Texas blues guitarist Sam "Lightnin'" Hopkins (1912–1982) to give voice to his anxieties. In the early 1950s he had devoted a few songs to the Korean War, and in the late 1960s he would focus on Vietnam. Contrary to the lyrics of his "War Is Starting Again," Hopkins had never been overseas to fight, and in 1961 at the age of forty-nine, was in no danger of it. Nevertheless he vividly portrayed the tension of the first year of Kennedy's presidency. As is so often the case in these war-related songs, the blues singer presents himself in the role of the Jody Man, the sexually predatory male who stays at home to look after the women the soldiers had to leave behind.

Oh, you know, this world is in a tangle, now, people, yes, I believe they're fixing to start war again,
Yeah, there's gonna be a mother's heart to worry, yes, there's gonna be a many girl to lose her friend.
Well, I got news this morning, right now they need a million men,
Oh, you know, I've been overseas once, poor Lightning don't wanna go there again.

sp: *Lord, have mercy! All right!*

Yeah, you know my girlfriend got a boyfriend in the army, that fool 'bout to go overseas,
You know, I don't hate it so bad, because, boy, you know there's a better break for me.
Oh, this world is in a tangle, yes, they're bound to have a war again.[25]

After World War II Germany had been split into two nations. Berlin, the old capital, could only be approached by a heavily guarded highway that ran a hundred miles through East German territory. Before the winter of 1961, 300,000 men had been called up, 40,000 of whom were sent to Europe. More than 100,000 tons of equipment were transported to Europe. Louisiana pianist Sonny Martin (1937–1969) sang that he had to go to East Berlin, in the "Air Force–U.S. Navy." Stanzas two and three are quoted here to show how the draft separated the soldier from his loved one.

> Well, Uncle Sam he's taking me from my baby, says he'll use me maybe,
> He wants to see me serve in the Air Force–U.S. Navy.
>
> Well, uh, diddley-oh and diddley-ay, I'll see my baby later,
> For I must go to East Berlin, in the Air Force–U.S. Navy.[26]

The draft led Mississippi blues guitarist "Big" Joe Williams (1903–1982) to revive part of Sonny Boy Williamson's 1940 "War Time Blues."[27] For good measure he also threw in a stanza from his own 1935 "Providence Help the Poor People," New Deal reference and all.[28] Big Joe was almost 58 when he recorded his 1961 "Army Man Blues," but the fear of death and the impossibility of taking care of loved ones that confront a draftee are poignantly evoked.

> Well, I heard a voice this morning, I never did heard before,
> Uncle Sam was calling us, said: "Big Joe, I swear you gotta go,
> To the army man, yeah, you know the United States been raising sand,
> (Yeah)
> Well, when you get twenty-one, boy, you know you're in the government's hands."
>
> I got a handful of nickels, pocketful of dimes,
> House full of children, nary one looks like mine,

> But I'm in the army, yes, I'm in the army, man. Well, I'm in the army, man, in the army, man,
> Well, the Yanks over there raising sand.

sp: Yeah!

> I got a big gun over yonder, hid way out in the woods,
> I got a big gun way in the European country, hid way out in the woods,
> If my gun don't do no good, boy, I swear I would drop a bomb.
>
> Well, now the rooster told the hen: "I want the hens all go lay,"
> Said: "No, but my man is in the army, boy, and I got to go work for the WPA."
> I'm in the army, man, yes, I'm over there raising sand,
> Yeah, when your age gets twenty-one, you're in the government's hands.[29]

When he recorded "Uncle Sam Don't Take My Man" in 1963, Snooky Pryor (1921–2006) adhered more closely to the text of Williamson's "War Time Blues," quoting several lines, but found room to include references to the unpopularity of the draft.

> Yeah, did you hear about the news up north? It was everybody's Santa Claus,
> Well, every time I pick up a paper, I can read something about the war.
>
> I can just hear women screaming and crying: "Uncle Sam, please, don't take my man,"
> Yes, the men ain't qualified for the army and the Man don't understand.
>
> Well, just look at them big guns yonder, them big guns hid out in the woods,
> (Look over yonder!)
>
> Yes, I believe I'll drop a bomb, 'cause a space ship won't do no good.

sp: Play it now! Oh, but just looka there![30]

The first line is rather enigmatic as Europe is not "up north" for a Chicago based bluesman. Perhaps Sonny Boy Williamson, whose phrase it is, had spoken from the point of view of his perceived audience which was mainly "down south." "It was everybody's Santa Claus" is probably an ironic way to say that everybody gets the same (terrible) present at the outbreak of war. Pryor criticizes "the Man" (who may be the president) for failing to understand that draftees are "not qualified for the army." Pryor was in the army in the South Pacific for three and a half years during World War II. In a 1993 interview with Norman Darwen he claimed to have composed the song himself while a soldier on duty.[31]

Snooky Pryor, Casimir Lyceum, Amstelveen, the Netherlands, 1 December 1973. Photo: Hans ten Have.

It is, however, an adaptation of the 1940 Sonny Boy Williamson original in which Williamson's "machine gun" is replaced by a topical "space ship."

If the lyrics of "I Thought the War Was Over" are to be believed, 1961 found the Texan pianist Teddy Reynolds (1931–1998) engaged in the same war plant work that he carried out in the 1940s. Such jobs had been highly prized back then, as they offered stable and relatively high wages and security of employment. However, although Reynolds is clearly determined to make the most of the situation while it lasts, he is quick to disassociate himself from its cause. "Mr. K" must be a reference to the president, although Reynolds may be economically referring to Khrushchev as well.

I thought the war was over, Mr. K. said: "That don't mean a thing,"
Well, this world is all mixed up, and you know I'm not to blame.

> Well, I'm working hard, baby; you gotta treat me like a king,
> Well, I'm back on my old war plant, y'all, and I'm doing the same old thing.
>
> Well, you can come back home, baby, if you promise to be good,
> 'Cause the last war, I gave you everything I could.[32]

Louisiana harp blower Jimmie Anderson (b. 1934) sings about receiving a draft letter from his local board in "Draft Board Blues." A local board consists of five citizen volunteers whose role, upon the announcement of a draft, is to decide which registrants in their community will receive deferments, postponements, or exemption from military service, based on the individual registrant's circumstances and beliefs.[33] Inevitably poor blacks had fewer grounds for deferment than most.

> I got a letter this morning, from Local Board 98,
> They said they wanted to see me and I'd better not be late,
> They say I'll take a trip, and, baby, all around the world,
> I know I'm not gonna like it, 'cause I miss you, little girl.
>
> ch: I got the draft board blues, yes, the draft board blues,
> I got the draft board blues, the blues I just can't lose.
>
> They said I can take my choice, the land, sea, or the air,
> But I know I'm gonna be lonely, 'cause, baby, you won't be there,
> But, baby, someday if I'm lucky, I'll be back, little girl,
> I'll keep thinking of you, baby, on my trip across the world.[34]

Blues guitarist Ellas Bates (b. 1928), also known as Ellas McDaniel, but better known as Bo Diddley, recorded "Mr. Khrushchev" in January 1962. In an interview with George R. White the artist remembered the circumstances:

> Durin' the time I wrote "Mr. Khrushchev," everybody in America was arguin' 'bout which schools black kids could go to, talkin' 'bout "black this" an' "black that"—but, when bullets an' bombs start fallin', they don't jump up an' say: "Oh, that's a white man, we ain't gonna blow 'him' up. We'll go an'

get all the 'niggers!'" Everybody's ass go! That's why I wrote the line: "We're fightin' over a six-wheel bus/That bald-head Khrushchev's plottin' on us." I was tryin'—in so many words–to tell people that we'd better start lookin' after one another. I was serious when I wrote that sucker—serious as a heart attack—an' I'm still serious about it, but I wouldn't dare play that song now. It's a little—uh—political, an' I got enough problems![35]

Why the issue was more problematic in the eighties when the interview took place than in the sixties remains a mystery. African-American activists often felt that JFK should take care of civil rights at home before embarking on foreign adventures "to save the world." Bo Diddley's song was recorded about eight months after the first wave of Freedom Rides. He thinks the country should unite in the face of Communist expansion.

Bo Diddley was strongly motivated to join the armed forces for a good cause, but in World War II he had been too young and he was never called up later.[36] After some standard chest beating there is a call for citizens to unite, which then leads to the bus reference. Bo Diddley concludes by observing that the army is no place for weaklings.

sp: Hup, two, three, four, etc.

I think I wanna go to the army,
I think I want to go overseas.
I wanna see Khrushchev,
I wanna see him all by myself.

ch: Hey, Khrushchev! (4x)

He don't believe that water's wet,
If he did he'd been a-stopped those jets.
JFK can't do it by his-self,
Come on, fellows, let's give him a little help.

We, as Americans, understand,
We gotta unite and protect our land.
We gotta keep on alert,
To keep our families from getting hurt.

> We're fighting over a six-wheel bus,
> Now, bald-headed Khrushchev's plotting on us.

sp: Hup, two, three, four, etc.

sp: Oh. Yeah.
> Oh, get in line now.
> Fix your collar there, boy.
> Oh, have mercy.
> Looka here!
> Shut up there and walk right.
> I want my mama!
> Your mama can't help you now!
> This is Sergeant Diddley's Army.
> There ain't no place like home!
> Oh, have mercy.
> I want you to recognize these stripes on my shoulder.[37]

Blues singer Luke "Long Gone" Miles (1925–1987) served in the U.S. Navy from 1943 to 1944. When he sang his "War Time Blues" in 1962 he was thirty-six years old, afraid of death, and hoping that he was too old to be drafted again. Here, as in many wartime blues songs, Sonny Boy Williamson's famous line about planes that climb like squirrels from his 1944 "Check Up on My Baby" is used.[38] The image had evidently stuck in the collective memory. Here it prefaces an allusive reference to satellites and/or intercontinental ballistic missiles.

> Well, you know the war is raging, it's raging more and more every day,
> And that's why I'm glad I'm growing older, so I can try to stay away.
>
> That's why I don't want no army, oh man, I don't wanna go,
> Well, when I get my examination card, I want the doctor tell me I'm too doggone old.
>
> Well, you know they got the planes, they got 'em climbing like squirrels,
> And the fellow they call Khrushchev, got them out of this world.

> *That's why I don't want no army, oh man, I don't wanna go,*
> *Well, when I get my examination card, Willie,[39] oh man,*
> > *I want 'em to tell me I'm too doggone old.*
>
> sp: *Go ahead, play it, Brown,[40] for me, boy, you know how I feel now.*
> *Back me up! That's what I'm talking about. Play that guitar, Willie.*
>
> *You know, I wouldn't mind going to the army, but they like to shoot and kill,*
> *And when I'm dead and gone, some woman be drawing my will.*
>
> *That's why I don't want no army, oh man, I don't wanna go,*
> *Well, when I get my examination card, boy, I want the doctor tell me I'm too doggone old.[41]*

In 1962 harp blower Billy Boy Arnold (b. 1935) also recorded a version of a war-related song from Sonny Boy Williamson.[42] At the time the song remained unissued. Both in Arnold's "We All Got to Go" and in the original recording of Williamson's "I Have Got to Go" Blind John Davis provided the piano accompaniment. The song painted a picture of an inexperienced lad who is impressed by his "in style" uniform and his "high class" superiors who behave as if they are kings. At the same time the African-American soldier's aspirations of flying a bomber plane are unrealistic.

> *Now, I want you to gather around, boys, we all got to go,*
> *Now, you know ain't no use in you worrying, you won't see your baby no more.*
>
> *Now, you got to wear a uniform, man, you got to be in style,*
> *(Now, you got to wear Uncle Sam's uniform, so you can be in style,)*
> *Now, you got to walk straight and carry a rifle, Uncle Sam wanna use you a while.*
>
> *Well, now, here come a man, a man with a crown, high class:*
> *"Well, now, you got to walk straight down, my boy, pick up your feet and don't let 'em drag."*

Ain't no use in you smiling at me, man, it ain't no use in you shaking my hand,
Now, I ain't gonna walk with you this time, I got to fly one of them bomber planes.[43]

Blues artist J. D. Short (1902–1962) was a disabled World War II veteran. While training with the 92nd Division in March 1943 (when he was forty!) he was injured on an obstacle course and discharged. The injury never healed completely and two toes had to be amputated.[44] Although he apparently had no experience on the battlefield himself, his song "Fighting for Dear Old Uncle Sam" is a harrowing account of the horrors of war. The song was recorded in July 1962, and although it is not clear from the lyrics if the threat of war during Kennedy's presidency had occasioned this song about World War II, it remains a possibility.

Tell me war is all over, yes, gonna be war right here,
Well, on account of so many women now, toting away the soldiers' monthly pay.

I may go down in South Pacific, going down in a European land,
Wheresomever I go down swinging, boys, I'm going down fighting for dear old Uncle Sam.

So dark was the night now, people, cold, cold was the ground,
Me and my buddies in some old foxhole, we had to keep our heads all down.

Well, machine guns and cannon roaring, boys, we was afraid to raise our heads,
You know if bayonets cost a many dollars, boy, now you know we'd have all been dead.

Yes, the first of the month now, salute the lieutenant and get our pay,
There's a little piece of paper laying on the side, sign it, send your wife home allotment pay.

Some say they'll be so glad, when the boys all come back home again,
You'll get so many soldiers on the place, the soldiers ain't gonna be your friend.

> *Honey, the war is all over, ain't nothing but a little shout,*
> *'Cause the war is all over, you just don't know what it's all about.*[45]

In July 1961 Ray Charles (1930–2004) recorded Percy Mayfield's composition "The Danger Zone," which was issued as the flipside of his number one hit "Hit the Road, Jack." Fear of total destruction through technology permeates this worried blues.

> *Sad and lonely all the time,*
> *That's because I've got a worried mind.*
>
> ch: *You know the world is in an uproar,*
> *The danger zone is everywhere, everywhere.*
>
> *Just read your paper, and you'll see,*
> *Just exactly what keeps worrying me.*
> *My love for the world is like always,*
> *For the world is a part of me.*
> *That's why I'm so afraid,*
> *Of the progress that's being made,*
> *Toward eternity,*
> *Every morning, noon, and night,*
> *Finds me hoping that everything's alright.*[46]

On 11 January 1962 Kennedy delivered his second State of the Union address to Congress. The threat of war and the resultant buildup of forces and armaments received special attention:

> We intend to have at all times the capacity to resist non-nuclear or limited attacks—as a complement to our nuclear capacity, not as a substitute. We have rejected any all-or-nothing posture which would leave no choice but inglorious retreat or unlimited retaliation.
>
> Thus we have doubled the number of ready combat divisions in the Army's strategic reserve—increased our troops in Europe—built up the Marines—added new sealift and airlift capacity—modernized our weapons and ammunition—expanded our anti-guerrilla forces—and increased the active fleet by more than 70 vessels and our tactical air forces by nearly a dozen wings.
>
> Because we needed to reach this higher long-term level of readiness more quickly, 155,000 members of the Reserve and National Guard were activated under the Act of this Congress.[47]

To blues singers the White House was a remote and far-off place, the stuff of fantasies. Taking as his point of departure Big Bill Broonzy's influential "Just a Dream,"[48] blues guitarist "Sleepy" John Estes (1899–1977), the only artist in this study who was born in the nineteenth century, recorded "It Was a Dream" on 19 April 1962. The song belongs to a group of blues songs from the late 1930s onward in which the singer is asked to come to the White House to help the president out or to become president himself. Of course, at the end of such songs this turns out to be either a dream or decidedly wishful thinking. When Broonzy found himself sitting in the president's chair, he was greeted by name and made to feel welcome. No such reception awaited Estes. In his afterthought, fear of total annihilation by an atomic explosion is expressed. The blind musician here employs some gallows humor for maximum effect.

> You know, I went to the White House, I sat down in President Kennedy's chair,
> He looked around, asked me how come I'm here.
>
> ch: It was a dream, it was a dream,
> You know, that was a dream, dream I had on my mind.

*Now, he throwed me out, I slipped back and got up on the chair,
I could hear him addressing Congress, what it's gonna be next year.*

*You know, I dreamed last night, I was a millionaire,
I got up and wrote a check, it wouldn't cash nowhere.*

*You know, United States got a bomb, bomb and burn us out in a week,
It go in the ground, 'bout eight foot deep,
You know it cook up eyes, you know what it'd do for me.*[49]

Khrushchev did not have a high opinion of the young president of the United States after the failure of the Bay of Pigs operation. Despite his much publicized intervention, Kennedy had also been unable to prevent the building of the Berlin Wall in 1961, another factor that surely must have influenced Khrushchev. As a result the Soviet Union felt safe in installing intermediate range ballistic missiles in Cuba. CIA aerial photographs led to the discovery of this buildup, and on 22 October 1962 Kennedy ordered a blockade to prevent further supplies reaching Cuba. In response, Khrushchev threatened to launch atomic missiles after a U.S. invasion. For a week the world held its breath.

At this moment Kennedy proved his leadership; in a complicated balance of interests, he took sensible measures and was so determined that the Soviet leader yielded to American pressure and removed its missiles from the island. In a secret communication Kennedy promised to remove Jupiter rockets from Turkey after four or five months.[50] The Soviet prime minister was now impressed by Kennedy's leadership, and the 5 August 1963 Limited Test Ban Treaty, banning atomic tests in the atmosphere, was a direct result of the favorable outcome of this confrontation. Khrushchev's long and emotional telegram to President Johnson immediately after Kennedy's assassination provided ample evidence of the respect that the latter had gained in the Kremlin by his handling of the Cuban crisis.

"Red's Dream" from 1962, during the Cuban crisis, was recorded by Louisiana Red, the best known of the many soubriquets used by blues guitarist Iverson Minter (b. 1936). It is yet another (albeit highly original) version of Big Bill Broonzy's "Just a Dream." In an epic confrontation on the floor of the U.N. General Assembly, Red publicly humiliates Castro and Khrushchev. Although the language used is not that of international diplomacy but rather that of the street corner, Red's braggadocio clearly supports Kennedy's tough stance. Red threatens to give Castro "a Georgia shave," which means he will cut his throat. Red is invited to Washington and uses the opportunity to press for political concessions. While the president is running the country, Red will "run the Senate," which perhaps implies that he is in the position of vice president. The idea of five top blues singers[51] sitting in the Senate is humorous but also reflects the campaign for wider recognition of black political aspirations: there had been no black senator since Reconstruction.

> ch: It was a dream, dream I had last night,
> I dreamed I went to the U.N., and set the whole nation right.
>
> I dreamed I called on old Castro, stood him on the floor,
> Looked him right in the eye, and said: "Boy, you got to go,
> I'm tired of your foolishness, and if you don't behave,
> I'm gonna grab you by your beard, give you a Georgia shave."
>
> Then I told old Khrushchev, sitting there looking bad:
> "Get that junk out of Cuba, before you make me mad,
> Dig up them missile bases, take them planes and all,
> Or I'll grab me a bat, use your head for the ball."
>
> Then into Washington they called me, and I went,
> There to be the guest, of the president,
> He said: "Red, I'm glad to see you, so glad you come down here,
> To help me run the Russians, from the western hemisphere."
> I said: "You can run the country, I'm gonna run the Senate,
> Gonna make a few changes, put a few soul brothers in it:
> Ray Charles and Lightning Hopkins, and a guy like Jimmy Reed,
> Bo Diddley and Big Maybelle, be all I need."[52]

Castro and his beard became a favorite subject for comedians, but Slappy White (1921–1995) explained why he could not follow suit:

> *Now, I could stand up here and say a lot of sarcastic remarks about Castro and his beard, but I couldn't do it. I wouldn't do it. A white*

comedian could do it, but not me. If I said something sarcastic about Castro and his beard I'd get a feeling Abraham Lincoln looking down, saying: "After all I've done for you!"[53]

Eddie (Big Blues) Carson (1923–1990) worked as a mechanic in Toledo, Ohio, by day and as a blues singer and emcee by night. In 1962 he recorded a blues-accompanied monologue, probably written in response to the Cuban Missile Crisis. It was issued on three different pressings, with a different title each time: "The Devastating Bombs" or "The Bloody Bloody Bombs" or "The Bombs of Destruction." Fear of total annihilation pervades Carson's recitation. The artist calls himself a "war orphan," which may imply that he lost his father in World War II.

> *You know, there is trouble all around the world today, and not a pretty, pretty sight to see,*
> *And rumors, rumors of wars, just to destroy humanity.*
>
> *That's why I'm writing you this letter in words, in words of a song,*
> *I wanna tell the world, the whole world of today: it won't be long.*
>
> *Now you know those bloody, those bloody, bloody bombs, that hangs high, high over our heads,*
> *They may someday, someday destroy the world, and make our own, our own death beds.*
>
> *Now you can hide, you can hide in your bomb shelters, and if you do, and if you do survive,*
> *You can see the world, the whole world of today, destroyed before your very eyes.*
>
> *Now, you know, I was a war orphan, and it hasn't been, hasn't been too long ago,*
> *But I've seen, I've seen what bombs can do, to this country, this country that I love so.*
>
> *Now, we've had, we've had too many wars, and there's many, many more to come,*
> *So stop, think a minute, won't you? The next might, just might be the one.*[54]

The Eisenhower administration had trapped itself and its successors into a commitment to Indochina. In 1961 the perceived threat of worldwide communist expansion accelerated American involvement in Vietnam. Kennedy was unprepared, as he had apparently not been fully briefed on recent developments by his predecessor.[55] At length, in November, he decided to send reinforcements, and by the end of the year there were over 3,000 American troops in Vietnam. Throughout the remainder of his period in office, overriding the objections of some of his most highly placed advisers, Kennedy continued to commit greater numbers of men and munitions to this theater of operations, although they never reached the levels requested by his generals.[56] By the end of Kennedy's thousand days there were 16,000 men in Vietnam.[57] His brother Robert, the attorney general, questioned America's continuing presence, but the President waded deeper and deeper into the war. On 1 November 1963, three weeks before Kennedy's assassination, the president of South Vietnam Ngo Dinh Diem was murdered by Vietnamese generals with American support, an act that would accelerate the rate of American involvement in the war.[58] During the Johnson and Nixon administrations dozens of blues and gospel songs on Vietnam were to be recorded. No such songs were recorded in the JFK years.

After his death the question of what Kennedy would have done about Vietnam had he lived became a contentious issue, to which, of course, no definitive answer is possible. The war in Vietnam is usually identified with the presidency of Lyndon B. Johnson, and Kennedy's role in increasing U.S. involvement is often forgotten, as a 1983 *Newsweek* poll showed.[59] However, even Kennedy's special assistant Arthur M. Schlesinger wrote: "No doubt he realized that Vietnam was his great failure in foreign policy, and that he had never really given it his full attention. But the fact that the Vietnamese seemed ready to fight had made him feel that there was a reasonable chance of making a go of it."[60]

Blues singers generally hail the young Democratic president enthusiastically. They hope for a better future in spite of the fear of atomic annihilation. The singers who comment on the draft had often served themselves, but for the first time these songs express fear and a general unwillingness to risk life in yet another war. This is in contrast to patriotic songs about participation in two World Wars and one in Korea.

There may even be some criticism of President Kennedy, who does not understand that the soldiers are not ready (Snooky Pryor) and who is unable to prevent yet another war (Teddy Reynolds). In this respect these songs may foreshadow the massive resistance to the war in Vietnam that was to become so evident under Kennedy's successor Lyndon Johnson. The many blues about Vietnam from the Johnson presidency sometimes reflect the unease about the war that would lead to perhaps the greatest failure in American foreign policy.

3

TWISTIN' OUT IN SPACE

In his campaign speeches John F. Kennedy criticized Eisenhower's leadership as ineffective and emphasized the need for change. Commentators noted, however, that the Democratic candidate was no radical and that many of his ideas were interchangeable with those of his rival, Richard Nixon. What set Kennedy apart from other politicians was his unaffected charm, his ability to project a favorable image in person and through the media. It helped, of course, that he was much younger than most heads of government and that he had a style- and fashion-conscious wife and a young family.

As the new president and his team settled down to formulate new policies, reporters sought to satisfy the curiosity of the public. The change of administration coincided with a revival of an old dance called the Twist. In November 1959 Hank Ballard (1927–2003) and the Midnighters had recorded the seminal version of "The Twist." At the time it was the latest in a long line of songs that promoted new dances, ones that were easy to do and had universal appeal. The Twist consisted of a few basic steps and movements, notably a suggestive gyrating of the hips. The success of the original recording, which entered the *Billboard* pop charts on 24 July 1960 and reached #28, was eclipsed by a later version by Chubby Checker, whose appearance on the television show *American Bandstand* on 6 August 1960 introduced the dance to a mainstream audience. Checker explained that the Twist was performed like putting out a cigarette with both feet while coming out of the shower and wiping your back with a towel. For a period in the early 1960s the Twist enjoyed enormous popularity.[1]

The White House is both the president's home and office, and along with the business of government many social events take place there. The formal atmosphere was lightened in 1961 when the historic East Room reverberated to the sound of the Twist, as performed by the orchestra of New York dance band conductor Lester Lanin. The President looked on as twenty-six-year-old Andrew Burden, who had the reputation of doing "the best Twist in New York Society," gave an energetic demonstration of how it was done. In order to avoid giving offense to conservatives, the press emphasized that the president had merely been an amused spectator.[2]

However, there were rumors that the First Lady had been dancing the Twist at this black-tie party in the White House. Such a report was still thought in 1961 to be inconsistent with the dignity of the Presidency, and press secretary Pierre Salinger firmly denied it. Later newspaper reports of Jackie Kennedy doing the Twist in Fort Lauderdale were the result of mistaken identity.[3]

This relatively trivial news item came to the attention of pianist-composer Sonny Thompson (1916–1989) and prompted him to write a song for his wife Lula Reed (b. 1927), which they recorded on 7 February 1962. Like the newspaper report, the song, "Do the President Twist," linked the dance craze with the young President in the White House, adding mention of his family, including baby John Fitzgerald Kennedy Jr., who had been born on 25 November 1960 (John and Jackie Kennedy's first child, Caroline Bouvier Kennedy, was born in 1957).

> Come on, baby, let's do the President Twist,
> Come on, baby, let's do the President Twist,
> Everybody's doing it, you go 'round and around like this.
> Come on, baby, let's do the President Twist.
>
> I wanna go to Washington, to see the President Twist,
> The cabinet members, they all insist,

Everybody's doing it, they go 'round and around like this,
Come on, baby, let's do the President Twist.

John, Jackie, and the baby too,
If they can do it, so can you,
It's a whole lot of fun, and a real good show,
'Round and around, then you go, go, go.

Even in society, they do the President Twist,
They move their bodies, and they swing their wrists,
Everybody's doing it, they go 'round and around like this,
Come on, baby, let's do the President Twist.[4]

Now that the first Roman Catholic president had been elected, people wondered if there would ever be a black president in the White House. Comedian Dick Gregory, who was to win 1.5 million votes himself as a candidate for his Peace and Freedom Party in 1968, was already dreaming

Freddy King, Vondelpark, Amsterdam, 15 December 1974.
Photo: René van Rijn.

of a swinging cabinet when he performed for a mainly white audience in San Francisco in July 1961:

> *And you heard what Bobby Kennedy said: "Thirty years from this year a Negro can become president. So treat me right, or I'll get in there and raise taxes on you. Now, if I was president, you talking about good living? Ooh, everybody would be swingers. That's right, first thing I'd do is repeal the Mann Act[5] and anything else that discouraged traveling in this country. I think I'd grab Satchmo[6] and make him a Secretary of State. Dizzy Gillespie[7] would be my vice president and I'd give you a job just so they won't say I'd been prejudiced, you know? That's what I would do my first day in office. My second day I'd take Georgia, North Carolina, Mississippi, Louisiana, Alabama, and make it a H-bomb testing area.[8]*

At about the same time that the Twist was gaining in popularity, rivalry between the United States and Soviet Russia was escalating. In the field of space exploration the Americans clearly lagged behind. Having successfully launched the world's first orbiting satellites and an unmanned moon probe, the Russians were the first to put a man in space when cosmonaut Yuri Gagarin orbited the Earth on 12 April 1961. On 15 May 1961 Navy Commander Alan B. Shepard became the first American in space, to be followed by Air Force Captain Virgil I. Grissom on 21 July 1961, although neither carried out a complete orbit. Not until 20 February 1962 did Lieutenant Colonel John Glenn surpass the Russian achievement by circling the Earth three times in Friendship VII.

Many blues artists (or their producers), even established ones like Muddy Waters[9] and Sleepy John Estes,[10] tried to cash in on the dance craze.[11] Although he was never able to repeat his earlier success, Hank Ballard reworked the Twist on a number of occasions. One variant, "The Float," recorded in 1961, seems particularly contrived.

> *I'm a spaceman sent from the moon,*
> *Shine up a missile and hear me zoom.*
>
> ch: *Let's float, eeh, let's float, let's float, let's float, baby, let's float!*
>
> *Now, lift your arms just like a bird,*
> *And listen for that magic word.*

sp: Hey now!

> Now, watch those planets go whizzing by,
> Float with me, we're going up high.

sp: Come on, baby, come on, baby, come on!

> Hey, Mercury, Mars, and Venus too,
> Floating with me, that's the thing to do.

> Now, my missile is down to Earth,
> I'm floating for all I'm worth.

sp: Come on, baby, let's go.
Come on, baby.

sp: Raise your hands high.
Go on, real high.
That's alright.[12]

New Orleans singer Robert Parker, who was to have a great hit with "Barefootin'" in 1966, began his recording career as an instrumentalist, but by the mid-1960s was riding high on a new wave of popularity as a vocalist, promoting a series of dances that went down well in local venues. In his 1962 recording "Twistin' Out in Space" he ingeniously combined two topical, crowd-pleasing themes. Recognition of Glenn's achievement gives way to a description of the celebrations, which are truly universal. Their rough-and-ready nature suggests that no one will be excluded.

> Way up in orbit they heard a man say:
> John Glenn is heading our way,
> Friendship VII is on track number five,
> I wanna be twisting when John pass by.

ch: They did the twist (way out in space). (4x)

Venus gave a twisting party, way out in space,
She invited Pluto, to twist the night away,
Pluto invited Mars, Mars invited Neptune,
Neptune invited Jupiter and Jupiter invited the Moon.
Way up there they had a jubilee,
The jockey folks[13] they had a jamboree,
They were drinking cider from a old tin cup,
They felt so good they got all shook up.[14]

    For many years blues singer Sam "Lightnin'" Hopkins had lived in Houston, which was also home to NASA's Mission Control Center. It may be that he felt an especially close tie with the astronaut, because on the very day of his mission Hopkins recorded a two-part "Happy Blues for John Glenn," which bears the hallmark of an impromptu improvisation. At his peak Hopkins had a remarkable ability to devise inventive and thought-provoking lyrics, which the greater length of the long-playing album track allowed him to use more fully.

    Blues researcher Mack McCormick, who co-produced the album, recalled the circumstances in his sleeve notes. By a happy coincidence studio time had already been booked to record a session on the very day of Glenn's return to Earth. Hopkins had gone to the recording studio that morning straight from his apartment, where he had been watching the news on his landlady's television. While the band set up their instruments, the blues singer sat in the solitude of his car making cryptic notes on the back of an envelope. Barely three hours after Glenn's successful return he had begun to put together a song to commemorate the event. In the studio those present were taken aback at the bleakness of the lyrics, although the first take was ruined when the amplifier developed a fault. While the necessary repairs were being made, Lightnin' took a few moments to study the latest newspaper reports. By the time the mechanical problem had been sorted out, his mood had lightened, the delay notwithstanding, to such an extent that the second take could be described as a "happy" blues when it was eventually released.[15]

> People all was saying this morning, with this on their mind,
> Said; "Ain't no living man can go 'round the world three times,"
> But John Glenn done it. Yes, he did it.
> He did it, I'm talking about, he only did it for fun.
>
> Half a million dollars made him feel so well,
> He got to eating his lunch and couldn't hardly tell.
> He said: "I feel all right," John Glenn said it,
> Everybody was laughing and they didn't regret it.
>
> It was a many prayer went up, praying that he would land,
> I looked at a schoolhouse full of 'em and they didn't know what to say.
> But they said: "Let him come back, God, please, let him land,
> You know that's the onliest man ever did it, and you is a helping hand."
>
> sp: I'm gonna turn out to be one to pray.
>
> I seed him when he left, but I didn't see him when he land,
> But I knowed he was doing all right, when they said it was OK to give him a great big hand.
> He'll be in on the next ship; they say he's on deck.
> His mother say: "I know my son's gonna make it, 'cause it ain't never been no mistake."
>
> You know, I'm gonna tell you something, this ain't lying:
> You know that man must have on his mind, flying.
> It ain't nobody will take that much time,
> Unless they're gonna build 'em ownself a airplane, and they gonna go flying.
> They told 'em: "Don't worry. This is true:
> You may miss me for a few minutes, but I'll be back to see about you."
>
> He did, yes he did!
> Yes, when he done it, they didn't know where he was at in a helicopter.

Lightnin' Hopkins, 12 November 1977, Rotterdam, the Netherlands. Photo: Rosemieke van Hauwe.

> You know, they tested that boy's body, they even test his heart,
> They knowed he was all right, when he was fixing to start.
> I believe he made it, he went around the world three times,
> You know, he went and got him a airplane, and he made up and then had it on his mind.
>
> sp: That's what he had on his mind.
>
> He didn't have no killing, he didn't have no digging,
> He just had it on his mind: flying.[16]

The song focuses on Glenn's heroism and single-mindedness, without mentioning his predecessors. The references to his pre-mission lunch and medical examination remind us of his humanity. If Hopkins was aware of the technical problems that imperiled Glenn's mission, there is no indication. During the second orbit there were problems with the heat shield. Flames engulfed the spacecraft on its reentry. When the California coastline came in sight the spacecraft went out of control for a while and fuel ran out. After splashing down into the Atlantic Ocean, Glenn endured a nerve-wracking wait until he was located and rescued.[17]

A fortnight after Glenn's successful return Little Willie John (1937–1968) recorded "Mister Glenn," an odd song written for him by songwriter Rudy Toombs (1907–1962), who died a few months after the recording. After a dubbed-on radio or television report about the astronaut being beyond Earth's gravitational pull, Little Willie John asks John Glenn if he can accompany him on his next space trip. Glenn had reported a "real fireball" outside when the capsule's rocket retropack broke off.[18] Little Willie John concluded that he must have seen some gorgeous space women from Venus, the Planet of Love.

> sp: John Glenn reports: "Zero G and I feel fine." He says the view is tremendous.
> Under current conditions John Glenn in the Friendship VII spacecraft is traveling at a velocity of seventeen thousand five hundred forty-five miles an hour and is in orbit.
>
> Tell me, Mr. Glenn, what did you see when you went up there?
> When they shot you in a rocket and zoomed you through the atmosphere?
> Is it true what they say of the stars above?
> Did you see a pretty maiden from the planet of love?
> Please, Mr. Glenn, Mr. Glenn.
>
> What about the things you saw floating all around your ship?
> If they were pretty girls, won't you take me on your missile trip?
> On your very next trip and I hope it's real soon,
> Drop me off at Venus on your way to the moon,
> Please, Mr. Glenn, Mr. Glenn.
>
> They say that the girls really grow about nine feet tall,
> Is that what you saw when you spoke of a fireball?
> You only had to make one trip 'round the world,
> Was the last true trip just to see those pretty girls?
> Mr. Glenn, Mr. Glenn.
>
> Now, Mr. Glenn, Mr. Glenn, on your very next rocket shot,
> Together you can ask and request astronauts,
> As we orbit the Earth in a big space ship,
> I wanna see those visions that made you flip,
> Mr. Glenn, oh please, Mr. Glenn.
>
> sp: Please, Mr. Glenn, I wanna go, Mr. Glenn,
> Mr. Glenn, Mr. Glenn, Mr. Glenn, Mr. Glenn.[19]

The New York–based pianist Johnny Acey (b. 1925) recorded "I Go into Orbit" in 1962. Here the blues singer again employs the topical event for a sexual metaphor. Every time he holds his outer space lover's hand, he goes into orbit.

        I'll be in the heaven, Lord, in an hour's time,
        'Cause when I'm with my baby, you know, I feel so fine.

        I'll go into orbit, every time she holds my hand,
        She's my outer-space lover, you know, I'm her little pilot man.

        Oh, you know, she's a looker, she can spend my gold,
        'Cause she's not just good-looking, my girl is a jelly roll.

sp: Oh, yeah!

        Well, you know that I love her, she's my pride and joy,
        Yes, I call her my little girl, she calls me her little boy.

sp: Walk on out.[20]

Emboldened by the success of the early missions, President Kennedy decided to throw his weight behind a new program, named Apollo, with a more ambitious set of objectives. On 25 May 1961 he appeared before Congress to deliver a special address:

    I believe that this nation should commit itself to achieving the goal,
    before this decade is out, of landing a man on the moon and returning

> him safely to the Earth. No single space project in this period will be more impressive to mankind, or more important for the long-range exploration of space; and none will be so difficult or expensive to accomplish.[21]

The new project was truly a bold undertaking, as it was impossible to predict whether the ultimate target could be met, even with a massive injection of resources, or whether the outcome justified the expenditure. Nonetheless, Congress voted to allocate the necessary funds. When Neil Armstrong walked on the moon on 20 July 1969, President Nixon hailed the episode as "the greatest week in the history of the Creation."[22]

Comedian Slappy White dreamt that he would be the first (black) astronaut to travel to the moon in a rocket. His sardonic humor was later transferred to white audiences. "I don't tell racial jokes to offend anyone," he explained later. "I try to create a little humor so that all people can laugh."[23]

> About three months ago my wife and I was honored at a testimonial for the Good Neighbor of the Year in Hyannisport, Massachusetts. You see, we were the last Freedom Riders. Lord, there is no more Freedom Riders. Every city in the south now has a Negro bus driver. You should see him trying to make a left hand turn with his arm out the back window. I got a call in Hyannisport, and it said: "Slappy White, we want you to come to Florida." I said: "To the Fontainebleau?"[24] They said: "No, Cape Canaveral." They said: "We want you to be the first to take a rocket to the moon." Slappy White the Astronaut! I'd like to be the first astronaut to go to the moon. I can just see the headlines on the papers: "White Astronaut." And I go down to Cape Canaveral, they put the space suit on me, carry me out to the launching pad, have the countdown, the blastoff, and I'd get in my rocket and I'd be flying along. I fly over New York and I'd go: "Hello, New York." Get over Chicago and I go: "Hello, Chicago." Get over Alabama and I go: "Pffff."[25] Yeah, they can't catch me now, boy. And can't no dog jump that high. And straight to the moon with two bags of money. You see, I figured I'd take a lot of money with me to the moon, because I know, if I be the first to land on the moon, right away the price of real estate is going to drop. And I buy the moon, so it'd be my moon. And I'd be walking around on my moon. And I look and see a figure coming to me, it's a colored man. And I walked up to him and I said: "Brother, I'm from the

planet Earth." He said: "You better get back home, 'cause up here Lincoln lost the election."[26]

Although some of the blues lyrics about the Twist and the space race are rather trivial, it is clear that both subjects were a source of escape and excitement in the early 1960s. In spite of the fact that there were no African-American astronauts as yet, space travel was the stuff of dreams for black and white alike. Looking back on the dance craze in 1968 Eldridge Cleaver compared the Twist itself to "a guided missile, launched from the ghetto into the very heart of suburbia. The Twist succeeded, as politics, religion, and law could never do, in writing in the heart and soul what the Supreme Court could only write on the books."[27]

4

THE WELFARE TURNS
ITS BACK ON YOU

In 1959 French record collector and journalist Jacques Demêtre (pseudonym of Dimitri Vicheney) paid a visit to the United States during which he made the acquaintance of many contemporary blues artists, including "St. Louis" Jimmy Oden (1903–1977). Oden, who had enjoyed a lengthy recording career, was known to European enthusiasts as the singer and composer of thoughtful lyrics like those of his most famous recording, "Going Down Slow," from 1941. At the time he was living in virtual retirement, his career having been interrupted by a serious road accident, and he was flattered by the attentions of his overseas visitor. As a result the two began to correspond on a more or less regular basis.

In a letter dated 2 June 1961 Oden described how he had been following current events. Details of President Kennedy's visit to France were being broadcast on television and Oden had been watching keenly: "The day that our President visited Paris, I've seen nearly every place he was to speak doing his mission over there. Mr. Kennedy is making a different world in this United States. We all are very proud of him, for he and his brother Mr. Robert Kennedy are waking up these people who seem to think that it's just a minority are human being. So they are putting the pressure on them like they should have had all the time. Now we have at least voted the right President in this time. Thank God a big change has been made already in the Deep South of this United States." A letter dated 14 December 1961 added: "Every week things are getting much better in this country, but it can be better. I should know I have been here all my life, but thank God it's changing pretty fast since Kennedy has been President. May God bless the Irishman, I believe he means right."[1]

By the end of the 1950s the rate of inflation had increased to 3.3 percent and unemployment stood at 7.0 percent. In his campaign speeches Kennedy had called attention to the fact that the economy was stagnating and promised to "get America moving again," though without committing himself to any specific program. One apparent casualty of the downturn was the Scotlandville, Louisiana, guitarist Herman E. Johnson (1909–1975), who recorded a number of songs for the researcher Harry Oster in April 1961, including "Depression Blues," which drew on personal experience. Having worked as a laborer for the big Esso refinery in Baton Rouge for fifteen years, he suddenly found himself out of work. By the time of the recording he had obtained a job as a janitor at the African-American Southern University in his hometown, but complained that it was impossible to make ends meet at $30 a week. Johnson blames his own unkindness for the loss of his woman.

> *I'm looking for a depression, in Nineteen and Sixty-one,*
> *And what grieves me so bad, I can't have no more fun.*
>
> *I been driving, I been walking, until my hands and feet is tired,*
> *And I've been going here and yonder, but I can't find no job.*
>
> *A man called me down in the alley, and I went down there by myself,*
> *That man had a little job and had give it to someone else.*
>
> *Then I went out on the railroad, my friend told me to go,*
> *He had all the men he wanted and he wasn't gonna hire no more.*
>
> *Now, I'll admit the times is hard, and that is everywhere you go,*
> *And all I do for my little woman, she just don't be pleased no more.*
>
> *I walked all night long, my poor feet is soaking wet,*
> *I was looking for that little woman, but I haven't found her yet.*
> *I was looking for that little woman, but I haven't found her yet.*

I don't take the daily paper, I don't have time to hear the news,
I'm just rolling, rolling, rolling with these depression blues.

I'm gonna take you for my friend, whoever you might be,
But if you hears of a job, will you break it down to me?

I'm feeling sad and lonesome, but, man, I've been sad all day,
Well, well, I had a sweet little woman, but unkindness drove
her away.

Well, it seem mighty hard, but I brought it all on myself.
But she was so kind to me, but I was loving someone else.[2]

Civilian unemployment rates, which never fell below 5.5 percent, and the poverty that afflicted millions in urban slums and depressed rural communities continued to cast a shadow over the Kennedy era.[3] Although he listened to advice from a variety of sources, two most influential members of the new president's team were Douglas Dillon, the Republican secretary of the Treasury, and Walter Heller, the chairman of the Council of Economic Advisors. At first he tended to steer a middle course between conflicting views, but as his knowledge of economics grew thanks to frequent meetings with the council, JFK came to agree with those who, like the British economist John Maynard Keynes, argued that recessions had to be fought by an expansion of the money supply. If the central bank were to put more money in consumers' hands, confidence would return and people would start to spend again.

Smoky Babe (Robert Brown, 1927–1976), a poor migrant farmer from Mississippi, was another of the blues artists recorded by Harry Oster in 1961. In "Hard Time Blues" he observed how severe the depression was by noting that this time the whites were unemployed as well. The final stanza may be his way to express his fears that whenever the depression is over the white people will be hired first again.

Well, now I say, you people, oh, you know times is hard,
Well, now while the depression is on, look like me and my baby
want to part.

Work done got scarce, I'm trying to make a living, peoples, I know,

Seem like my baby, she want to put me out, she want to drive me from her door.

I ain't just all alone, there is others too,
I see both white and black walking the road, trying to find something to do.

Well, we don't know how everything is going to be,
I say the way this segregation going on, all I can say, Lord, have mercy on me.[4]

Jimmy Lee Robinson (1931–2002) recorded "Times Is Hard" in Chicago in 1962. The song evokes a picture of an unemployed man at the end of his tether who is in danger of losing his house and his girlfriend as a result.

Times is getting harder, baby, times is getting harder, baby,
times is getting harder, baby,
Well, I'm broke, well, I'm broke, well, I'm broke, well, I'm broke.

My landlord gave me a calling, I couldn't pay my rent,
I was looking for my baby, found she done and went.

ch: *Times, times is getting harder,*
I ain't got no money, can't even find a job.

My baby been a-nagging, for days at a time,
I can't buy her clothes, I ain't got a dime.

[62]   The Welfare Turns Its Back on You

> My heels sticking out, toes on the ground,
> Can't find a job, can't even leave this town.[5]

At the president's recommendation Congress passed an area redevelopment bill, an omnibus housing bill, a farm bill, a rise in the minimum wage, the liberalization of Social Security, temporary unemployment benefits, and benefits for dependent children of unemployed parents, all in a single 1961 sitting.[6] However, these measures, which were followed by a cut in personal income tax, seem to have had little immediate effect on the economy or the lives of most African-American citizens.

Using the stage name King Karl, the Louisiana singer Bernard Jolivette (1931–2005) enjoyed local popularity as a performer of ballads, but when he recorded the blues song "Hard Times at My Door" in Nashville, Tennessee, in 1962, producer Ernie Young gave him the pseudonym "Chuck" Brown. When I talked to him over the phone a few months before his death, he was disillusioned with the recording business but proud that he had written all his songs himself. When I asked him what his opinion of President Kennedy was, he replied that Kennedy had done a lot of good things and stated: "that is why he was assassinated."[7]

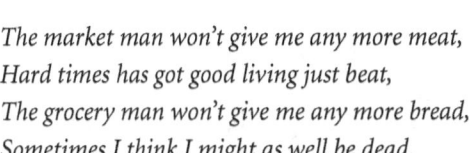

> The market man won't give me any more meat,
> Hard times has got good living just beat,
> The grocery man won't give me any more bread,
> Sometimes I think I might as well be dead.
>
> ch: Hard times, ooh, hard times,
> It's so hard, hard, hard, yeah, hard time is on.
>
> Furniture man came to pick up his bed,
> And pulled the pillow right from under my head,
> He even took his dinette set:
> Pretty soon there'll be nothing left.
>
> All I had left was a living room suite,
> And a dinette wasn't built for two,

But this-a morning when I came home,
Too sad that it's gone too.

Something better give somewhere,
Or my babe might thought of being unfair,
And that's something that I couldn't bear,
For she's all that-a I've got left.⁸

The targets of this tirade were the butcher, the grocer, and the furniture man, but when the Los Angeles–based singer King Solomon recorded "Inflation Blues" in 1962, he hinted that forces were at work that were beyond the power of any mortal to control. In the early 1960s inflation was low, but this was little comfort to those laid off as a result of the economic downturn.⁹ King Solomon uses the term "inflation" (as so many blues singers do) as a general term to embody what he is complaining about. Thus "inflation" is being appropriated from the vocabulary of economics and used as a general term for policies that are perceived as leading to recession and as having adverse effects on working-class African Americans.¹⁰

sp: Lord, Lord, Lord!

Woke up this morning, didn't have a dime,
Landlord's crying: "Rents are behind!"

ch: *I don't know, oh, I don't know,*
I've got to move, Lord, I've got to move, away from here.

Tried to get her just to give me a little more time,
Bills piling up on me, 'bout to lose my mind.

Oh, I had a good job, making good money,
I bought myself a, a big fine car,
I got laid off about a month or two,
I drawed all my unemployment, Lord, oh, what I'm gonna do?
Peoples crying: "Ain't got a dime,
Can't even make my car note on time."

Oh, I've got to move, baby, I've got to move away from here,
Lord, for sure, honey, I don't know what to do about (my) machine,
Pack your things now, woman, I know we gotta split the scene.
Ah, ah . . . ![11]

Muddy Waters, Groningen, 21 October 1976. Photo: Sem van Gelder.

The Welfare Turns Its Back on You

Muddy Waters (real name McKinley Morganfield, 1915–1983) enjoyed a lengthy and successful recording career, during which he seldom committed his thoughts on current affairs to wax. However, in 1962 the lyrics of "Tough Times" elicited an impassioned vocal from him.

> *I can't stay awake for worrying, ah, you know I can't sleep for crying,*
> *Oh, you know I can't find a job no place, to take care of this little woman of mine.*
>
> *Tough times, tough times, and I don't know what to do,*
> *Well, if times don't get no better, Mr. President, I'm gonna have to move in the White House with you.*
>
> *Tough times, tough times, and people don't know what to do,*
> *Well, you know you is my president and the whole world is depending on you.*[12]

Although Muddy Waters refrained from explicit criticism of the president, there is no mistaking his sense of frustration. Kennedy's campaign speeches had aroused expectations that were becoming difficult to satisfy. Unemployment among African Americans, "the last hired and the first fired," continued to run at an inordinately high level, roughly two and a half times higher than among whites.[13] Although a system of welfare benefits was in place, claimants already stigmatized by their dependency felt further resentment at having to justify themselves to unsympathetic bureaucrats. Singer-guitarist Freddie King (1934–1976) gave voice to these feelings in his 1962 recording "(The Welfare) Turns Its Back on You."

> ch: *Now, whatcha gonna do when the welfare turn its back on you?*
> *Yes, you'll be standing there stranded, yes, there ain't a thing that you can do.*
>
> *Now, you look all through your house, yet you can't even find a piece of bread,*
> *Oh yes, sometime you begin to wonder, yes, if you ain't better off dead.*

> *You have to go down to the welfare every month to report,*
> *And some of the things they'll say to you, it will surely get your goat.*
> *If you tell 'em you're sick, you'd better have a bad cough,*
> *Because if you don't, they'll be ready to throw you off.*[14]

Rev. Al Sharpton (b. 1954), one of the candidates for the Democratic nomination in the 2004 presidential race, lived in a poor New York neighborhood during the Kennedy administration. In one of his sermons he remembered the dependency on the welfare system: "You know, back in the days when I grew up in Brownsville, I was on welfare. In those days, they used to make us get in line to get the welfare peanut butter ... the little chips and can goods ... and the welfare cheese in the long brown box."[15] Emanuel Laskey (1945–2006) had some success with his "Welfare Cheese" in 1963. The big blocks of surplus cheese handed out by the welfare stores became proverbial for the low-quality food the poor were supplied with. In Laskey's humorous song the man behind the welfare counter gradually becomes identified with President Kennedy himself.

> ch: *Yeah, yeah, yeah, now!*
> *I say, hey, hey, hey, yeah, yeah, now!*
> *Eh, my-y-y-y-y-y, yeah, yeah, yeah!*
>
> *I said: "Early in the morning, 'bout the break of day,*
> *We make it on down Commodity way."*
>
> *Oh, but Mister, eh, Mister, won't you please, now,*
> *Send me some of that welfare cheese?*
>
> *I said: "You don't have to wear satin and silk,*
> *To get that old pack Commodity milk."*
>
> *I said, "Uh, baby, baby, baby, can't you hear,*
> *We all get that stuff out here?"*
>
> *Oh, but Kennedy, oh, Mister, won't you please, now,*
> *Get me some of that welfare cheese?*
>
> *I said, uh, "Calling Mr. Kennedy, it's an emergency,*
> *Hand me some of that welfare cheese."*[16]

Although President Kennedy introduced a number of measures to stimulate economic growth and relieve poverty, it was not until after his demise that they began to take general effect. Some of his "New Frontier" goals had not been achieved as Congress rejected increased federal aid for education, medical care for the elderly, and major tax cuts. However, the minimum wage was increased, there was some modest success in urban reform, and his medical plans would eventually be enacted as Medicare and Medicaid.

5

MARCH ON, DR. MARTIN LUTHER KING

The vast majority of performers whose lyrics are discussed in this book hailed from "down south," the states below the Mason-Dixon Line where segregation and disenfranchisement were still vivid reality in the early 1960s. Although many chose to leave, few traveled as far as the pianist Memphis Slim (Peter Chatman), who finally settled in Paris, France, during 1962. For those who were prepared to listen, he could draw upon a great fund of anecdotes to illustrate what it was like to live in the southern states. The codes of behavior that governed everyday life were a constant source of humiliation and distress. It was unwise to defy the system as the threat of violence was never far away. Memphis Slim had already recorded some candid commentary on racial oppression in March 1947, but that recording, which he made together with Sonny Boy Williamson and Big Bill Broonzy, was issued pseudonymously.[1] Slim's monologue with piano accompaniment, "Down South," was recorded in a Chicago studio after Kennedy's election in November 1960. He mentions a senator and governor of Mississippi, Theodore Bilbo,[2] and the former mayor of Memphis, Big Boss Edward Crump,[3] as examples of typical southern racists. From

Memphis Slim, De Bajes, Amstelveen, the Netherlands, 2 April 1971. Photo: Courtesy Guido van Rijn.

the mid-1950s on, attacks on rock and roll by white segregationists had shown their fear of integration, and Slim concludes his story with a pragmatic observation.

> *Down South, my native.*
> *Don't get me wrong, I'm not bragging, but I'm very glad, I'm very happy,*
> *Because being born in the South, you get so much experience.*
> *If you make it away from the South, you got it made.*
> *Mr. Bilbo, Mr. Crump, and all those guys out to get you.*
> *But I had a brother; as you know, I'm six foot four; my brother called me "Shorty."*
> *My brother was born above the Mason and Dixon Line: Newark, New Jersey.*
> *My brother came down to visit me, you know.*

Being a good sport I had to carry him around, to the back door, Down South.
This was where the Southern cross the Dog, Moorhead; I know all you boys are familiar with this.

So while in the pool room shooting a little pool,
My brother, he always had a mind of his own,
He gets hungry, you know, he steps next door to a bus station,
Not noticing the sign where it says "Colored Only."
He goes in the wrong side, so they say.
But my brother wasn't used to that kind of stuff, you know.
So the guy says: "What can I do for you, boy?"
Said: "I'd like a hamburger."
So the guy, he knew my brother didn't know what he was doing, he told him,
He says, "We don't serve Negroes."
My brother says: "Wonderful, I don't eat 'em either, give me a hamburger."
So he got the hamburger!
So I say that to get to say this, it takes nerve.

Another kid went down south with me, visiting my old home town,
So we goes to the commissary.
Arbee Stidham, he never been south before.[4]
So the guy, I know how to act, the guy says: "Oh, Peter, how you feeling?"
"Fine, Mister Ed."
"What can I do for you?"
I said, "Give me a pound of those cheese, if you please."
Said: "Wonderful, Peter, wonderful. I see you haven't forgotten your learning."
"What else can I do for you?" I said, "Give me a box of crackers, if you please."
"Good old Peter, good old Peter."
So Arbee wanted some Camel cigarettes, so he said: "What can I do for you fellow?"
Arbee said, "Give me a pack of Camel cigarettes."

So Mr. Edwards tried to help Arbee.
He said: "If you, if you." You know he's trying to tell Arbee to say: "If you."
He said: "What you mean? Gimme a pack of Camel cigarettes."
He said: "I know, but, if you, if you."
He said, "Yeah, if you got 'em; if you haven't, I'll go next door."
Boy, this guy's scaring me to death.

But you know, the funny thing about Down South, all kidding aside, it's so silly.
My mother, your mother, they feed the guys down there, you know,
Put diapers on them, raise them, then they don't want to eat with you.
They raise them, then when they become seventeen years old,
They want you to say, "Mister" and "Mrs."
Some people call it prejudice, but I call it just plain ignorance.

Yes, Down South.
Only one solution to it, though: that's youth, the young people see it different.
Like a guy told me, he says, "You know, rock and roll has got to go."
He was about fifty-four years old. I said, "You'll, I bet you'll go before rock and roll.
Because the young people was the ones that brought rock and roll in,
And they gonna last much longer than you. They're seventeen, eighteen and nineteen."
This guy's fifty-four. He says, "I'll see rock and roll go."

So the moral of the story is: "If you can't beat them, join them."
That goes for Down South.[5]

Slim's survival technique consisted of turning the other cheek, of temporizing in the hope that conditions would surely improve when the reactionaries were swept away. Yet at the same time there were others who were prepared to offer themselves as martyrs in the cause of progress.

Blues artist and former boxer "Champion" Jack Dupree (1909–1992) said that his mother and father had both been killed by the Ku Klux Klan.

When he had the chance to leave the United States in 1959, he made his home in Europe. In a 1976 interview he made an important statement: "I don't know anything about politics and that thing but I have seen the mess they have done out of people's life. I've seen these things, so when I sing I can really sing what's going on. If I stand on a box and tell people of all the wrong in the world, people wouldn't listen. But if I sing it on records all around the world everybody will know. That's the way we have to get our message out in the world to the people. That's why the people around the world know so much about us and our living. We couldn't stand up like the white man and speak. If we did, we would be killed or put in jail. But we could do it in singing. When we sing, they listen."[6] In October of 1961 Dupree recorded a monologue with piano accompaniment. "Free and Equal" was recorded in Copenhagen, Denmark, where he felt secure enough to speak out on Jim Crow.

> sp: You know I often have people asks me, where was I born? I tell 'em: "New Orleans," which New Orleans bears a great name around this world. Very good people come from New Orleans. A nice place to come from. Musical world, with a feeling to everybody, that's why they like New Orleans. But those places for me, is out the book. As long as it's the southern states and down south, it's out the book for me. Because I struggled and struggled hard, to try to get a break. I couldn't never get a break. I was a great man—to myself, but to nobody else. But maybe someday them people down there will straighten up, 'cause how could they live in this world with all that hate in their minds and THEY even hate somebody or somebody else care for you? They make it miserable for other people.
>
> But, you know, someday things is gonna change. Maybe it'll be better in the by and by. Of course we don't say the whole America is the same, for there's lots of places we can get by and we do pretty good. Now you take like New York, Chicago, Detroit, California. We could live in those places, but that's not the thing in life we want. If we vote, we wants to live happy, all over the world, where we can go anywhere and be happy. We don't wanna go in one place where the law is that you can't come in and eat, you can't sit down and talk to nobody, you gotta go around the back to get a sandwich, like they handing it out

the window to a dog! We don't want that, we just want to be free. We want to have a soul's salvation, we want to be free! We don't want nothing they got. We just want happiness. We don't wanna rob 'em or nothing. That's all we wanna do, is live like people. I want my people to live too. Life is misery. Every time you read the paper, your heart aches for the poor people that's there that can't get away.

So maybe someday, when you pick up the paper you'll see where things done changed, where everybody is free, and everybody is happy. But I think until that day, and when that day comes, I'll be gone along before. I may be six feet down in the ground, but maybe that day'll come to the other people, and I hope it'll come someday.

So, I leave those few words with you from the bottom of my heart, how I feel about my home that I can't go to and be in peace. But until we meet again someday, I wanna say: "Live while you're living."[7]

Kennedy's narrow margin of victory in the 1960 election had been partly due to his popularity among African Americans. He claimed that he was also held back by his unfamiliarity with the issues of desegregation and civil rights. Harris Wofford, one of Kennedy's speechwriters, reported him as saying: "You know, I'm way behind on this, because I've hardly known any blacks in my life. It isn't an issue that I've thought about a lot . . . I've got to learn a lot, and I've got to catch up fast."[8]

In the early days of Kennedy's presidency, civil rights remained low on his list of priorities. Indeed, the administration would continue for some time to respond to each racial conflagration on an ad hoc basis, intervening as unobtrusively as possible and fearful of alienating the support of southern, white Democrats in and out of Congress. Meanwhile the president built bridges with prominent members of the African-American community. In 1961 a dinner was given in Kennedy's honor at the Hollywood Palladium in Los Angeles, and the entertainer Nat "King" Cole was invited to perform. After dinner Cole apologized to the assembled guests for having to leave early, as he wished to attend a debutantes' ball at the L.A. Hilton Hotel where his daughter Carol was appearing. Later that evening the president himself made a surprise appearance at the ball, explaining that "Nat sang at our dinner tonight, so I thought I'd reciprocate. I'm grateful to you girls for letting an itinerant president come and visit your party."[9]

Such gestures, of course, cost little, but any hopes Kennedy might have entertained that the civil rights issue would somehow go away were dashed by a series of major confrontations that the administration could not afford to ignore.

On 1 February 1960, before JFK was elected President, four black students entered the local Woolworth's store in Greensboro, North Carolina, seated themselves at the segregated, white-only lunch counter, and ordered sodas, coffee, and doughnuts.[10] When no one served them, they refused to leave. The store closed early, but on the following day the four returned and resumed their protest, joined by twenty others. News of the demonstration quickly spread, and in a short time "sit-ins" were taking place in nine southern and a few northern states. Although demonstrators were routinely insulted, threatened, and assaulted and some were even thrown in jail, mostly on trumped-up public order charges, such was their determination that in many cases perplexed store owners eventually gave in.

"With NAACP leaders," 12 July 1961. Photograph by Robert Knudsen, courtesy the John F. Kennedy Presidential Library and Museum, Boston. (KN-18353)

Although Martin Luther King Jr. had not started the sit-in demonstrations, he soon found it a tactic that he could use to good advantage. "Jail for Martin Luther King," said the caption of an October 1960 photo in the *Chicago Defender* showing him driven to jail in a police car. "Dr. King Jr. and 23 other Negro integration leaders remained in jail rather than post bond pending trial on charges they violated Georgia's new law aimed at stopping sit-in demonstrations against segregation. King, leader of the 1955–6 Montgomery, Alabama, bus boycott which won integrated seating on city buses for the Negroes in Alabama's capital city and over 700 others staged sit-ins at eight downtown stores and set up pickets at some of them Wednesday. The sit-ins were apparently the first moves in a stepped up program to crack barriers in the South."[11]

Two years later the sit-ins were still topical. Over the preceding decade B.B. King (b. 1925) had been one of the mainstays of the Bihari brothers' various record labels, but in 1962 he signed a contract with ABC-Paramount. The A-side of his very first single for his new employer was titled "I'm Gonna Sit In Till You Give In." Other bluesmen had recorded songs in which they threatened to take strike action in order to get their way with uncooperative girlfriends; B.B. King found a way of expressing his determination that was novel and would also resonate with his perceived audience.

> sp: Ever since the world began, men have received the right to live
> from God above,
> But there is only one right that you can give, that is the right for
> me to have your love.
> That's why I'm gonna sit in till you give in and give me all of
> your love,
> No use resisting, I'll keep insisting, stop your conniving, girl,
> I ain't jiving.
>
> ch: Yes, I'm gonna sit in till you give in and give me all of your love.
> Yes, I'm gonna sit in till you give in and give me all of your love.
> Night time, daytime, sunshine or rain, I'll be riding that old
> freedom train.[12]
> Yes, I'm gonna sit in till you give in and give me all of your love,
> Tonight at eight, in the morning at four, you'll find me sitting at
> your front door.[13]

The immediate reaction to the Greensboro sit-in exceeded expectations. More radical members of the civil rights movement put forward a plan of action that they hoped would ultimately force the federal government to act. Segregated interstate travel was prohibited by law, but without the intervention of the federal authorities, efforts to enforce the law had proved unsuccessful.

In the wake of the Greensboro sit-in, a body known as SNCC (Student Nonviolent Coordinating Committee) was established on the campus of Shaw University in Raleigh. Teams of activists were dispatched to various communities throughout the South to organize demonstrations against segregation and to encourage potential voters to exercise the franchise.

The Congress of Racial Equality (CORE) proposed a new journey dubbed the "Freedom Ride." It was to be a symbolic journey through the South to New Orleans; once aboard the bus, the whites would sit in the back and the blacks would make a point of sitting at the front. Furthermore, at stops where they encountered segregated facilities, the whites would go into the area reserved for blacks and vice versa. As this was sure to provoke a violent reaction among white southerners, their voyage would be an extremely hazardous one. Accordingly, when the riders set out on 4 May 1961, leaders of the movement made sure that the president, the attorney general, and the head of the FBI were forewarned.

The blind street singer Arvella Gray (real name Walter Dixon, 1906–1980) recorded "Freedom Bus" for his own Gray label in 1965. Gray singles were sold by the artist on Maxwell Street or the nearby corner of Halsted Street in Chicago. The idealism of the Freedom Riders and their trust in God shine through this encouraging song.

> ch: We are riding on a freedom bus; we are riding on a freedom
> bus,
> Like our money say, "In God We Trust"— we are riding on
> a freedom bus.

> *One by one we have made a stand, we are riding through this barren land,*
> *Like our money say, "In God We Trust"; we are riding on a freedom bus.*
>
> *One by one we have seen the light, we are willing to do what is right,*
> *Like our money say, "In God We Trust"; we are riding on a freedom bus.*
>
> *We are learning from our neighbors true, each one doing just what he can do,*
> *Like our money say, "In God We Trust"; we are riding on a freedom bus.*
>
> *Help our fellow man to see the light, let him know that we doing right,*
> *Like our money say, "In God We Trust"; we are riding on a freedom bus.*
>
> *Help our fellow man to know the truth, let him know that we're not uncouth,*
> *Like our money say, "In God We Trust"; we are riding on a freedom bus.*[14]

The flip side, "Freedom Riders," gave evidence of the same Christian patriotism. Gray told blues writer Cary Baker that he was arrested for singing this "apparently politically titilating [sic] protest song."[15]

> ch: *Lord, we are the freedom marchers, we have broken the ice,*
> *We are the freedom marchers, we have broken the ice.*
>
> *We are brothers of this great America, bound together with peace and love,*
> *Strengthening in this heavenly fire, placing our hopes on the Heaven above.*
>
> *We are sisters with true mortality, standing behind our men folk true,*

> *Helping make this great America, just as the foreparents used to do.*
>
> *We are people in this great America, and bound together in peace and love,*
> *Strengthening in this heavenly fire, placing our hopes on the Heaven above.*
>
> *We are people of all creation, of any race and creed,*
> *Shoulder to shoulder with pride and justice, sowing and sharing the harvest seed.*
>
> *Come what may, anything we'll say,*
> *We are the freedom marchers today,*
> *We are the freedom marchers today.*[16]

When the first group of Freedom Riders reached Anniston, Alabama, a mob of 200 Ku Klux Klan members stoned the bus and slashed its tires. While the tires were being changed, an incendiary device was thrown inside and the passengers assaulted. The second group got no further than Birmingham, Alabama, where they too were beaten up with the connivance of local officials. Bull Connor, Birmingham's public safety commissioner, had seen to it that the police were nowhere around.

A party of SNCC students from Nashville, veterans of a local sit-in campaign, volunteered to continue the ride. After making their way to Birmingham, they were arrested by local police and escorted back across the state line. Undeterred, they returned to Birmingham, where they found local officials more accommodating, thanks to the intervention of Attorney General Robert Kennedy. At length they boarded a Greyhound bus and reached Montgomery, where their journey came to an abrupt end when, denied police protection, they were viciously assaulted by local vigilantes. As further attempts were made to complete the symbolic ride to New Orleans, the focus of resistance shifted to the neighboring state of Mississippi, where those who braved the mobs were arrested and corralled through the local penal system.

The freedom rides took place on the eve of Kennedy's conference with Khrushchev in Vienna. They caused deep international embarrassment, and this may help to explain why the Freedom Rides were

Louisiana Red, Montreux, Switzerland, 11 July 1975. Photo: Job Zomer.

successful. In September 1961, after a petition from Robert Kennedy, the Interstate Commerce Commission enacted regulations that enabled the federal government to enforce the Supreme Court ruling that desegregated interstate travel.

With the climate of public opinion gradually changing, there was greater inducement for relatively conservative sections of the record industry to enable outspoken opinions to be heard. Born Iverson Minter in Vicksburg, Mississippi, in 1936 and orphaned at the age of three when his father was killed by the Ku Klux Klan, bluesman Louisiana Red was an accomplished and much-traveled singer and musician. In October 1962 he was given an opportunity to record in depth and responded with an impressive collection of songs, some of which leaned on personal experience, while others like "Red's Dream" and "Too Poor to Die" mined a rich vein of humor and fantasy. There is nothing original or controversial in the theme of leaving the South, which recurs in numerous prewar commercial issues; what is unusual about "Ride On Red, Ride On" is the note of explicit and bitter criticism. Although Red portrays himself traveling in the opposite direction, passing the segregated towns of Shreveport, Louisiana, and Little Rock, Arkansas, it is quite likely that the song was inspired by the hardships endured by the Freedom Riders.[17] The bus he boards departs from New Orleans, which was the intended destination of the riders. Far from detaining him, the local segregationists are keen to see him go and he is only too happy to comply, given the indignities he has to endure. Red offers no comment on the civil rights movement, but it is evident that without the intervention of the federal government, little progress can be made.

"Woodmen, Spare That Tree!" Courtesy *Chicago Defender*, 8 September 1962.

The White Citizens' Council (= Louisiana Red's "Citizens' Commission") had been established in Greenwood, Mississippi, shortly after the 1954–5 *Brown v. Board of Education* decisions were rendered. Sister branches had spread throughout the South with the aim of maintaining segregation. Red sings that the councils paid the fares for those African Americans who were ready to leave the South.

> sp: Board!
>
> > Ride on, Louisiana Red, ride on!
> > Left my home in Vicksburg, started traveling north,
> > Made it to New Orleans where the bus was taking off,
> > Citizens' Committee, giving away the fare,
> > "You don't like the South, boy, just go on away from here."
>
> ch: Ride on, Louisiana Red, ride on,
> > Ride on to your freedom, make the Northern states your home.

*Then we rode into Shreveport, where we were supposed to eat,
And when I got my sandwich, I had to eat it on the street.*

*We rolled into old Little Rock, had made another state,
Where it took the whole U.S. army to make one school integrate.*

*Now, I'm here in New York, and I'm doing fine,
Having me a ball above the Mason-Dixie line.*

sp: *Yes, my home, I ain't going down there no more!
Same thing in Georgia!...*[18]

Chuck Berry traveled across the United States from east to west in his February 1964 recording "Promised Land." On his way to the "promised land" of California, Berry's "poor boy" leaves from Virginia and passes through or over North and South Carolina, Georgia, Alabama, Mississippi, Louisiana, Texas, New Mexico, and Arizona (although the last state is not mentioned).

*I left my home in Norfolk, Virginia, California on my mind,
I straddled that Greyhound, and rode him into Raleigh, and on across Caroline.*

*We stopped in Charlotte but bypassed Rock Hill, we never was a minute late,
We was ninety miles out of Atlanta by sundown, rolling out of Georgia state.*

*We had motor trouble that turned into a struggle, halfway across Alabam',
And that 'Hound broke down and left us all stranded in downtown Birmingham.*

*Right away I bought me a through train ticket, riding cross Mississippi clean,
And I was on that Midnight Flyer out of Birmingham, smoking into New Orleans.*

Somebody help me get out of Louisiana, just help me get to Houston town,
There are people there who care a little 'bout me, and they won't let the poor boy down.

Sure as you're born, they bought me a silk suit, put luggage in my hand,
And I woke up high over Albuquerque, on a jet to the promised land.

Working on a T-bone steak a la car-tee [sic], flying over to the Golden State,
When the pilot told us in thirteen minutes he would set us at the terminal gate.

Swing low sweet chariot, come down easy, taxi to the terminal zone,
Cut your engines, and cool your wings, and let me make it to the telephone.

Los Angeles, give me Norfolk, Virginia, Tidewater four-ten-o-nine,
Tell the folks back home this is the Promised Land calling, and the poor boy's on the line.[19]

When Berry wrote this song in 1962/3 he was serving time on a morals charge in St. Louis and had great difficulty getting the use of a road atlas, which the prison authorities feared would be an aid to escape rather than songwriting.[20] The place names on Berry's route are all landmarks on the historical map of the civil rights movement. The most notorious spots are bypassed (Rock Hill) or crossed without stopping (Mississippi); Albuquerque is flown over and no effort is spared to escape from Atlanta, Birmingham, and New Orleans. The Greyhound bus breaks down in downtown Birmingham, Alabama, the worst possible place for an African American to be stranded. The Midnight Flyer train takes him through Mississippi "clean" (i.e. nonstop), but terminates in New Orleans, Louisiana. From there Berry escapes to Houston, Texas, where friends put him on a jet to Los Angeles. The jet is compared to the "sweet chariot" of the old spiritual, carrying slaves home to the promised land.

The significance of most of the places on Berry's musical Freedom Ride has been outlined above. In 1958, schools in Norfolk, Virginia, that were about to integrate by court order were seized and closed as a result of the massive resistance movement led by Senator and former Governor Harry Byrd.[21] Raleigh, North Carolina, was the scene of sit-ins and desegregation efforts, and Rock Hill, South Carolina, was where the Freedom Riders first encountered white resistance in May 1961.[22] When Freedom Riders John Lewis and Albert Bigelow got off the bus in Rock Hill and headed toward the white waiting room, they were stopped and beaten up by a group of white men. Albuquerque, New Mexico, though not usually thought of as a center of civil rights activism, was the scene of a remarkable direct action campaign between 1947 and 1950 by University of New Mexico students against segregated facilities near their campus.[23]

The efforts of SNCC met with a particularly positive response from African Americans in the rural town of Albany, Georgia. In November

"From Every Walk of Life." Courtesy *New York Amsterdam News*, 7 September 1963. Artist: Melvin Tapley.

1961 an organization known as the Albany Movement had been set up, whose leadership included prominent members of the local black community. Within a few days SNCC workers Charles Sherrod, Cordell Reagon, and Charles Jones were arrested while attempting to use white facilities in the local bus terminal. This event began to attract media attention, which soon escalated as further arrests followed, notably on 11 December when 267 demonstrators, mostly students from the black high school, were rounded up and thrown into jail. At this point, with the protest threatening to lose momentum, the leaders of the Albany Movement decided to seek the help of Dr. Martin Luther King Jr.

"Don't You Think You're Moving Too Fast!" Courtesy *Chicago Defender*, 18 May 1963.

Dr. King arrived in Albany on 16 December and his presence lifted the spirits of the protesters. That same evening he led a mass march to the City Hall, where he was arrested on the orders of Police Chief Laurie Pritchett, along with many others. By now over five hundred demonstrators were languishing in jail. However, if they had hoped to overwhelm the local police by weight of numbers, the tactic proved unsuccessful, as Chief Pritchett contacted all the jails he could find within a thirty mile radius and assured himself of an enormous capacity that far surpassed his requirements. Since remaining in jail served no useful purpose, Dr. King allowed himself to be bailed out on 18 December.

In 1962 the demonstrations and the arrests continued. When he returned for his trial on 10 July, Dr. King was finally sentenced to a $178 fine or 45 days in jail. To the dismay of the local and federal authorities alike, for whom his imprisonment was a considerable embarrassment, he elected to serve the prison term.

The *Chicago Defender* reported on the event under the headline "Mystery Donor Pays Jail Fines of Dr. King, Rev. Abernathy":

> "Southern integration leader Dr. Martin Luther King Jr. was released from jail Thursday after serving only two days of a 45-day sentence. The fine that had been levied against King on conviction of an integration incident last year—and which he had refused to pay—was put up mysteriously by an unidentified benefactor. Albany Mayor Asa Kelley announced that King and the Rev. Ralph Abernathy, also an Atlanta minister and integration leader, had been released because the fines had been paid. He claimed "no communicable knowledge" of who paid the fines. However, the Justice Department was reported to be deeply involved in the release. A spokesman said Atty. Gen. Robert F. Kennedy had given a "full report" on the King case to his brother, President Kennedy, and the White House was being kept informed of developments.[24]

Pritchett also refused to say who had paid the fine, and King had been outsmarted by him once again.[25]

At his 1 August 1962 press conference Kennedy made his position clear in reply to a journalist's question: "Let me say that I find it wholly inexplicable why the City Council of Albany will not sit down with the citizens of Albany, who may be Negroes, and attempt to secure them in a peaceful way, their rights. The United States government is involved in sitting down at Geneva with the Soviet Union. I can't understand why the government of Albany, City Council of Albany, cannot do the same for American citizens."[26]

Mayor Kelley declared that Kennedy had "sided with the blacks" and on this pretext refused to negotiate. The president subsequently received a large number of threatening letters, all of which were investigated by the Secret Service. A typical example, posted in Los Angeles, read: "We are sick of the dirty black Catholics. The next bomb will be for you, Mr. Kennedy."[27]

During their imprisonment, many of the SNCC activists tried to reinforce solidarity in the time-honored fashion of singing freedom songs appropriate to their situation. One such song was "Oh Pritchett, Oh Kelley," co-written by Bertha Gober and Janie Lee Culbreth and based on

"Rockin' Jerusalem,"[28] which Gober recalled singing as a member of her high school choir.

> ch: Oh, Pritchett, oh, Kelley,
> Oh, Pritchett, open them cells.
>
> I hear God's children, crying for mercy,
> Hear God's children, praying in jail,
> Hear God's children, you know they're suffering,
> I hear God's children, praying in jail.
>
> Bond's getting higher, praying in jail,
> Bond's getting higher, praying in jail,
> Bond's getting higher, praying in jail,
> Bond's getting higher, praying in jail.[29]

The Albany campaign ended inconclusively, with both sides claiming victory. Dr. King vowed that he would continue his campaign in Albany but was stopped by an order from Federal District Judge J. Robert Elliot. As Judge Elliot had been appointed by the Kennedy administration, Dr. King was disappointed in the president.[30] The Albany Movement was a humiliating defeat for Martin Luther King and changed hardly anything for local African Americans.

At a June 1963 show at New York's Club Harlem, comedian Slappy White described a humorous Freedom Ride of his own from New Orleans to Pittsburgh, Pennsylvania. White describes escaping jail in Albany, Georgia, and finding a room in the "Talmadge Hotel," ironically named after Herman Eugene Talmadge, the racist former Governor of Georgia:

> I've been doing pretty good here of late, thanks to the Urban League. No, they booked me down in New Orleans. I had a wonderful time in New Orleans. Only had to pay one-way transportation. When I left New Orleans I had to open at the Holiday House in Pittsburgh. In order to make a Sunday opening I had to fly. I don't like to fly because I'm nervous on planes. And I'm sitting on the plane, nervously looking out the window and the pilot come running down the aisle with a parachute strapped to his back. He said: "Ladies and gentlemen, don't be alarmed, but we have a

little trouble with the landing gears and I'm going on ahead to warn them at the airport."

Well, we finally landed, though; a stewardess brought us down. And I decided not to fly any further. I figure I'd rent me a car and I'd drive from New Orleans through south on into Pittsburgh, see? So I let her put me in the driver's seat. And it like to broke my leg.

Well, I'm driving along, I'm doing pretty good, you know, and I have no trouble. I get to Albany, Georgia. A police gave me a ticket for speeding and I was fixing a flat! I was gonna slip him a little money, he said: "Do I look like a crooked cop?" He said: "I am as honest as the day is long." I said: "Here is twenty." He said: "Wasn't that a lovely sunset?"

One police wanted to carry me to jail for having my windshield wipers going the wrong way on a one-way street! Boy, and he was giving me a hard time. I was just standing there, listening to him. But you see, every year, when I work here at the Club Harlem, I do a free show for the Atlantic City police department and they gave me a badge. And he kept giving me a hard time, so I eased my hand in my pocket and I pulled my badge out and I said: "What shall I do with this?" (pause) After he told me, (pause) I'm glad they didn't give me a plaque.

Oh, I must have drove 500 miles. I was so tired and sleepy I say: "The first hotel I see, I will pull in and check in for the night and then leave the next day." I was really tired and I see this big hotel, Hotel Talmadge. Good. Walked up then to the desk clerk and I said: "I like to have a room." He said: "Why, sure, we have no racial prejudice in this hotel. Sign right there and I'll put you in a room with running water." Now, how was I to know that Running Water was a Seminole Indian? He said: "And furthermore, we have a colored bellboy here." I said: "Lot of hotels have bellboys that's colored." He said: "Green?" His name was Pete Moss.[31]

Well, I finally made it, though, went on into Trenton. When I got to Trenton I got a phone call at the house, it said: "Slappy, you gotta come right back down south, there's a lot of property in your name was willed to you. Come on down right away and see about it." I said: "I'll be right down as soon as I say a little prayer." And I knelt down and I said: "Lord, there's a lot of property in my name in the South; shall I go there and see about it?" The Lord said: "Go down and see about your property." I said: "Lord, are you going with me?" He said: "As far as Virginia."[32]

In 1962 Rev. Ben Gay, an associate of the SNCC movement, was recorded by Alan Lomax for the documentary *Freedom in the Air: Albany, Georgia 1961–2*. In his sermon "As the Eagle Stirreth Her Nest," Gay urged the people of Albany to continue to bear the sacrifice necessary in the fight for equal rights. He pointed out that Attorney General Robert Kennedy was abroad at that specific moment. How could Kennedy explain what was going on in Albany? How could the United States claim to lead the free world when it had not straightened itself out with regard to segregation?

> "As an eagle stirreth up her nest, fluttereth over her young, spreadeth abroad her wings, so the Lord did lead."[33]
> Now that's my interpretation of this movement, that it's a part of God's divine program to bring His Kingdom into this world. You see, you can't have the Kingdom of God with segregation, discrimination, and lines of demarcation zones, because God looks upon us as all being one. Not until that is an actual fact in this world will we have the Kingdom of God. The world is in a turbulent condition. Not only are we experiencing this change and this revolution here in Albany or in Georgia or in the United States, but this thing is worldwide.
> The writer of the scripture that I just read uses the analogy of an eagle stirring her nest. It is said that the mother eagle becomes active and restless when it's time for the young to take their wings. Somebody in Albany, they said that it's time that Albany have some democracy here. It's time that we move out of the old ruts of life and begin to contend for the things that all Americans ought to have. So they stirred up Albany, as an eagle stirreth her nest. (applause)
> The eagle builds its nest out of thorns, and these thorns are laid parallel with the nest and woven in with feathers and straw. But when it's time for the little ones to, to get out of that nest, then the old mother eagle goes there and pulls those thorns up into the nest and makes the nest uncomfortable for those that ought to be up and going. We saw somewhere that there was a democracy, that on the other side of the

fence that there were those enjoying the privileges of life. That there were those who were enjoying life in its richest blessing. And somebody came and turned the thorn up in this nest of segregation where we were sitting complacent and, and at ease and the nest of thorns have been turned up and all Albany is uneasy now. (applause) Because an eagle has stirred her nest.

And in Albany, movement has come to Albany to stir her up. And by stirring up the Negroes in Albany, all of Albany is now reeling, by the impact of this great request we're making just to be first class citizens, just to be as anybody else, just to walk the streets with dignity and with pride and with honor. (applause) All we're trying to do is to help America to preserve herself, her better self.

Another example in point is that of Jonah. And you know, sometimes there is a mission out there that needs to be done for the sake of God's Kingdom. In the case of Jonah, Nineveh was on the brink of eternal ruin. All that she needed was somebody to go out and point the way to that great city to come back to God. Albany, Albany, Georgia, is on the brink of ruin. Nobody thought, not even you here, had any idea, that the commissioners downtown, the officers elected by you and by me to govern the City of Albany, nobody knew that they would take and ignore 38 percent of the populace of Albany in the manner that they have done. (applause) So Albany was on the brink of ruin. She couldn't be a part of God's Kingdom with that kind of heart. So God has called upon us to go down and point this city back to God. And by the help of God we're gonna do that. (applause) And as we do it, and as we do it, we're gonna do it in love, we're gonna do it in dignity, we gonna do it in pride.

God is no doubt using the Negro to a great extent to help save this nation. I know that Attorney General Kennedy is abroad now, and he is having to apologize for many things that happened, mainly here in Albany. But, but the time will come, when, when this, this world will look to America as she'll straighten up. But she can't lead the world, when most of the people of this world are people of color, by downing the Negro. They ask the question: "What about the Negroes in Albany, what about the Negroes in Alabama and Mississippi and all the other places? If you can't give them their rights, you cannot speak to us." (applause) Isn't that right, ladies and gentlemen?

God went with Jonah, even in the belly of the great fish. God went with Abraham and protected him. God is saying to us today, in this hour that: "Lo, I'm with you always, even till the end of the world." And you know, sometimes people become stirred. When they're stirred and really stirred, they become stirred to the extent that they will give the supreme sacrifice. Patrick Henry[34] was stirred to the extent that his soul cried out within him: "Either give me liberty or give me death." Jesus was so stirred by the sins of the world that he said: "Greater love than this hath no man, that a man would lay down his life for his friends,"[35] and he went out on Golgotha's Hill and died for the sins of the world because he was stirred by the sins of the world.

I read an article the other day and it said: "Everything shines, everything shines by perishing." And it went on to say: "A candle, the sun, and even me, there are many sacrifices that you may be called upon to bear before this battle is fought to the victory." But I want you to understand that, that whenever, whenever I am deprived of something that I want or something that I need, that I can't go in town to get it because I am cooperating with the movement, I want you to realize that everything shines by perishing. This sacrifice that you have, you, you're giving of yourself, but, but the giving of yourself is activeness, shines far beyond anything that you can imagine. Light a candle if you will, and the light that you get from that candle is coming from the, the wax of that candle and as it burns the candle is perishing. Everything shines by perishing. I am told that the sun is burning itself out at a rapid rate of speed, it's shining by perishing.

And even you and me in this Albany Movement, if we are to be a significant part, we got to shine, we got to give of ourselves, and when we give of ourselves, we're shining, not only in Albany, but to the world around, saying that the Negro can do without, the Negro can stand together, the Negro can protest together, defend what he think are right and justly his. (applause) We gonna stand together for ourselves.

Hallelujah,
Ain't no harm in keeping your mind set on freedom, Hallelujah.[36]

In January 1961 James Meredith (b. 1933), a sophomore at the all-black Jackson State University, contacted Medgar Evers (1925–1963),

Mississippi's field secretary for the National Association for the Advancement of Colored People (NAACP). Meredith wanted to transfer to Ole Miss, the all-white University of Mississippi. Evers advised him to contact Thurgood Marshall (1908–1993), who was later to become the first African-American Supreme Court justice. Meredith's academic credentials were checked, and on 3 September 1962 a federal district court ordered the University of Mississippi to admit him. Mississippi Governor Ross Barnett went on statewide television to proclaim that "there is no case in history where the Caucasian race has survived social integration." "Miss. Governor Faces Jail for Barring Negro Student," was the headline in the *Chicago Defender*.

> *Several hundreds [sic] students cheered loudly when the governor walked out of the alumni house flanked by state troopers and other law enforcement officers. "His application was denied," Barnett told newspaper men and students. Immediately after making his statement the governor got into an automobile and drove away. Meredith, flanked by U.S. marshals, also got into an automobile and was driven off the campus. During the 20 minutes Meredith was in the room the students sang "Dixie" and chanted "We want Ross. We want Ross." "Go home nigger," many of the students shouted as Meredith entered his car.*[37]

Secretly, however, Barnett tried to negotiate with President Kennedy on 30 September 1962, suggesting that if the federal government used armed force to compel Meredith's registration, the governor might save face. JFK rejected this devious proposal and threatened to make the telephone call public. Intimidated, Barnett allowed James Meredith within the walls of the University building. When the president announced on television that this had happened, rioting on campus went totally out of control. A hundred and sixty federal marshals were injured and twenty-eight people were shot, two of them fatally.[38]

The *Chicago Defender* wondered what kind of a man the fiery governor was: "His speeches, many of them prepared with the help of White Citizens' Council leaders, never fail to win applause in Mississippi when they promise a continuance of 'our way of life.' Barnett is one of the last of a breed that has seen the likes of such men as Bilbo, Thurmond[39] and others who hold their segregationist beliefs in greater reverence than the constitution. Fortunately, it is a breed that is fast fading from the public scene."[40]

Amid the dramatic events of 1963, those in Birmingham, Alabama, during the spring were particularly significant in moving public, and eventually federal, opinion in favor of civil rights legislation. The city was chosen as a target area because it was an important business center with a 40 percent black population. In January Alabama's new Governor, George Wallace, proclaimed in his inaugural speech: "Segregation now! Segregation tomorrow! Segregation forever!" In response Rev. Martin Luther King, Rev. Fred Shuttlesworth, and Rev. Ralph Abernathy developed Project "C" (for confrontation). Money was raised, maps were drawn, and detailed plans were made.

On 2 April Birmingham's racist commissioner of public safety, Theophilus Eugene "Bull" Connor, was defeated in a mayoral election by a more moderate candidate, Albert Boutwell, but Connor insisted on completing his term of office as commissioner until 1965, so that power remained in the hands of outright segregationists. Through April more and more demonstrators were jailed.

Blind singer Al Hibbler (1915–2001) was in Birmingham to support the protest. Television showed him next to Dr. King. Pressure was put on another blind singer, Ray Charles (1930–2004), to join Hibbler, but Charles refused.[41] In his autobiography he tried to defend himself:

> I figured that if I was going to pick up my cross and follow someone, it could only be a cat like King. Yet I couldn't see me doing any marching. And I told that to Martin personally. A reporter once asked me why my name didn't appear in ads protesting one cause or another. Was I soft on the issues? he wanted to know. No, I said, I just don't believe that my name—as a musician or an entertainer—can do very much. Besides that ain't my way. I didn't march for a couple of reasons. First I wouldn't have known when to duck when they started throwing broken beer bottles at my head. And secondly, I'd defeat Martin's purpose. My temperament just wouldn't stand certain treatment.[42]

In spite of Charles's explanation, his drug addiction at that time also may have played a role in his reluctance to participate in the march.

King defied a federal injunction to halt the Alabama protests. Dressed in blue jeans and a white shirt open at the collar he explained to some twenty newsmen: "In the past we have abided by federal injunctions out of respect for the forthright and consistent leadership that the federal judiciary has given in establishing the principle of integration as the law of the land. However, we are now confronted with recalcitrant forces in the Deep South that will use the courts to perpetuate the unjust and illegal systems of racial separation."[43] He said that his attorneys would attempt to have the temporary injunction set aside and that he and his top aide Rev. Ralph Abernathy planned to lead a demonstration that Friday.

On 12 April, a symbolically selected Good Friday, Rev. King was arrested. In the margins of the *Birmingham News*, King began to write his classic "Letter from a Birmingham Jail":

For years now I have heard the word "Wait!" It rings in the ear of every Negro with piercing familiarity. This "Wait" has almost always meant "Never." We must come to see, with one of our distinguished jurists, that "Justice too long delayed is justice denied." We have waited for more than 340 years for our constitutional and God-given rights. The nations of Asia and Africa are moving with jetlike speed toward gaining political independence, but we still creep at horse-and-buggy pace toward gaining a cup of coffee at a lunch counter.

Perhaps it is easy for those who have never felt the stinging darts of segregation to say, "Wait." But when you have seen vicious mobs lynch your mothers and fathers at will and drown your sisters and brothers at whim; when you have seen hate-filled policemen curse, kick, and even kill your black brothers and sisters; when you see the vast majority of your twenty million Negro brothers smothering in an airtight cage of poverty in the midst of an affluent society; when you suddenly find your tongue twisted and your speech stammering as you seek to explain to your six-year-old daughter why she can't go to the public amusement park that has just been advertised on television, and see tears welling up in her eyes when she is told that Funtown is closed to colored children, and see ominous clouds of inferiority beginning to form in her little mental sky, and see her beginning to distort her personality by developing an unconscious bitterness toward white people; . . . then you will understand why we find it difficult to wait.⁴⁴

Dr. King's willingness to undergo imprisonment for the sake of his beliefs prompted Bob Starr (b. 1932, real name Carl Tate) to record an enthusiastic tribute to "The Jail House King" in 1963:

> *Luther King is the man to know,*
> *You hear his name everywhere you go,*
> *Half his time is spent in jail,*
> *He knows the lock on every cell.*

ch: *He's a jailhouse king,*
> *Oh, he's a jailhouse king,*
> *And all the people should shout and sing:*
> *"Hallelujah to the jailhouse king!"*

> *The people call him a new boss man,*
> *Fighting for freedom in this land,*
> *And when they throw old King in jail,*
> *He just teaches what the Scripture tells.*

> *He's sending hatred into the sod,*
> *Teaching all mens the image of God,*
> *And when he's told: "You're going too far,"*
> *He says: "We want freedom, and we want it now!"*

> *I don't want no blood stains,*
> *Just our freedom in this land,*
> *And when injustice is at an end,*
> *You'll see that all races will be friends.*[45]

From his cell Dr. King managed to send a telegram to President Kennedy: "I am deeply grateful to you for taking time out of your Easter weekend to telephone my wife concerning the Birmingham situation. Your encouraging words and thoughtful concern gave her renewed strength to face the difficult moments through which we are now passing. Such moral support greatly enhances our humble efforts to make the American dream a reality."[46]

A few days later Robert Kennedy asked singer Harry Belafonte (b. 1927) to bail King out of jail. Belafonte acquired $5,000 from influential friends, and both King and Abernathy were released.[47]

On 2 May civil rights demonstrators, including many students and schoolchildren, began to march into the city. By the end of the day almost a thousand of them were in Birmingham's jails. Eugene "Bull" Connor, the quintessential southern racist lawman, roughly arrested protesters and used high-pressure water cannons and police dogs against peaceful black marchers, including children. Photos and films of these brutal actions shocked the world. Governor Wallace sent in the Alabama National Guard, and the Ku Klux Klan declared that King's "epitaph could be written here in Birmingham." Immediately after this declaration, a KKK bomb exploded near the hotel room King had just left.

As blues guitarist John Lee Hooker appreciated, Birmingham had become a decidedly dangerous town. In his May 1963 "Birmingham Blues" he sang that he dare not go down to the city alone. Unable to accept the motivations of the racists, he insisted, "A man is just a man," affirming the equality of all before God.

> *I ain't going down, Birmingham by myself,*
> *If I go, will take someone with me.*
>
> *Get me a airplane, fly over Birmingham,*
> *Drop me a bomb, keep on flying on.*

Feel so bad, I read about Birmingham,
Although I know one thing: a man is just a man.

God made this land, and this land,
Is no one, no one's land.
And God made everybody equal, equal, equal,
I don't know why Birmingham,
Treat, treat the people the way they do,
But I ain't going down, Birmingham by myself,
I 'clare I ain't. Yeah!
One thing I do know:
Our president, he is doing everything he can,
Make every man equal right,
It takes time, I do know,
But one day: Birmingham, Mississippi,
Georgia, Tennessee, Kentucky,
All them states,
Arkansas, will fall in line.[48]

"Birmingham Blues" was released as a single on Vee-Jay Records, a black-owned company based in Chicago. It seems likely that owners Vivian and James Bracken would have had some idealistic commitment to the song's message, but it is also true that the changed climate of the early 1960s may have made them believe it was now commercially safe, indeed lucrative, to issue such material.

In "Birmingham Blues" Hooker's apparent willingness to drop a bomb on Birmingham put him rather outside the ranks of the nonviolent army, which was forging a revolution in the South. Nevertheless, coupled with the song's aggressive delivery, such sentiments reflected the new militancy unleashed by the early movement. Equally significant was Hooker's thoroughly favorable view of President Kennedy's handling of the civil rights issue. Hooker's conviction that Kennedy "is doing everything he can, make every man equal right," was an opinion broadly shared by many in the African-American community although it might have raised a few eyebrows among movement leaders in Birmingham and beyond.

Baseball hero Jackie Robinson, who had supported Richard Nixon during the 1960 campaign, was not pleased with the president's record on race either. Robinson had a regular newspaper column, and in mid-May 1963 he commented:

> The fact is that the problems created by the tense Birmingham, Ala. situation lie smack on the doorsteps of the White House. Lie down with dogs and you are due to arise with fleas. . . . Anyone who follows this writer knows that we have consistently voiced the belief that the President is not "for real" on the civil rights issue—that he is a clever tokenist. But tokenism will not satisfy the swelling chorus of indignation which is directed against an Administration which talked big and bad to the steel industry and to Fidel Castro, but fails to take action when Negro ministers and teen-aged Negro children are knocked to the ground by high-pressure water hoses and bitten by police dogs.[49]

Meanwhile Medgar Evers, who had assisted James Meredith in his historic enrollment at Ole Miss, had moved to Jackson, Mississippi. In the spring of 1963 he wrote Mayor Allan C. Thompson that the NAACP was determined to stop racial inequality in Jackson. On 12 May the racist mayor reacted on television with a downright refusal to meet members of the NAACP. A week later Evers used the same medium for his response, in which he eloquently denounced the strict segregation in the city, with its 40 percent black population. On 28 May the NAACP organized sit-ins at the Woolworth lunch counters in Jackson. That same night a Molotov cocktail was thrown at Evers's home. Protest demonstrations led to arrests. Field secretary Evers needed bail money for those arrested. When the NAACP told him that they had insufficient funds, Evers used his own resources, and asked singer Lena Horne to give a benefit concert in Jackson. Both Horne and Evers delivered civil rights addresses at the concert, which took place on 7 June 1963.[50] Evers told the audience: "I love my children and I love my wife with all my heart. And I would die, and die gladly, if that would make a better life for them."[51]

Even those leaders frustrated by the slow and grudging rate of federal action rejoiced when, five days later on 11 June, Kennedy made a moving television address accepting the moral righteousness as well as the constitutional legitimacy of African-American demands for equality, and pledging his administration to comprehensive civil rights legislation.

Kennedy's speech was delivered as Governor George Wallace of Alabama was standing in a doorway to block the attempt of two black students, Vivian Malone and James Hood, to register at the University of Alabama.

> And when Americans are sent to Vietnam, or West Berlin, we do not ask for "Whites Only." It ought to be possible therefore for American students of any color to attend any public institution they select without having to be backed up by troops. It ought to be possible for American consumers of any color to receive equal service in places of public accommodation, such as hotels and restaurants and theatres and retail stores, without being forced to resort to demonstrations in the street, and it ought to be possible for American citizens of any color to register and to vote in a free election without interference or fear of reprisal. . . . But this is not the case. A negro baby born in America today, regardless of the section or the state in which he is born, has about one half as much chance of completing a high school as a white baby, born in the same place, on the same day; one third as much chance of completing college. Are we to say to the world, and much more importantly, to each other, that this is the land of the free, except for the Negroes? That we have no second-class citizens, except Negroes? That we have no class or caste system, no ghettos, no master race, except with respect to Negroes?[32]

Black activism had finally compelled Kennedy to act decisively on civil rights. The president had woken up, and the "new presidency" was born. The moral indignation that had been so sorely missed during the first two years in the White House finally appeared in 1963, only a few months before the president's death. One of those watching John F. Kennedy speak on television about the country's moral crisis was Mrs. Myrlie Evers. After the speech Mrs. Evers went to bed. Just after midnight she heard her husband come home. The car door slammed, followed by the deafening sound of gunshots. Neighbors put Medgar Evers on a mattress and rushed him to the hospital where he died that same night. As a veteran, Medgar Evers, who went ashore at Normandy and won two Bronze Stars, was laid to rest at Arlington National Cemetery.

An NAACP official told Congress that Mississippi leader Medgar Evers was killed because the United States government followed a policy of "too little and too late" in safeguarding the civil rights of Southern

"Running Wild!" Courtesy *New York Amsterdam News*, 30 November 1963. Artist: Melvin Tapley.

Negroes.[53] In a front-page editorial the *Chicago Defender* wrote: "The entire state of Mississippi stands guilty of the cold-blooded murder of Medgar Evers ... inspired and perpetrated by decades of racist ideology that finally resulted in one addle-brained brute ending the life of a dedicated man."[54] UPI reported from Jackson: "Club-swinging violence broke out here during a demonstration inspired by the murder of civil rights leader Medgar Evers."[55] The *Defender* organized a Medgar Evers Memorial Fund to help educate the three Evers children.[56]

On 21 June 1963 President Kennedy welcomed the Evers family at the White House. With them was Medgar's brother Charles, who was designated to take over his slain brother's job as field secretary for the NAACP. The president presented son Darryl (9) with a model PT boat and daughter Reena (8) with a charm bracelet with a PT boat engraved on it.

The sit-in movement of the 1960s, like other protest campaigns, produced a very large number of "freedom songs." Groups like the Carolina Freedom Fighters, the CORE Freedom Singers, and, most famously, the SNCC Freedom Singers from Albany, Georgia, were recorded by dedicated civil rights activists like Guy and Candy Carawan from Highlander Research and Education Center in Tennessee. Although many albums of freedom songs were issued, the artists themselves have generally been neglected by blues and gospel experts because they were not "dedicated gospel recording artists," as gospel discographer Robert Laughton explained.[57] As a result, they are not to be found in the standard blues and gospel discographies, and we are at a loss for information about recording dates and locations, and in many cases even the identities of the singers themselves. Sometimes their identities may have been withheld for their own protection.

"With Medgar Evers Family," 21 June 1963. Photograph by Cecil Stoughton, courtesy the John F. Kennedy Presidential Library and Museum, Boston. (ST-323-2-63)

At a SNCC conference in Atlanta in either 1964 or 1965, the SNCC Freedom Singers recorded a "Ballad of Medgar Evers" about the assassination. It was composed by Rev. Matthew A. Jones Sr., who based it loosely on the ballad "Jesse James." Jones had structured the song so that the chorus was open to congregational singing.

> *In Jackson, Mississippi, in Nineteen Sixty-three,*
> *There lived a man who was brave,*
> *He fought for freedom all of his life,*
> *But they laid Medgar Evers in his grave.*
>
> *He spoke words of truth for all men to hear,*
> *Black and white alike for to save,*
> *Then a hate-filled white man, named Byron de la Beckwith,*
> *Laid Medgar Evers in his grave.*

He taught words of love, dignity, and freedom,
He died before he'd be a slave,
Then a high-powered rifle tore out his heart,
And laid Medgar Evers in his grave.

Medgar had some company in his heavenly home,
Those little children from Birmingham,
Like Christ they died for you and for me,
They died for you to be free.[58]

Although his identity seems to have been common knowledge, it was not until 1994 that the assassin, Byron de la Beckwith, a member of the Citizens' Council of Greenwood, Mississippi, was sent to prison, where he died in 2001. Despite convincing evidence from forensic science, juries in two previous trials failed to return a guilty verdict.

On 19 June 1963, President Kennedy sent Congress the promised bill that became the Civil Rights Act of 1964, which prepared the way for the 1965 Voting Rights Act and offered federal protection to African Americans seeking to shop, to eat out, and to be educated on equal terms. The African-American press reported: "Senate Democratic leaders predicted that President Kennedy's civil rights bill will have more than 50 co-sponsors—a majority in the Senate. They also mapped plans to prevent it from being tied up in committee. These developments came as the tough new civil rights proposals touched off what promised to be one of the most bitter Congressional battles in decades."[59] Pressuring Congress to adopt this bill, and consolidating the huge upsurge in protest activities, major civil rights, labor, and religious groups came together to organize a massive Washington demonstration.

On 10 March 1963 Rev. C. L. Franklin, Martin Luther King's favorite preacher,[60] moved his church into a renovated theater on Linwood and Philadelphia on Detroit's West Side. President Kennedy was one of those who sent a congratulatory telegram. The events in Birmingham caused Franklin to become active in the freedom movement of the Motor City again. To focus attention on racial problems in Detroit and to raise funds for the Southern Christian Leadership Conference (SCLC), a major march was organized. Dr. King asked all Detroit ministers to send telegrams affirming their support to Rev. Franklin. In an 8 June interview with the

Detroit News, Franklin bluntly stated: "We comprise nearly 30 per cent of the population [of Detroit], for example, but 70 per cent of us live in sub-standard housing. Our demonstration will serve as a warning to the city that what has transpired in the past is no longer acceptable to the Negro community. We want complete amelioration of all injustices. This is new leadership."[61] On 23 June 1963 between 125,000 and 200,000 African Americans marched through the segregated shopping center. Those who were lucky found their way into Cobo Hall. After some speeches and songs by Ramsey Lewis, Dinah Washington, Jimmy McGriff, Erma Franklin, and the Four Tops, Martin Luther King delivered the main speech that foreshadowed his famous "I Have a Dream" speech in Washington, DC.[62]

Next the mass choir sang songs dedicated to the memory of Medgar Evers and a special offering collected a scholarship fund for the Evers children. Rev. Franklin had reason to be proud of his efforts and subsequently organized a program to end segregation in jobs, housing, and schools in Detroit.[63]

Gospel singer Dorothy Love Coates (1928–2002) worked with Dr. King from 1959 to 1961 and was arrested on more than one occasion for championing civil rights. She worked voter registration drives, and almost lost her life in the Newark riots of 1967.[64] As she was fond of telling church audiences: "The Lord has blessed our going out and our coming in. He's blessed our sitting in, too."[65] In 1964 she recorded "The Hymn" with her Gospel Harmonettes, a monologue with piano accompaniment and congregational response. As a "born again" Christian she did not doubt the existence of God, as so many Americans did when a church had been bombed and the President assassinated. On 15 September 1963 four young girls attending Sunday school at the Sixteenth Street Baptist Church in Birmingham, Alabama, were killed and twenty others injured when a bomb exploded. The church had been a center for civil rights meetings, and the blast occurred a few days after courts had ordered the desegregation of Birmingham's schools. Dorothy Love Coates had been born and raised in Birmingham, hence the reference to her children being cared for by her mother while she was on the gospel highway.

> We're living in a mean world, we're living in perilous times, all over this world today. Cities are filled with hostility, brutality, and some of the most

ungodliest things you've ever seen in your life. I get word about my children sometimes, and I call home very often to talk to my mother. She said: "You go on and sing your song, we're telling God and God is fighting our battle." My Lord.

When the president was assassinated, the nation said, "Where is God?" When the little children lost their lives in the church bombing, the nation said: "Where is God?" But I got the answer for you today: God is still on the throne and He's got all power entrusted in His hand. And in God's own time and in God's own way he's gonna make everything all right. You better set your house in order, because His patience is wearing out and He's gonna raise Him up a nation that shall obey.[66]

At seventy-four, A. Philip Randolph (1889–1979) was the Nestor of the civil rights movement. As long ago as 1941, he had planned a massive march on Washington, but when President Roosevelt issued Executive Order 8802 and installed the Fair Employment Practices Committee in response, the march was called off.[67] In 1963 Randolph thought it was high time to revive the old idea. Eleven percent of African Americans were unemployed as against 5 percent of white people, and where the average annual earnings for an African-American family were $3,500, a white family earned $3,000 more.[68] Randolph also felt that the time was ripe because the American public had been shocked to see televised images of fire hoses and police dogs aimed at black protesters.

Kennedy was afraid the march would erupt in violence and did his best to prevent it. However, when he understood how strong the determination of the organizers was, he yielded to their pressure and gave them his support. The president's endorsement had a beneficial influence on the pacifist character of the march.

Blues singer Bob Starr recorded a civil rights single for the Hollywood-based Fable label in 1963. Evoking both Abraham Lincoln and Medgar Evers, the A side, "The Freedom March," was one of the many calls to march.

> *Old Abe Lincoln signed the Bill of Rights,*
> *All men was free to see the light,*
> *A hundred years later, they started to strike,*
> *That's what sent off the freedom march.*
>
> ch: *So march, children, march! March, children, march!*
> *March from the north; march from the south,*
> *The news is traveling all over Earth,*
> *So, march, children, march! March, children, march!*
>
> *Well, some are young and some are old,*
> *Some are timid and some are bold,*
> *But they all are marching for the freedom goal.*
>
> sp: *March, children! March, children!*
> *You heard what they said about Dixie:*
> *"In Dixieland where I was born,*
> *On one early frosty morn."*
> sp: *Just march!*
>
> *Well, Medgar Evers, a noble man,*
> *Was fighting for freedom in this land,*
> *Was shot in the back for this cause,*
> *Now, don't let his death suffer a loss.*
>
> sp: *Come on, children, march, children. Fall in!*
> *Come on now, children, let's march, we gotta go!*[69]

The plan was to call up 100,000 people from all over the country, but the success of the march was such that ultimately 250,000 people attended it, a quarter of them white.[70] Among the musicians who entertained the crowds on 28 August 1963 were gospel singer Mahalia Jackson (1911–1972) and blues artist Josh White (1914–1969). In 1961 White had been invited to the president's inauguration and had appeared in the fundraising television program "Dinner with the President,"[71] a showcase hosted by JFK to raise money for the Anti-Defamation League of the B'nai Brith.[72]

A favorite song was the traditional "I Shall Not Be Moved," often adapted for the purpose. Here it is as "We Shall Not Be Moved," recorded in August 1963 by the SNCC Freedom Singers with Rutha Harris as the lead singer. The sleeve notes say this song "was used throughout the union drives to organize black laborers during the 1930s and 1940s."

> ch: We shall not, we shall not be moved,
> Just like a tree that's planted by the water,
> We shall not be moved.
>
> Oh, we're on our way to victory, we shall not be moved,
> Just like a tree that's planted by the water,
> We shall not be moved.
>
> Oh, segregation is our enemy, Lordy, it must be removed,
> Oh, just like a can of garbage in the alley,
> It must be removed.[73]

The Boston-based Mighty Sons of David, whose lead singer was Ernest Frazier, recorded "March On Dr. Martin Luther King" for an unnumbered "Freedom Songs" 45 r.p.m. record in 1963.[74] Significantly, its control number is preceded by the abbreviation MLK. This song is simply a list of all the places where Dr. King should march for equal rights. The B-side of the "Freedom Songs" record by the Mighty Sons of David, "We Want Freedom in This Land," was also recorded in the year of the March on Washington.

> ch: We want freedom in this land,
> We want freedom in this land.
>
> We've been up and we've been down,
> Sometimes level with the ground.
>
> We've been 'buked and we've been scorned,
> Give up right for the wrong.
>
> Oh, I said, listen, everybody, there's something you ought to know,
> Dr. Martin Luther King got freedom on the go,
> They are marching everywhere,
> Having trial here and there.
>
> We've been 'buked and we've been scorned,
> Give up right for the wrong.

We've been up and we've been down,
Sometimes level with the ground.

Shout about freedom in this land,
Shout about freedom in this land.

Sometimes right, sometimes wrong,
One day I'll get my starry crown.

Moan about freedom in this land.
Moan about freedom in this land.

Sometimes up, sometimes down.[75]

The *Chicago Defender* printed Dr. King's speech in its entirety and commented: "Rarely has history witnessed a more moving, dramatic or eloquent moment than the hour when America's foremost civil rights leader, Rev. Dr. Martin Luther King, Jr. delivered his brilliant address on the steps of the Lincoln Memorial with the brooding countenance of the Great Emancipator looking down on the 300,000 people assembled."[76]

The day ended with a visit of the Big Six of the civil rights movement to the president in the White House. They are, from left to right in the photos made of the occasion, James Farmer (national director of the Congress of Racial Equality), Whitney Young (executive director of the National Urban League), Martin Luther King Jr. (president of the Southern Christian Leadership Conference), John Lewis (president of the Student Nonviolent Coordinating Committee), A. Philip Randolph (president of the Brotherhood of Sleeping Car Porters), and Roy Wilkins (executive secretary of the National Association for the Advancement of Colored People). This appears to be the only occasion at which Kennedy and King were photographed together.

In an editorial, the *New York Amsterdam News* pledged its support: "We herewith, salute these men and we formally accept them as our leaders. And as we accept them, we urge others to do the same. In these six men we have the flower of a great people. They are the best of our breed. We do not need more. We should not accept less. What is needed now is for all of us to get behind them into a reality of the great American dream."[77]

On the same page Roy Wilkins, one of the Big Six and rather critical of MLK, wrote that it was not a great day simply because of the

"With MLK and Other Civil Rights Leaders," 28 August 1963. Photo: Courtesy United States Information Services.

"joy-giving" music (Mahalia Jackson) or the "good" speeches (Martin Luther King), but "because of the people themselves—more than 200,000 of them who came to Washington from every corner of this nation and from overseas. They came, white and black, to say to the nation's capital and to the world that freedom must ring throughout the land, in Mississippi as well as in Minnesota."[78]

On 28 August 1963, the March on Washington marked the symbolic culmination of the early movement. As the nation heard Martin Luther King's "I Have a Dream" speech, with its thinly veiled hints that far more radical African-American activists waited in the wings should America continue to ignore the nonviolent movement's demands for equality, public support for Kennedy's proposed civil rights bill was growing.

Less than three months later, on Friday 22 November 1963, John Fitzgerald Kennedy, the youngest president ever, the president who had been seen to promise so much, drove into Dallas, Texas.

6

THE DAY THE WORLD STOOD STILL

As the Great Emancipator who actively supported the Thirteenth Amendment to the Constitution which abolished slavery, Abraham Lincoln has always been held in high esteem by African Americans, and yet recorded blues contain few references to him.[1] One notable exception is the extended tribute "Ballad to Abraham Lincoln" recorded by John Lee Hooker on 9 March 1961. As in other recordings from this period in which Hooker commemorates historical events, such as the flood that devastated Tupelo[2] or the dancehall fire in Natchez, Mississippi, that claimed the lives of bandleader Walter Barnes and many of those present,[3] the narrative is spoken, rather than sung. Although it is likely that this composition was prompted by the 4 March 1961 centenary of Lincoln's inauguration, it was certainly also inspired by the escalating civil rights confrontation in the South. Hooker notes ominously that Lincoln paid the ultimate price for his efforts to reconcile the warring parties.

> *Do you remember the great president?*
> *His name was Abraham Lincoln.*
> *Around a hundred years or more ago,*

The North and the South didn't like each other.
Abraham Lincoln, oh, tried to pull them together.
The North and the South they fought.
Abraham Lincoln freed the South, freed the slaves,
But although he got assassinated, trying to pull the North and the South together.

That's been a long, long, long, long time ago,
Way, way before my time, before your time,
But he was a great man.
The South fought the North,
Because the South didn't know,
But the North felt sorry for the poor slaves.
Oh, Abraham Lincoln, he got assassinated,
Trying to bring the North and South together.

Although he succeeded in freeing, freed the South,
Lord, but you know I'm very thankful for him, what he did,
I'm very thankful, people, today,
For a great president, you know he died, died for me.
I have a right to live here. Oh, yeah.
I don't remember him, but I read books about him,
What a great man he was, he freed the South,
Although he got assassinated doing it, mmm.[4]

On Friday 22 November 1963 John F. Kennedy, the thirty-fifth president of the United States, was killed by gunshots while riding in a presidential motorcade through Dallas, Texas. It was experienced by many people as the day the world stood still.

In the days following Kennedy's assassination, the *Chicago Defender* published a cartoon that depicted a solitary black man standing on Freedom Road, waving goodbye to both Lincoln and Kennedy.[5] The caption read, "Good-bye, Dear Friend." Even more complimentary was an article by Simeon Booker in *Ebony* entitled "How JFK Surpassed

Abraham Lincoln." Booker argued that Kennedy had prepared the ground for full integration of African Americans into the American scene. "While Lincoln fought slavery he was also opposed to giving Negroes social and political equality. Just before his death in 1865 he recommended suffrage only for Negro veterans and Negroes who were 'very intelligent.' President Kennedy, on the other hand, did not apply standards to Negroes differing from those for whites."[6]

During a 1970 tour through Europe with the American Folk Blues Festival, Champion Jack Dupree was recorded in concert in Frankfurt, Germany. In his "School Day," a remake of his 1961

"Good-bye, Dear Friend." Courtesy *Chicago Defender*, 7 December 1963. Artist: Eugene.

"Schoolday Blues,"[7] Dupree reminisced on the effect of segregation on African-American education. He asked the white German audience not to look down on him for his illiteracy. Seven years after Kennedy's assassination Dupree had not forgotten him and still equated him with Abraham Lincoln.

Lord, I never went to school, not one day in my life,
I had to work hard every day, every day of my life.

Well, the people all told me, I ain't nothing but a white man's slave,
And conditions ain't no better, slave out all the day.

I can't read, I can't write, I can't even sign my name,
It's a low down dirty, low down dirty shame.

I know you people glad, I know you glad you ain't none of me,
I know you have hard times, but you don't have times like me.

I don't have no education, I ain't nothing but a fool,
I say, don't blame me, people, 'cause I never went to school.

Well, it wasn't but two men in the world ever tried to free me,
That was Abraham Lincoln and President Kennedy.[8]

In his inaugural address President Kennedy had declared: "United, there is little we cannot do in a host of cooperative ventures. Divided, there is little we can do—for we dare not meet a powerful challenge at odds and split asunder." After the president's assassination these words rang in Brother Sidney Harris's ears. On "My Friend Kennedy" he mourns the loss of a righteous President who had fought for human freedom.

Sleep on, my friend,
What God says surely will be,
Sleep on, my friend, (oh)
President John F. Kennedy, (oh yeah)
While here on this old Earth, (oh yes, you did)
You fought a mighty good fight, (oh yes, you did, oh yes, you did)
And for every nation, (oh yes)
You stood for the right, (oh yes, you did)
In Nineteen Hundred and Sixty-one, (oh Lord)
President Kennedy, he took the seat, (oh yes, he did)
He started telling about the rights of men, (oh, help me to tell the story, Jesus)
To all that, eh, he would meet, (oh, help me, Lord)
No, no, respect a person,
Then he fought to make the goal, (oh, help me, Jesus)
About the rights of freedom, (oh, yes)
For every, every living soul, (oh, Lord)
He said, together we would stand, (oh, yes, he did)
And divided we surely would fall, (oh, yes, he did)

President Kennedy knew that there was only one God,
Just one God, who was born over us all, (oh, help me, Jesus)
Sleep on, sleep on, my friend, sleep on, sleep on,
Surely, what God said was true, (oh, yes, he did)
You fought for the right, (oh, yes, you did, Lord)
You fought a good fight, (oh, yeah, Lord, you did)
You fought a good fight, President John F. Kennedy.[9]

The same lines from the inaugural address were quoted by the Dixie Hummingbirds when they made their television debut on *TV Gospel Time* in Washington, DC, in 1964.[10] Kennedy's assassination prompted composer and baritone vocalist James Emerdia Walker (1926–1992) to add a special verse to "Our Prayer for Peace," a song loosely based on his "A Prayer for Tomorrow," which he had recorded with the Southern Sons.[11] That 1953 song contained the line: "Together we stand, child, and divided we fall." The reason why gospel singers favored the phrase that much might be found in its ultimate source in Mark 3:25: "And if a house be divided against itself, that house cannot stand."

Shortly before his death James Walker remembered: "President Kennedy was assassinated—I think it was on a Friday—and that Saturday I wrote a verse about the assassination. And we were in Jamaica, New York, and boy, when I did that verse, people was really going wild—because it had just happened."[12]

> *Lord, teach us how to love each other,*
> *Mmm, every creed, Lord, and every color.*
> *Let every, let every man know, Lord, let them know that it is a sin,*
> *To hate his brother because of the color of his skin.*
>
> sp: *And then, while you're talking to him, don't forget to tell him this:*
>
> *For you to guide, Lord, guide our mind and tongue,*
> *Oh, keep our hands, oh Lord, please, don't let our hands do any thing wrong.*
> *Oh, please, Father, let all of this hatred cease,*
> *Then let us all live down here together, Lord, let us all live in peace.*

sp: There is one thing happened that shook the nation, listen:
In Nineteen Sixty-three, we all know it was on the twenty-
second of November,
Tragedy that happened way down in Dallas, Texas,
Oh, I do believe the whole world will forever remember.

Listen: President Kennedy, the one who fought so hard for the human race,
By the hands of a mad, evil man, today Kennedy is sleeping cold in his grave,
He was only trying to tell the world this: "Jesus died, yeah, to save us all,"
He said: "Together we, together we stand," oh, he said: "Divided we'll fall."
Oh, Jesus, oh, Father, let all of this hatred cease,
Lord, if it's your will, let us work and go to school together, Lord, let us all go in peace.[13]

The most memorable passage in President Kennedy's 20 January 1961 inaugural address was paraphrased by Rosie Wallace and the choir of the First Church of Love, Faith and Deliverance in "Take Courage": "And so, my fellow Americans: ask not what your country can do for you—ask what you can do for your country. My fellow citizens of the world: ask not what America will do for you, but what together we can do for the freedom of man." For inspiration Evangelist Rosie Wallace also turned to the magnificent promise of the prophet Isaiah.[14] At the time of writing, Mrs. Wallace (b. 1935) is still pastor of the church she founded, the First Church of Love, Faith and Deliverance in Philadelphia.[15]

They that wait upon the Lord shall renew their strength,
They shall mount up with wings as eagles.
They shall run and not be weary; they shall walk and not faint,
So take courage, my fellows, and be strong in your faith.

Ask not what your country can do for you,
Rather what can you for your country do.

And for those with whom you walk each day.
So take courage, my fellows, and be strong in your faith.

Let's destroy hatred, malice, bigotry, and greed,
And all those things on which destruction feed.
And let's walk hand in hand behind those who are brave,
And take courage, my fellows, and be strong in your faith.

God has blessed our country to be strong and brave,
We have never been defeated, nor have we been enslaved.
So, together every nationality and race,
Take courage, my fellows, and be strong in your faith.[16]

In a 2005 telephone conversation, Mrs. Wallace had the following to say about President Kennedy: "He was a people's president. By that I meant he was conscious of the needs of people who are below the line of the middle class, those kinds of people, grassroots people, who were not rich people. He had a heart for those kinds of people, and I think he was a great man, a good president, a great negotiator. I am sure he had help in his administration, but he was great. I only remember the good things. I don't remember all the bad things they write afterwards. That's not my concern, other than him being my president."[17]

The assassination of President Kennedy led to a worldwide outpouring of grief, but two public opinion polls conducted in the United States shortly afterwards suggested that African Americans believed themselves to be the most profoundly affected of all. In a national survey people were asked to compare their own reactions against a perceived norm. Overall, 30 percent believed that they were more upset than "most people," but 49 percent of African Americans thought they were more upset. Two thirds of African Americans, against 38 percent of all respondents, agreed with the statement that they were "so confused and upset, they didn't know what to feel." Furthermore, half of the African Americans surveyed, compared with one fifth of the total sample, "worried how this might affect my own life, job and future."[18]

For the Sensational Six of Birmingham, Alabama, 22 November 1963 was "The Day the World Stood Still." This song is an adaptation of one of the best-loved Isaac Watts hymns, "The Day Is Past and Gone." Dr. Watts (1674–1748) was the "father of English hymnody."

> *November the twenty-second, Nineteen Hundred and Sixty-*
> *three,*
> *That is the day the whole world stood still, when the newsman*
> *said these words:*
>
> *"President Kennedy has passed and gone."*
> *President Kennedy has passed and gone,*
> *Oh, he died for you and me,*
> *The reason it happened, I just can't see.*
> *I'm so sorry to say that President Kennedy has passed,*
> *Our president has passed and gone.*
>
> sp: *I was so sad that day!*
>
> *The whole world began to mourn,*
> *The whole world began to mourn.*
> *No matter what faith or creed,*
> *We surely lost a friend we need.*
> *I'm so sorry to say, that President Kennedy has passed,*
> *Our president surely has passed and gone.*
> *Oh, Lord!*[19]

The early morning of Friday 22 November 1963 found President Kennedy in his hotel room in Fort Worth, Texas. As he prepared for the thirteen-minute flight to Dallas, he addressed some prophetic words to his wife and his special assistant, Kenneth O'Donnell: "If anybody really wants to shoot the president of the United States, it's not a very difficult job—all one has to do [is] get [in] a high building someday, with a telescopic rifle, and there would be nothing anybody could do to defend against such an attempt." Kennedy had gone to Texas to gather support for the 1964 elections, because he was aware that his policies were arousing considerable resentment among his opponents. Only a month before Adlai Stevenson, U.S. ambassador to the United Nations and a former presidential candidate, had been spat at and cursed during a visit to Dallas. Factional squabbles among local Democrats presented further problems for the Kennedy administration. An extra day had therefore been added to the original itinerary to allow for a motorcade through Dallas.

James Brewer, Blues Estafette, Utrecht, the Netherlands, 19 February 1983. Photo: René van Rijn.

Although the fateful day started cold and cloudy with some rain, the weather cleared up as the president flew from Fort Worth to Dallas. Blind James Brewer (1921–1988), a guitarist who had traveled from Mississippi to St. Louis in the 1940s and on to Chicago in the 1950s, took the weather as an omen in "Why Did He Have to Go?"

Well, oh well. Well, oh well, oh well,
Well, we lost a good president, why did he have to go?

President Kennedy, he was a mighty good man,
Well, going throughout the country, serving every woman and man.

It was one cold, cloudy day, when our president went away,
Well, he left us alone, doing the best we can.

Well, I wonder why, why did he have to go?
Well, he's gone, he's gone, but his work must go on.

> *President Kennedy, man, we all know he gone,*
> *Well, he left his country, what are we gonna do?*
>
> *I remember, when he first took the seat,*
> *Well, jobs began to open up, work turne d out so neat.*[20]

Brewer's view of Kennedy's employment record is also interesting. It is true that there had been some early economic success, mainly through the efforts of Kennedy's economic advisor Walter Heller,[21] but not until he read Michael Harrington's *The Other America* in 1963 was Kennedy really convinced of the urgent need for economic reform.[22] Ever since FDR the hallmark of a good president was his ability to create jobs, and JFK must have done just that because he was a good president, or so James Brewer thought.

When the presidential plane arrived at the Dallas airport, Love Field, at 11:35 a.m., fears of a hostile reception appeared to be unfounded, for an enthusiastic crowd had gathered to welcome the president. He and Mrs. Kennedy took their places in the rear of a blue 1961 Lincoln convertible, while Texas Governor John Connally and his wife occupied the jump seats in front of them. The President preferred to travel with the limousine's bubbletop removed so that he could see and be seen. Instead of proceeding directly along Main Street to Industrial Boulevard, where he was due to address a group of local businessmen and civic leaders, the motorcade was obliged to make a number of slow turns through Dealey Plaza, on a route that had been widely publicized in the Dallas newspapers of 19 November. To turn from Main Street via Houston Street into Elm Street, the presidential limousine had to slow down to five miles per hour, in full view of hundreds of windows in the adjacent buildings. Philadelphia-based blues guitarist Bill Jackson (1906–poss. 1982) sang about the fatal route in his "The 22nd Day of November."

> *On the twenty-second of November, in 1963,*
> *In the old city of Dallas, down Texas way,*
> *It was on that day, our president was slain.*
> *Now, wasn't it sad, sad, when our president was slain?*
>
> *Now, it was on, on a Friday, just one o'clock,*
> *Oh, the president and his party rode down Mockingbird Lane,*

And his dear wife sat beside him, all dressed in pink,
They were on their way to the Trade Mart, when three rifle shots
                                                        rang out.

Oh, they rushed him to the hospital, but the doctors couldn't do
                                                        no good,
And when they said that the president was passed, tears began to fall,
Now, wasn't it sad, sad, when our beloved president was slain?[23]

On the sixth floor of the Texas School Book Depository a sniper was waiting. At half past twelve three rifle shots were fired. The first missed the car and hit the pavement, but the President stopped waving and turned to the right, as the Abraham Zapruder film shows in frame 160.[24] Governor Connally turned around to see what was going on. The second shot (Zapruder frame 223 and fired 3.4 seconds after the first) hit the president in the throat. His arms went up horizontally across his body at shoulder level because of a reflex caused by the bullet hitting a nerve. The throat wound was minor. Had the driver accelerated instead of coming to a virtual halt, the president's life might have been saved. Four and nine-tenth seconds after the second shot, a third one blew out the right side of the President's brains. A piece of bone was later found on the ground, and Mrs. Kennedy reflexively climbed onto the back of the car to retain another part.

The limousine was rushed to Parkland Hospital. The president and the governor were carried in. Connally had been shot in the wrist and chest, but was not seriously wounded.

Ollie Hoskins, lead vocalist of the Dixie Nightingales, wrote "Assassination" for his gospel quartet, who sang that when the news came on the radio both the rich and the poor cried.

> *Assassin in the window, down in a Texas town,*
> *(Lord, have mercy!)*
> *He waited till he saw him, then he shot the President down.*

> ch: Oh, oh, what a shame it was! (3x)
> He shot the president down.
>
> The world became a sphere of solitude and sadness, rich men
> and poor men cried,
> When the news came on the radio, that President Kennedy had
> died.
>
> He was a man of honor, a man who had pride,
> A man who faced responsibility, had equality in his eye.[25]

Anyone old enough to remember knows where they heard the news of Kennedy's death. Blues singer B.B. King recalled seeing the news on television in a hotel room:

> The word was out there was a young senator who might become president. He was a handsome gentleman, and the ladies liked him. Usually when you've got the ladies on your side, it helps. I think he had most of the ladies on his side. But then he had a lot of the men too. The band and I were on the bus. We were just pulling up to the Persian Hotel in Chicago, Illinois.[26] We were playing poker. We had the TV on—a local station. We thought we'd lost everything. I hadn't felt that way ever, the way he made me feel. Being a citizen, you love your country, and you love the president and you stand behind him, but when John F. Kennedy came in, you wanted to help. That's what he made you feel like. "Ask not what your country can do for you, but what you can do for your country." My God, that stirred me up. The things he did in office made me love him forever. He made it possible for black kids to go to schools that had been closing the doors on them. It wasn't always thinking in terms of politics. It wasn't always the smartest thing to do, but it was the right thing to do. He did more for black people than President Truman did. Knowing that, just thinking about it now, I almost cry again. He gave us confidence that the country loved us too. We felt like real citizens. He gave us a feeling to fight for our rights. I thought it would probably be like that for the rest of my life.[27]

Perry Tillis (1919–2004) is one of the many blues artists who crossed over to gospel music. Very late in his life, when he had become a bishop

Perry Tillis, Samson, Alabama, 18 July 2004. Photo: Kevin Nutt.

in his own church, he was still performing every first and third Sunday at the Our Savior Jesus Holiness Pentecostal Church in Samson, Alabama. Bottleneck guitarist Tillis became totally blind in 1954. In 1971, eight years after the assassination, he recorded "Kennedy Moan" at his home outside Elba in southeast Alabama. A few days before his death in 2004, Tillis remembered "Kennedy Moan": "Them songs would bring money, you know, too! People pay me to play that. He was my president. One thing he did, he made it better for the colored man in some ways. Me myself, I tell you, I ain't never had it bad. I always have got along with white folks and colored. I always would go with them to their house. I eat with them, I sleep with them. But a lot of folks couldn't do it. I thought one of the best things he ever done while he was president was when he and his brother got Wallace out of the schoolhouse door."[28]

ch: *Well, wasn't it sad, President Kennedy's gone?*
The man we trusted is done gone on.

Well, in Nineteen Hundred and Sixty-three,
Just as God would have it to be,
The man went out in Dallas, Texas,
He was shot by a sniper, was a boy suspected.
The twelve-thirty bell began to tone,
The whole wide world was left to moan.

Great God almighty, while he was alive,
They tell me his wife, she stuck by his side.
All indication showed that he was dead,
In her lap she held his head,
The bloody stockings that she had to wear,
She grieved so much, she didn't know it was there.

Well, 'bout twelve-thirty, getting out of bed,
I heard the news, that the man was dead,
Started to grieve, and began to moan,
Our best president is done gone on.[29]

Tillis sings about "a sniper, (who) was a boy suspected." Lee Harvey Oswald had been a sharpshooter with the U.S. Marines. Marine documents show that he was a very good shot and prove that a target eighty-eight yards away was well within his ability. The 6.5 mm Mannlicher-Carcano rifle that he had bought by mail order was known for its fast loading and fast firing. Three shots within 8.3 seconds would have been no problem for a well-trained marksman.

Mahalia Jackson (1911–1972) had campaigned for JFK and sang the "Star-Spangled Banner" at his inauguration.[30] A week after the assassination the undisputed queen of gospel music recorded a moving "In the Summer of His Years," with a muffled drum as the only accompaniment. The song emphasized that by killing

The Day the World Stood Still

this young president, Oswald also killed the realization of an American dream. Laurraine Goreau, Jackson's biographer, wrote that Columbia had rushed her into the studio to cut the Kennedy memorial single. "Other editions had been questioned for taste, but not Mahalia Jackson's," Goreau added.[31]

> A young man rode with his head held high, under the Texas sun,
> And no one guessed that a man so blessed would perish by the gun,
> Lord, would perish by the gun.
>
> A shot rang out like a sudden shout, and Heaven held its breath,
> For the dream of a multitude of men rode with him to his death,
> Lord, rode with him to his death.
>
> Yes, the heart of the world weighed heavy, with the helplessness of tears,
> For the man cut down in a Texas town, in the summer of his years,
> in the summer of his years.[32]

One of the other versions (MGM 13203) was advertised on a full page of *Billboard* of 14 December 1963. It was recorded and released by Connie Francis for the benefit of the J. D. Tippit fund. Tippit was the police officer who was killed by Lee Harvey Oswald forty-five minutes after the Kennedy assassination.

The same issue also featured an ad for the "inspired" Toni Arden version on Decca 41576, and under the headline "BBC Kennedy Broadcast Is Hot Item" the ethics of the song and its recorded versions were discussed extensively. Some radio stations thought it was "poor taste to capitalize on such a tragic situation":

> The controversy was not an outgrowth of Tin Pan Alley activity. Two Britishers wrote the song as part of the BBC tribute. Herbert Kretzmer wrote the words and David Lee the music. Lou Levy, president of Leeds Music, happened to be in a London apartment when the program was performed over the BBC. He felt the song was a great piece of material and he acquired the copyright. Several artists, according

to Levy—among them Connie Francis, queried the BBC to ascertain the
publisher—and in this way the initial disks were cut. Levy notes he made
no effort to promote the song—he merely urged that artists bear in mind
the dignity of the material and exercise care in their choice of material for
the flip side. Even if the publisher wished to stop the flood of records, this
was impossible owing to the compulsory or automatic license provision
of the Copyright Act. Publisher Lou Levy and singer Connie Francis will
donate their royalties to the family of Patrolman J. D. Tippit, who was shot
in the Dallas tragedy, and to worthy causes. ABC-Paramount will donate
a portion of the royalties to charities, and possibly others will take similar
action. Levy stated in part: "No one has ever been able to explain the creative process. Whatever magic is involved . . . touched two young songwriters in London . . . when the news about President Kennedy came to them
over the air it was part of the BBC's tribute" . . . But songs are not made
just to be sung and heard." They are created to be sung again and again.
And so many fine artists have recorded this song: Connie Francis, Mahalia
Jackson, Toni Arden, Kate Smith, Millicent Martin. Translations are being made in many languages; it is a song to be heard 'round the world . . .
It will be a part of every remembrance . . . royalties are being donated by
many of those involved . . . Our part in making this song is small, but we
feel well rewarded." As the week closed, discussion reached a high point,
centering around the theme of what was the proper role of the music-record industry—and the radio industry-with regard to "event songs," in
this specific instance a song dealing with one of the most tragic events in
the nation's history.[33]

Six years later, in 1969, when Martin Luther King and Bobby Kennedy had also been killed, Mahalia Jackson recorded another tribute. "Abraham, Martin and John" was written by Dick Holler, who was awarded a Million-Air certificate in 2002 on the occasion of the three millionth time a performance of his song was played.[34]

Blues guitarist and factory worker Avery Brady (1912–1977), who had come from Clarksdale, Mississippi, to Chicago, was one of the many American citizens who were sent home early from work on 22 November 1963. Here is part two of Brady's 1964 "Poor Kennedy."[35]

> *Well, you know, early one morning, friend of mine walking down the street,*
> *Well, he didn't even know that was his last, last step he's making in the street.*
> He was so nice and kind, trying to help all poor people to meet.
>
> *You know, the devil standing at the stairs, stick a gun in his hand,*
> *Well, poor Kennedy, this is your last time.*
> *He say: "Ooh, Lord," fell way over in his wife's loving arms.*
> *Well, I feel so bad, didn't even finish my day's work.*

sp: *Yes, sure, the whole truth. I got off early that day too!*

> *Well, it seemed so sad in the morning, men over all across town,*
> *Baby, and all them womens and mens, crying 'bout poor Kennedy dying.*
> *I didn't even had no mind, no mind to stay in your town.*
>
> *Lord say: "Goodbye Kennedy, you are going home."*
> *(I believe he was a Christian man.)*
> *Well, you know everything he said, tried to help the poor people in their homes.*
> *I don't know how, just, I don't know how the time going to be now,*
> *Well, our best President is gone, poor Kennedy is gone home.*

sp: *I hate it too.*[36]

Brother Thermon Ruth (1914–2002) had come to New York from South Carolina in 1922.[37] With the Harmoneers, a pseudonym for the Harmonizing Five, he recorded "That Awful Day in Dallas" a week after the murder. This song is an adaptation of Ruth's 1941 recording "What a Time."[38] For Ruth, as for the Sensational Six, everything stopped at the moment the president was killed. His mind wandered to the impossibility of replacing this "voice to love."

> ch: *Wasn't that an awful time in Dallas? What a time, what a time!*
> *When a shot struck by surprise, and our president lost his life,*
> *Wasn't that an awful time in Dallas? What a time, what a time!*
>
> *Well, stop still, people, and listen to me:*
> *I wanna tell you 'bout a tragedy,*
> *November twenty-second, Sixty-three,*
> *In a day that will always stay with me.*
> *On Friday at noon in Dallas town,*
> *A bullet struck, that struck him down,*
> *Oh, with the president, when he lost his life,*
> *Eh, by his side was Jackie, his wife.*
>
> *When the world got the news, it went in shock,*
> *They tell me that everything did stop,*
> *He left the people feeling sad,*

> We lost the best president we ever had.
> A man of courage, who stood for right,
> Oftentimes he had to fight,
> A voice true loving has been stilled,
> A chair is vacant that can't be filled.[39]

Blues pianist Otis Spann (1930–1970) referred to the assassin as a "disinteresting person" in "Sad Day in Texas." He may either mean an uninteresting person of no consequence, or a disinterested person, someone who does not care about anything. Ever since the assassination, conspiracy theories have been very popular. How could someone as inconsequential as Oswald kill the president? The fatherless Oswald had always been a lonely boy who needed attention. According to Robert Oswald, his brother killed the president because he wanted to be somebody. Recent research by people like Gerald Posner and Mark Obenhaus has it that Oswald worked alone and that he fired all three shots.[40]

> You know, it was a sad day in Texas, when my president passed
>   away,
> He didn't get a chance to talk; he didn't know he was on his way.
>
> Know he left home happy, know the man he looked so gay,
> When a disinteresting person put my president away.
>
> sp: Have mercy!
>
> Only man I ever, ever loved in my life,
> Was my President Kennedy, and I also loved his wife.
>
> I feel sorry, I feel sorry, feel sorry for myself,
> Know we'll never have another president, and I don't want
>   nobody else.[41]

The Southern Bell Singers recorded "The Tragedy of Kennedy" in November or December of 1963. It is an adaptation of "Atlanta's Tragic Monday" by the Echoes of Zion, a 1952 song about an incident when people were poisoned by bad moonshine.[42] Kennedy is hailed as a champion of the poor, and the song ends with the marvelous observation that Jesus is a president too. This phrase had previously been used by Otis Jackson in his 1946 recording "Tell Me Why You Like Roosevelt."[43] The Southern Bells correctly state that Parkland Hospital is only five minutes from the Texas School Book Depository. Consequently the limousine reached the hospital at 12:35. At first Mrs. Kennedy would not let her husband go, but once he had been placed on a stretcher he was rushed inside. He was still breathing, and doctors connected him to a respirator. A tracheotomy was performed, but John F. Kennedy was pronounced dead at one o'clock.

> sp: My mind is on a day, a day that we should never forget:
> Friday, November the twenty-second, Nineteen Hundred and
>   Sixty-three,
> President Kennedy lost his life!
> It makes me wanna sing a song that sounds like this:
>
> ch: Lord, I know it was sad, (So sad one Friday evening!)
> Lord, sad. I know it was sad. Lord have mercy now!
> President Kennedy lost his life!
>
> Well, he was down in Dallas, Texas, to speak to a thousand or
>   two,
> Man from a tall, tall building, killed a man: he was good to you.
>
> Well, they rushed him to a hospital, only five minutes away,
> People standing in the lobby, and they didn't know what to say.
>
> Well, this is what I did, when I first heard the news:
> I said: "Lord, God Almighty, what we poor peoples going to do?"
>
> Well, let me tell you, people, what we'd better do,
> Keep our mind on Jesus, for he's a president too.[44]

Another gospel group, The Birds of Harmony, performed a "Tribute to a Great President." The author of this recitation, who is probably a member of the group, is given as Edward Lightner. He remembers that when he heard the news on the radio, he could not fathom what had happened. One thing all the gospel singers are certain of is that their president was welcome in Heaven.

> sp: This is our tribute to a great president, John Fitzgerald Kennedy.
>
> sp: It happened November twenty-two, Nineteen Hundred and Sixty-three,
> A man whose name was John Fitzgerald Kennedy.
> I was listening to a radio station,
> When I heard the news that shocked the nation.
> I also read in the newspapers how it had happened,
> It said that he was killed by an assassin.
> I do not know what causes such a thing,
> But God knows why the bells of freedom ring.
> They took this great man's life,
> Who has now left behind two darling little children and a very sad, sad wife.
> And when he was slain, Lord, so many of us said: "This could not be,"
> For he believed that no matter what creed or color,
> That we are all under our Heavenly Father as sisters and brothers.
>
> And when he gets to the Golden Gate, let them open wide,
> And let John Fitzgerald Kennedy walk inside.[45]

Gospel singer Brother Will Hairston (1919–1988) was a member of Love Tabernacle Church in Detroit. His recordings are characterized by the frequent use of topical and political allusions. "I take to heart whatever happens to people, and then sing about it," he explained in a 1968 interview.[46] During one of Hairston's church programs the congregation was roused to such a frenzy that someone mentioned afterwards that it looked as if a hurricane had been through the church. From that moment on, Brother Will was known as the "Hurricane of the Motor City." The hit record that would have meant that he could leave the Chrysler plant on Eight Mile Road in Detroit never came about, but his recorded legacy

Brother Will Hairston and unknown pianist in a Detroit recording studio, unknown date. Photo: Courtesy Mrs. Willie Hairston.

affords some insight into a wide range of topics such as the gruesome fate of Emmett Till, his enthusiasm for Martin Luther King and President Kennedy, and his horror of the war in Vietnam. "Since it is history that he records, rather than emotions, controversy is almost nil," interviewer Rita Griffin commented, failing to note that black pride necessarily includes pride in African Americans' history of struggle and achievement in the face of racism.

Brother Will Hairston's eldest daughter Sandranette interviewed her mother and kindly shared her own memories of her father: "My father always, even before retiring from the Chrysler plant in Detroit, read the newspaper from cover to cover, followed by reading the Holy Bible and lastly he watched the 11:00 p.m. news. Dad would always tell me: 'You have to read the paper every day, so you will know what's happening in the world.' Dad gathered information from the media, radio, television, and newspapers. He took factual information, rhymed the facts, and put music with it. He was a rapper way ahead of his time. Dad had a lot of hobbies, which included writing and composing songs about current events that affected the African-American community during our many struggles."[47]

In 1964 Hairston recorded "Story of President Kennedy." As usual, Hairston uses the newspaper as his source. After the assassination, Oswald, who is here equated with Satan again, had fled from the Texas School Book Depository where he had been a clerk for five weeks. The police noticed an employee on the second floor drinking a Coke, but did not arrest him. Twelve minutes after the shots, the building was sealed off for investigation. By that time Oswald had calmly walked off. Half an hour later he killed Dallas police officer J. D. Tippit with three bullets from the Smith and Wesson .38 revolver he had bought in January that year. Oswald next slipped into the Texas Theater on Jefferson Boulevard, where he was arrested. He denied the killings and claimed that he was "a patsy," a person

Brother Will Hairston and unknown pianist performing for WJLB, Detroit, unknown date. Photo: Courtesy Mrs. Willie Hairston.

who was set up by conspirators to take the blame for it. Less than forty-eight hours after Oswald's arrest, Jack Ruby, operator of the Carousel strip club, shot the suspected assassin dead. The murder was broadcast live on television. According to his brother Earl Ruby, Jack, who was devoted

The Day the World Stood Still [131]

to the President, was apparently infuriated by the triumphant smirk on Oswald's face.[48]

> *This is a story of one so great, listen:*
>
> *I said, hush, America, and don't you cry,*
> *You know President Kennedy was born to die,*
> *And if you read your newspapers and if you read them well,*
> *You'll know about a story that I'm bound to tell,*
> *I wanna tell you a story that we all should believe,*
> *How President Kennedy had died for you and me,*
> *He campaigned high and he campaigned low,*
> *But he said one day: "I won't campaign no more."*
> *He won the election for Sixty-one,*
> *He knew that his troubles had just begun,*
> *In Nineteen Hundred and Sixty-two,*
> *He was almost finished setting up his crew,*
> *In Nineteen Hundred and Sixty-three,*
> *He was almost to set United States free,*
> *But, oh, wait a minute, let me tell you again,*
> *Right in the picture old Satan stepped in,*
> *And I don't know, people, but I been told,*
> *In Dallas, Texas, the motorcade rolled,*
> *The time of day was just about one,*
> *There stood Oswald, he had a gun,*
> *The motorcade rolled down the streets that day,*
> *He was only one hundred yards away,*
> *The peoples heard a sound, it was all around,*
> *And they began to lay on the ground,*
> *He shot the president right through the head,*
> *He slumped to the floor and he fell dead,*
> *So they tell me his wife began to moan:*
> *"My God, my God, how long he been gone!"*
> *And they tell me his wife began to cry,*
> *She pulled off her ring and she bid him goodbye,*
> *Oswald was running and hiding his face,*

> But he couldn't find no hiding place,
> Oswald he could not find no peace,
> So he pulled out his pistol and he killed a police,
> Woh, Oswald, what you have done?
> You killed our president; you know that was wrong,
> You killed my bread in a starving land,
> But that's all right, I'm a-holding His hand,
> Oswald looked around, I saw him standing by himself,
> Up stepped Jack Ruby and shot him to death,
> And I don't know the time Jack Ruby arrived,
> But he shot him on TV, at the time it was televised.[49]

Brother Will Hairston's comparison of Kennedy with Christ ("he died for you and me") is most remarkable. As the Southern Bells had also done, Hairston remembered the president as someone who had kept starvation away from the hungry poor.

After a hurried autopsy without the aid of a forensic pathologist, Kennedy's mortal remains were returned to the White House. The day before the funeral blues singer "Mississippi" Fred McDowell (1904–1972) recorded a version of Blind Lemon Jefferson's best-known song "See That My Grave Is Kept Clean."[50] It has often been recorded under the title "Two White Horses." As McDowell's version was called "Six White Horses,"[51] it is highly likely that McDowell had the next day's state funeral in mind when he recorded his version of the song. He may have heard of the elaborate preparations and thought them a fitting tribute to the deceased president. The execution of the song is not up to McDowell's usual level, and we can conclude that it did not belong in his standard repertoire; this is his only recording of it.

The funeral took place in Washington, DC, on Monday 25 November 1963. The coffin, draped in the Stars and Stripes, was carried on the caisson that had been used for FDR's coffin in 1945. It was drawn by six white horses, and a Marine walked behind the coffin carrying the President's personal flag, showing the American eagle holding an olive branch. Next came Black Jack, a riderless horse carrying empty boots reversed in the stirrups, in token that the warrior would not mount again. Then followed the motorcade. A skirl of bagpipes accompanied the coffin as it was carried into St. Matthew's Roman Catholic Cathedral. The pontifical requiem mass was performed by Richard Cardinal Cushing, who had officiated at the marriage of John and Jackie Kennedy, spoken at his inaugural, and christened the children. When the coffin was carried out of the church, Jacqueline Kennedy bent over to her son John, who had his third birthday that very day, and asked him to salute his father.

Blues singer Avery Brady "closed his job" in the factory to watch the funeral on television. Here is the first part of his "Poor Kennedy."

Well, I know, my poor Kennedy, riding down the street in his car,
Some poor enemy shoot him down, that he fell in his wife's arms.

Well, I, mmm, ah, that hearse, way down the road, that I give up,
        I will go,
Poor Kennedy, going down, down in the ground.

Mmm, things was sad, they was blue, then I closed my job,
Sat in the room, looked at the coffin, passing on by, marching to the
        grave.

Well, my Kennedy, tried to be, be for the poor, like for the rich,
But some gun, shoot him down, put him in the ground.

Yeah, all I have to say 'bout Kennedy:
"I will meet you, in that heaven, some old day."
Mmm, feel so bad 'bout Kennedy is gone,
Gone on down, down in the ground.[52]

Mississippi-born blues guitarist "Big" Joe Williams (1903–1982) revived and updated the classic "His Spirit Lives On," which he had recorded in memory of President Roosevelt in 1945.[53] Now John F. Kennedy, the "best president we ever had," was Joe's subject. Williams recorded "A Man Amongst Men" twice. In the 1964 version he explained how Kennedy stood out among his fellow men. Williams mentioned the fighter airplanes from the navy and the air force that crossed the sky during the burial. Air Force One followed them. Stanza six about the rooster and the hen, which occurs frequently in Williams's recorded work notes that even the animal kingdom was disturbed because of the president's death. The expression

Big Joe Williams, Zodiac, Amstelveen, the Netherlands, 24 March 1973. Photo: Hans ten Have.

"A Man Among Men" was also used in a poem by James Darey in the *Chicago Defender* published in the days after the assassination: "people all over are mourning the death of a man among men."[54]

> *I just imagined seeing President Kennedy, when he rode down in Dallas town,*
> *I saw that mean old sniper, when he carried the President down.*
>
> ch: *Never be a man, just like President Kennedy was,*
> *He was a man amongst men, traveled four corners of the world.*
>
> sp: *Sad words to say, boys! Too sad! Think, boys: best president we ever had!*
>
> *I just saw that President Kennedy and the governor of Texas was shaking hands,*

> He said: "If I don't get my plans through, Governor, President Johnson will be the next man."
>
> I went home and I put on my television, looked at Washington town,
> I saw six white horses, carrying President Kennedy to the burying ground.
>
> Wasn't it sad we got the news, President Kennedy was dead?
> Church, here I'm coming to you, flying airplanes and jets over my head.
>
> President Kennedy traveled by land, traveled across the sea,
> Helped the United States, and I knowed he was good to me.
>
> Now, you know the rooster told the hen: "You hens ought to go lay,"
> Said: "No, President Kennedy's dead, I ain't got nowhere to stay."
>
> Well, my heart struck sorrow, tears come falling down,
> When they carried President Kennedy, laid him down in his burying ground.
>
> sp: Sad words to say about President Kennedy! Never'll be another![55]

In the second version of "A Man Amongst Men," recorded a year later, Williams only used the chorus and stanzas one, three, and six of the first version. That this tribute to JFK was an update of an earlier one to FDR became clear when Williams allowed an outdated reference to the CWA (Civil Works Administration) of the winter of 1933–34 to slip in.[56]

The flag was folded and handed to the former First Lady. After a twenty-one gun salute, the cardinal said a prayer and Mrs. Kennedy lit an eternal flame. It was a crisp and sunny afternoon when John F. Kennedy was laid to rest on a gentle slope in Arlington National Cemetery.

In "J.F. Kennedy's Reservation," Ronda Mitchell and Mrs. Lovell, two gospel singers from Chicago, referred to seven milk-white horses. In addition to the six horses that drew the hearse, a seventh had led the cortege. Every confidence could be placed in Kennedy's "reservations to his home on high." A saintly president like Kennedy could not but go to heaven, having "made his peace with God":

> On the twenty-second day of November, Nineteen Sixty-three,
> Our assassinated president left all this world in grief.
>
> On the twenty-fifth day of November, just about twelve
>   o'clock,
> Those seven milk-white horses had to march by the clock.
>
> ch: He packed up, made his reservations (3x), to his home on high.
>
> Now, I want the world to listen, and try to understand,
> Mr. Kennedy made his peace with God, while traveling through
>   this land.[57]

Jimmy Brewer accompanied his wife Fannie (1920–1980) on "When We Got the Message." Her song gives evidence of the emotions that had overwhelmed the biggest television audience up to that time when it watched the two Kennedy children at the funeral: Caroline Bouvier Kennedy and John Fitzgerald "John-John" Kennedy Jr. When John-John made a soldier's salute to his father's coffin the world wept:

> John F. Kennedy was our president, whom we dearly loved,
> He was assassinated in the South, southern land below.
>
> ch: President, president, how we loved him so,
> And we'll want to know, how he had to go.
>
> He traveled over land and sea, traveled there for you and me,
> Traveled through the countries shaking every man's hand.
>
> He was down in Southern Texas, on a mission there,
> Riding in his motorcade, when they shot him down,
> Oh, how my heart did bleed, and my eyes were full of tears,
> When we got the message that our president was dead.
>
> He left a darling wife, a little girl he called Caroline,
> Yes, he had a little boy, that he would call John-John,

> *Oh, how my heart did cry, the day she stood beside,*
> *When she lit the burning flame to let us know he's alive.*[58]

Three reigning monarchs and twenty-two presidents came to accompany Kennedy to his grave. There are many reasons why Kennedy's death had such a huge impact, among them that this was the first assassination of a president since McKinley's in 1901, that it happened in the middle of Cold War tensions, and that it was the first such event in the age of mass media. Another aspect that must be considered important is the charisma of the family. In 1960 Mahalia Jackson explained why she was going to vote for John Kennedy by saying that she thought he could "put a little more sun and a little more hope in people's lives."[59] At the inauguration Kennedy had held Mahalia's hands when he thanked her for her song. Her biographer explains: "It was his blue eyes that held her, though. They looked deep into hers, and she felt the magnetism."[60]

Mississippi blues singer Son House (1902–1988) recorded a song called "President Kennedy" in 1965. He also observed the magic of the Kennedy family and concluded that "they must have been born that way." House had used the melody of this song in 1942 when he recorded it as "American Defense," a patriotic waltz about World War II.[61]

> *Mmm, Mr. Kennedy was born,*
> *But now he is gone,*
> *To never return any more.*
> *Made me feel sad,*
> *And he's the best friend we had,*
> *He's for the rich and the poor.*
>
> ch: *Now, I can't but shed tears,*
> *It'll last me for years,*
> *His memory still rings in my ears.*
>
> *Now, this I agree,*
> *Had a great family,*
> *They all seemed so happy and gay.*
> *From adults to a child,*

They all seemed to have a smile,
They must a-have been born that way.

Mmm, now God bless little John,
That little Caroline respond,
And also their mother dear.
His father and mother,
Sister and brother,
They must been born that way.[62]

Accompanied by pianist Otis Spann and harmonica player Slim Willis, Mississippi-born mandolinist Johnny Young (1918–1974), who had been living in Chicago since 1940, described his reaction to the news of the president's death in "I Tried Not to Cry." In his inaugural speech Kennedy had said: "If the free society cannot help the many who are poor,

Johnny Young, American Folk Blues Festival, The Hague, the Netherlands, 21 October 1972. Photo: Paulus Zwaga.

The Day the World Stood Still   [139]

it cannot save the few who are rich."⁶³ The black population considered that the president kept this promise. Young's statement "he was for the rich, and he was sure for the poor" would have pleased Kennedy.

> *I tried and I tried, but the tears keep on coming on down,*
> *I tried not to cry, but the tears keep on flowing on down,*
> *Our president is dead and gone, and the people can't be satisfied.*
>
> *He traveled 'round the world, preaching things he wants you to hear,*
> *This is his life story, and I want everybody in Chicago to hear.*
>
> *We weeped, we cried, we said things all night long,*
> *Although we know we was making a mistake, because the president was dead and gone.*
>
> *He was for the rich, and he was sure for the poor,*
> *Don't you know, you know, he won't come back no more?*
>
> sp: *I want everybody to listen, listen what I will have to say:*
> *I want everybody to listen, Lord, it brung tears from my eyes,*
> *When a young man dead and gone, and the world can't be satisfied.*
>
> sp: *Lord, have mercy! My song is not completed, but I just have to say: "Goodbye!"*⁶⁴

Johnny Young said that his song was not completed, so it was no surprise when an unissued sequel was released as late as 1994. "Tribute to J.F.K." elaborated on some of the sentiments discussed before. Young had "peace of mind" when Kennedy was his president, but after the assassination he could not stop crying.

> *President, president, president, this is a story for him today,*
> *A young man had to be shot down this way.*
>
> *He was for the rich and he was for the poor,*
> *He was a wonderful man, people, can't you know?*
> *He was for civil rights; he was for it day and night,*
> *You know he was a president, but really all right.*

> He talked; he talked all over town,
> Only thing he talked about almost, giving you justice and peace
>   of mind.

sp: J.F. Kennedy, J.F. Kennedy, J.F. Kennedy, J.F. Kennedy,
Young president too, honest to God. He really was an honest man.
It brung tears in my eyes too, and everybody, it seemed they
   began to cry.

sp: My story is complete now, I gotta say goodbye,
I will have to say goodbye right here,
I'll tell you the reason why:
Because tears still coming in my eye.⁶⁵

At the funeral the Irish Guard paid their respects with Kennedy's Irish background in mind. The Harold Bowen Singers remembered the Irish descent of the "heaven-sent hero" when they recorded a demo 45 called "Dear President" at Sam Phillips's Memphis recording studio.

ch: Dear President, we miss you, oh, how we miss you,
America salutes you with love so true.

John F. Kennedy, from Irish descendants he came,
Making his way to the hall of fame.
A man of unity,
Love and purity.
For people he done his best,
John F. Kennedy stood the test.

John F. Kennedy, your living was not in vain,
You helped so many in the hour of stress and strain.
Deep down in our hearts the work shall remain.
A great hero and president,
John F. Kennedy was heaven-sent.

May the good Lord bless and keep you, till we meet again!⁶⁶

John F. Kennedy visited numerous countries during his "1,000 days" in office. In 1961 he went to Canada, France, Austria, the United Kingdom, Venezuela, Colombia, and Bermuda. In 1962 he was in Mexico and the Bahamas, and in his final year he traveled to Costa Rica, West Germany, Ireland, the United Kingdom, Italy, and Vatican City. The First Lady charmed foreign audiences with her linguistic accomplishments (French in Paris and Spanish in Mexico), and the president captivated the citizens of Berlin with the phrase "Ich bin ein Berliner."[67] The fact that Kennedy had "traveled around the world" occurs in many of these blues and gospel lyrics. The visits were all shown on television and broadcast on the radio, and they evidently made an impression on black Americans. James and Fannie Brewer were convinced the president had traveled there "for you and me" in their 1964 "I Want to Know Why."

> *John F. Kennedy was our president,*
> *We all loved him, yes, we did.*
>
> ch: *I want to know why, I want to know why, I want to know why.*
>
> *They assassinated his body, in the southern land,*
> *But we know, never can.*
>
> *It was one cold, cloudy day,*
> *That's when our president went away.*
>
> *He was a good man, we all know,*
> *We know he's a good man, we all know.*
>
> *He was the best president we ever had,*
> *Yes, he traveled all through the land.*
>
> *He traveled over land and sea,*
> *Know he traveled there for you and me.*[68]

Blues guitarist John Lee Granderson (1913–1979) had come to Chicago in 1928. Record producer Pete Welding (1935–1995) wrote of Granderson's Kennedy tribute, "A Man for the Nation," that it contained "restrained and finely detailed singing and playing. His subdued, though no less impassioned, approach reflects both the more 'musical' blues of the Tennessee area from which he hails and his own thoughtful, deliberate character."[69] While his guitar imitates the ringing of the church bells, Granderson sings about God welcoming Kennedy to heaven. The final "Amen" is most unusual and almost turns this blues song into a gospel recording.

> *I'm gonna tell you about a man, who made the nation rock,*
> *He was a man for the nation, yes, he really did his part.*
>
> *He was a man, worked for the nation, and his work was one hundred percent,*
> *And when the people heard about what happened, they were sad about the way he went.*
>
> *You just wait for a little while, and then you will see,*
> *Just what I mean, about Mr. John F. Kennedy.*
>
> *He could hear those bells a-ringing; he could hear those angels moan,*
> *He could hear a loud voice ringing, saying: "Kennedy, you're welcome home."*
>
> sp: *Amen!*[70]

On the day of the assassination Granderson had been driving from Chicago to visit his sister in Ellendale, Tennessee, when his car broke down. That day and the following he composed his Kennedy tribute while repairing his car. When he returned he sang it for Pete Welding, who told him he would like to record it. A few days later Big Joe Williams said he had also composed a song about Kennedy's death. When several other singers informed Welding that they had done so as well, he decided to record as many of them as possible. In 1964 eleven memorial songs were recorded for a unique album on Testament. Its title is *Can't Keep from Crying: Topical Blues on the Death of President Kennedy*. Thirty years later, in 1994, these Kennedy tributes were issued on a Testament CD with two additional unissued songs, making a total of thirteen by eleven different artists.[71]

The president was sanctified by blues and gospel singers. In "A Light That Shines" evangelist Rosie Wallace mourned the setting of his sun,

but rejoiced in the shining light that would prevail. She also sang that Kennedy was "esteemed by foe." Khrushchev's son Sergei remembered that his father was "very upset" that Kennedy had died, not only because of the potential for vast international instability, but because of his great admiration for him.[72]

His work is done,
Gone-a down his sun,
A light prevails,
That will not fail.

He led us well,
Until he fell,
But he left behind,
A light that shines.

Admired by friend(s),
Loved by kin,
Esteemed by foe,
Where'er he'd go.

He led indeed,
With dignity,
And he left behind,
A light that shines.

A light of hope,
And courage strong,
A light of faith,
Though the road be long,

For there was he,
For you and me,
And he left behind,
A light that shines,
Oh, and he left behind,
A light that shines.[73]

The Sensational Six of Birmingham, Alabama, called for liberty in "Let Freedom Ring." Like so many gospel singers before them they drew analogies between African Americans and the children of Israel enslaved in Egypt. A difference in skin pigmentation does not justify oppression, they argued: all men are made in God's image. As Martin Luther King Jr. had done in his 1963 "I Have a Dream" speech, the gospel group used the "let freedom ring" device for their catalogue of oppressed places in which Dallas, Texas, takes a prominent final position.[74]

An obscure gospel group called Little David and the Mighty Gospel Supremes recorded the song "Beloved Kennedys" for S Star Records in 1968. This gospel record was probably bootlegged for the calypso market by another obscure artist who called himself Lord Hummingbird and His Gospel Singers. His real name was Alberto Riberio, and the "Beloved Kennedy" that was issued on his own Hummingbird label is the Little David recording. As the lyrics refer to the Kennedy brothers John and Robert, the title of the song should actually be in the plural.⁷⁵

Another tribute was recorded by Jimmy Brown, who was born in Jackson, Mississippi, in 1910 and moved to St. Louis in the 1940s. Brown's rough-hewn vocal on "He Was Loved By All the People" was accompanied by his own idiosyncratic violin playing that is so integral to the total performance that the "lyrics" quoted below give no clue to the total effect.

> Our President Kennedy, he was loved by, with all the peoples around,
> Day and night they was around, weeping and moaning,
> In the rain they was weeping, in the rain they was crying, all around,
> The countries and cities, he was loved by the people, all 'round the town,
> The whole world compliment the man, 'cause he was the man,
> He was the man.
> Wonderful man, a great man, the world did love,
> Got invitations all from 'round the world,
> 'Cause he was loved by the world.⁷⁶

Gospel singer Doris Ann Allen, one of the vocalists of the Jewel Gospel Singers, composed "The Modern Joshua," a song that was recorded exactly one week after the assassination, one of eight African-American gospel tributes to JFK recorded by Savoy Records on Friday 29 November 1963. Allen compared Kennedy to Joshua, the successor of Moses. Joshua crossed the River Jordan and conquered Canaan, the promised land of the Jews. In chapter six of the book of Joshua the city of Jericho is conquered. The Lord gave the directions.⁷⁷ Like Joshua the president had walked around the walls. In this case the Jewel Gospel Singers hope the walls of hatred, deceit, prejudice, defeat, ignorance, fear, and bigotry will come tumbling down.

> ch: Oh, John, John Kennedy, our modern-day,
> Our modern-day Joshua,
> And just like old Joshua,
>   He marched around the walls,
> And, eh, bit by bit,

> They commenced to fall,
> But they assassinated Kennedy,
> > Whatcha gonna do about my Lord?
>
> I know He's tired
> > Tired of our wicked ways,
> He's so tired,
> > Tired of these evil days,
> And He's tired,
> > Tired of our evil ways,
> Well, now this old world is in a sinful state,
> You better mind how you deal with God's children,
> Wouldn't want Him to turn His back on you,
> They assassinated Kennedy,
> > Whatcha gonna do about my Lord?
>
> Come on around the wall,
> > Till the walls come tumbling down,
> Let's march around the wall,
> > Till the walls come tumbling down,
> March around the wall,
> > Till the walls come tumbling down,
> Till they come tumbling, tumbling down.
>
> We'll march around hatred, around deceit,
> Walls of prejudice, defeat,
> The walls of ignorance, of fear,
> The walls of bigotry and then love will appear,
> Well, they assassinated Kennedy,
> > Whatcha gonna do about my Lord?[78]

In blues and gospel music Kennedy was not only equated with the Old Testament Joshua, but especially with the New Testament Jesus. John Lee Granderson played subtle accompaniment for Chicago housewife Mary Ross on her composition "President Kennedy Gave His Life." In the last stanza John Kennedy is almost equated with the Savior: the manmade nails in Christ's hands are compared to the manmade bullet in Kennedy's head.

> You know the Bible tells us, we're going to reap just what we sow,
> After we leave this old world, we gotta face our God, you know.

ch: *President Kennedy, gave his life, gave his life,*
(Yes he did!)
President Kennedy gave his life, for his country, children, and wife.

> When President Kennedy was shot down, oh, how the nation did mourn,
> But I believe that somewhere in glory that he's living on.
>
> God chose President Kennedy; he put a message in his heart and in his hand,
> God gave him the message to pass on, to the people of his land.
>
> Man, born of a woman, bears hardships and woes,
> There's only one way to be born, but it's so many ways to go.
>
> Jesus died on Calvary Cross, with nails in the palms of his hands,
> The president died with a bullet in his head that was made by man.[79]

A group of prisoners from Ramsey Farm in the Texas state prison system under the direction of lead vocalist Johnnie H. Robinson made the same comparison. In their "Assassination of the President" Jesus is whipped up the hill to be nailed on the cross and Kennedy rides down the street to be shot by a gun. The final stanza finds the singer realizing that he has started a new song in the "dying mother's last words" convention. It indicated the helplessness that so many African Americans felt after the assassination. Who will now feed the hungry?

> Oh, wasn't it sad?
> I wanna tell you about a day, children, wasn't it so sad?
> I don't believe you know what I'm talking 'bout, children.
> I tell you: wasn't it sad?
> I wanna tell you about November the twenty-second,
> Oh, wasn't it sad?
> And oh, wasn't it sad? Aaah, my, my, my, my, my, my, my, God!

I wanna tell you a long time ago, children,
    What you wanna say?
When they whipped Him on up the hill,
    Yes, they did.
They whipped the man on up the hill,
And they begin to nail Him on the cross,
    Yes, they did.
I'm gonna tell you about a day, that you never will forget:
    Lord, have mercy!
The man was riding down the street,
    Yes, he was.
Riding down the street in a long black car,
    Yeah!
And, oh, wasn't it sad? Lord, my, my, my, my, my, my, my, my, my God!

They tell me that the little children began to running and crying,
    Yes, they did.
And they had tears all in their eyes,
    Lord, have mercy!
I heard somebody cry, said: "Lord, have mercy now!"
    Yes, they did, Jesus!
I do believe the president is gone on home,
    Yes, they did.
Do you believe what I'm saying, that man is gone?
    Yeah!
A great man has passed away,
    Yes, he has.
And, oh, wasn't it sad? Aaah, my, my, my, my, my, my, my, my, my, God!
    One more thing I wanna tell you now, son:
Yeah, what is that?
    I wanna tell you about the woman who was on her dying bed one day,
On her dying bed,
    The same day that they assassinated the President, I believe it was,
Yes, it was.

> *There was a little girl, she was running around, she was hollering,*
>
> Yeah.
>
> *She asked her mother, said: "Mother,"*
>
> Yeah.
>
> *Said: "Who's gonna wake me up in the morning?"*
>
> Yeah.
>
> *She asked her mother, said: "Mother, who is gonna feed me in the morning?"*
>
> Yeah.
>
> *Her mother looked at her and this is what she said:*
>
> *"Aaah, Lord."*
>
> *Lord, Lord, Lord, Lord, Lord, Lord, Lord, Lord, Lord, oh!*
> *Take me home,*
>
> *Yes, she did.*[80]

"Jackie Don't You Weep," Little Junior and the Butler-aires implored in 1964. Just like Jesus, the president was not dead; God led him to a better land and his spirit would live on. Although Kennedy was "rich and highly educated," Little Junior, like other singers, both religious and secular, saw him as the best friend the poor man ever had. When Junior sang that Kennedy "brought peace with the foreign land," he must have had the Soviet Union in mind. Why he sang that "Oswald lost his nerve" remains obscure; perhaps he simply needed a rhyming word for "curve."

> *You know his time had come and he had to go.*
>
> *The president was rich and highly educated,*
> *Nineteen Sixty-three, he was assassinated.*
> *Now, President Kennedy was a great, great man,*
> *For he brought peace with the foreign land.*
> *He did the things that he knew was right,*
> *Things that was pleasing in God's sight.*
>
> ch: *I said: "Jackie, oh Jackie, don't you weep no more," (3x)*
> *And I know his time had come and he had to go.*
>
> *Listen! I wonder how Oswald felt,*
> *An innocent man that he killed.*

> He shot the President, as he rounded the curve,
> That's when Oswald lost his nerve.
> Feel the shot struck the president's head,
> Jesus made up the man, his dying bed.
> He's not dead; for his spirit will live on,
> For my God heard when the president groaned.
> He took the president (Lord have mercy!) by the hand,
> To lead him on to a better land.
> And I know we'll miss him, oh, so bad,
> For he was the best friend that a poor man ever had.[81]

As late as 1974 Brownsville, Tennessee, guitarist "Sleepy" John Estes (1899–1977) continued to sing his "President Kennedy Stayed Away Too Long." Estes first recorded the song as "I'm Going Home" in Copenhagen in October 1964, during the third tour of the American Folk Blues Festival. It was later issued as "Blues for JFK." It is an adaptation of another Estes song, "I Stayed Away Too Long,"[82] about being homesick in Europe. Here the chorus still switches between "I stayed away too long" and "he stayed away too long," but from 1969 onward all other versions use the latter phrase. The blind artist employs some poetic associations of ideas in this song, with the news of the President's death conceived as a "seabird singing a song to me" and the six white horses drawing the coffin as "six little children to lead poor Sleepy John around."

> sp: That's Willie Dixon playing![83]
>
> Late one Friday evening, everything was sad,
> We lost the best president we ever had.
>
> ch: I'm going home, going back home, I stayed away too long.
> (I'm going home, he started home, he stayed away too long.)
>
> I heard the news in the air; I wondered what could it be?
> Nothing but the seabird,[84] singing a song to me.
>
> He rode from town to town, holding up for right,
> Some old low-down rascal stole the president's life.

sp: *I hear you, I hear you, I hear you, man, I hear you!*

Mrs. Kennedy got a home, a mansion, nine months is all she need,
And then she fly back to Washington, DC.

sp: *Play it! I got a long . . . , Willie . . .*

Every night, 'fore I lay down,
I pray to the Lord for six little children, to lead poor Sleepy John around.

sp: *Only about two more verses. Hold it for me, Hammie, too!*[85]

White horses and cars, all in a row,
I think Mr. Kennedy have a right to his long white robe.

sp: *One more time, I gotta go, Hammie!*

They checked my blood pressure (I was worried that day), a hundred and three,
Nothing but salty water, I had drinked right out o' the sea.[86]

In later versions of the song Estes refers to Jackie Kennedy's summer residence as her "millionaire home on the island" where she "no place have a fire." He probably refers to Hammersmith Farm in Newport, Rhode Island, which was the home of Hugh D. Auchincloss III, Jackie's stepbrother. Jackie grew up there, her wedding reception took place in it, and John Kennedy made it their summer residence from 1961 to 1963. The house has twenty-eight rooms and no fewer than fourteen fireplaces,[87] so Estes may have been referring to the central heating system that makes fireplaces obsolete.

Sleepy John sings that Jackie flew back to Washington, DC, for the three winter months. In December 1963 she bought 3017 N Street, a fourteen-room colonial house in Georgetown. Mrs. Kennedy and her two children lived there for a year before moving to New York.[88]

It may be wondered how the final stanza of "I'm Going Home" relates to the rest of the Kennedy song. The key to understanding this obscure connection is to be found in the 1968 Estes recording "Newport Blues."

That song explains that Sleepy John Estes was thinking of his performance at the Newport Folk Festival on 25 July 1964. He explains that he was so nervous about appearing before eighty thousand people that his blood pressure rose to 103. The doctor told him not to worry and jokingly said it must have been the salt water Estes had drunk from the sea! While on Rhode Island he must have spent time at the shore, and may have been at Hammersmith Farm. From there on his mind perhaps drifted to the Kennedy assassination and the fate of the President's wife and children.

> *As soon as I reached Rhode Island, I went out on the island beach,*
> *Nothing but them big whales and alligators sure enough waving at me.*
>
> sp: *Talk to me now, y'all take your time!*
>
> *Out in the park, they called us up on the stage,*
> *You know, I felt just as shaky (as) any man could be,*
> *About eighty thousand people, they're gazing at me.*
>
> *I saw a great crowd of people, I'm a wonder what is going on,*
> *Wasn't nobody but, but a viewing Mrs. Kennedy's millionaire home.*
>
> *In Mrs. Kennedy's millionaire home, she ain't no place have a fire,*
> *Nine months and she's going back home.*
>
> sp: *Boy!*[89]

Here is a version of the Sleepy John Estes Kennedy tribute from 1969. It now appears in its ultimate shape as "President Kennedy Stayed Away Too Long." New to this 1969 version, and in all the later ones, is a stanza about the 1964 elections. Estes was clearly afraid that the Republican candidate Barry Goldwater would win the presidential elections. "If Goldwater get it, we won't have no home" is a rare reference to the Arizona senator in blues and gospel music. Goldwater was painted as a dangerous extremist by the incumbent Johnson administration, which unofficially countered Goldwater's slogan "In your heart, you know he's right" with the line "In your guts, you know he's nuts." Fortunately for Estes, "Landslide" Lyndon Johnson defeated Barry Goldwater by winning in forty-four of the fifty states.

> *Late hours, everybody was sad,*
> *We lost the best president we've ever had,*

ch: *But he gone, gone back, he stayed away too long.*

> *Rode from town to town, holding up for right,*
> *Some low-down, took the president's life.*

sp: *How 'bout it, John?*

> *Everybody vote, they don't know what's going on,*
> *If Goldwater get it, we won't have no home.*

> *Mrs. Kennedy got a mansion on the island, stays nine months,*
>   *all she needs,*
> *She have another mansion, since she reached Washington, DC.*

> *When I went on the stage, shaky as I could be,*
> *'Bout eighty thousand people, had their eyes on me.*

sp: *Hold it in, John! Cut off, man! You cut it off!*

> *White horses and a cart, all in a row,*
> *I think Mr. Kennedy have a right, to his long white robe.*[90]

Although vibraphone player Lionel Hampton (1908–2002) had campaigned enthusiastically for his old friend Richard Nixon in 1960, he was greatly distressed when Kennedy died. In his biography Hampton explained how the assassination and Kennedy and Johnson's 1964 Civil Rights Act made him jump party lines.

> *It was hate that killed President Kennedy. How I mourned that man's death. I was for Richard Nixon in the 1960 election, but Gladys and I both felt that President Kennedy was working to help black people. And we were honored when he and Mrs. Kennedy invited us to a special Lincoln's birthday celebration at the White House. Sammy Davis Jr., and*

[154]   The Day the World Stood Still

> Noble Sissle, and a number of civil right leaders were also invited, and it was an occasion as special as any inaugural event I'd played there. I had the invitation framed and put up on display in our living room. Looking back, I believe it was President Kennedy's assassination that spurred me to start working on the administration, doing whatever I could to help President Johnson. I may be a Republican, but I'm first of all an American, and I thought that what President Johnson was doing was good for the country. So in 1964, when he ran for election as president, I jumped party lines to support him. I had nothing personally against Barry Goldwater—in fact, we were good friends—but Johnson had signed the 1964 Civil Rights Act and said, "We shall overcome," and he was the man I wanted to support.[91]

The introduction of the 33 r.p.m. long-play (LP) album in 1948 by Columbia Records afforded the opportunity to record full sermons using both sides of the record. Hitherto sermons had necessarily been truncated or divided into several parts to fit the limited space of the 78 record. In the 1960s many of these were reissued on LPs, and newer recordings of sermons profited from the new medium. In the 1960s, with political consciousness rising among African Americans, many sometimes quite militant sermons were recorded on LP. Except for a fine study of Rev. C.L. Franklin's sermons by Jeff Todd Titon,[92] little work has been done on the transcription of these fascinating sermons, which give a vivid insight into the effect of the political process on African-American churchgoers.

Rev. Omie L. Holliday (1924–1987), from Houston, recorded a sermon called "The Assassination of President Kennedy and the Crucifixion of Jesus" in the Greater New Pleasant Grove Baptist Church in Houston in 1966 or 1967. Many of the themes already discussed return in this sermon. Again Kennedy's assassination is compared to the crucifixion of Christ. Kennedy was "Christ-like," Holliday clearly states. He paints a picture of twentieth-century man: armed with scientific knowledge, but lonely and confused. The Reverend was convinced that Kennedy was "a friend of the Negro," as he had placed himself "at the head of" the civil rights revolution. Many comparisons were made between Christ and Kennedy and the most important question for both remained: "Why did they have to die?" According to Holliday, Kennedy died so that the Americans could see "the sin of segregation" and "the blackness in their own hearts." Holliday's view that Kennedy's death helped Lyndon Johnson get a much stronger civil rights act is interesting and probably true. The deification of Kennedy is almost complete here, although Holliday hesitated about Kennedy having "the power of the grave."

PART ONE

In John, the third chapter and the fourteenth verse, we find these words: "And as Moses lifted up the serpent in the wilderness, even so must the Son of man be lifted up." "And as Moses lifted up, lift up, the serpent in the wilderness, even so must the Son of man be lifted up."

I have been moved to talk with you briefly tonight about the assassination of President Kennedy and the crucifixion of Jesus. There has been much speculation and books written about the life and death of our late president, but none of them seem to deal with the humanity and the religion of the man. To me John Fitzgerald Kennedy, the thirty-fifth president of the United States, was one of the most brilliant statesmen of our time. He was born rich, yet humbled himself with love in his heart for all mankind. He was Christ-like. He took the oath of office and accepted the responsibility as leader of this great nation at a time when our country faced crises too numerous to mention. He courageously accepted what he called "the challenge of the twenties."[93] He realized that the twentieth-century president is summoned to live and serve in a grand and awful time. This is a century of crises in which mankind is caught between the thrusts of two efforts. Our civilization is experiencing the dying groans of the old order and the birth pains of the new. The twentieth century is a century of bewildering contradictions. Armed with scientific knowledge and technological skill we have produced countless gadgets to enhance our comfort and conveniences. Discoveries in nuclear energy has [sic] made it possible for man to probe into outer space and bring faraway planets within our reach. We have the resources with which to ascend into the heavens or to make our bed in hell.

W. H. Auden has called the twentieth century "an age of anxiety."[94] The sickness of society is seen in man's, eh, in man's strange ways and his alienation from God, social divisions and man's attempt to escape from himself. Twentieth-century man is a lonely creature, wrestling with the anxieties and the doubts, meaninglessly guilt and death. He is haunted by the failures of the past, perplexed by the problems of the present, and fearful about the uncertainties of the future. Man is thrust into a world of mass culture. Manipulated by hidden, eh, persuaders,[95] robbed our, us of selfhood and made a slave of superficial conformity. He is confused about who he is. He does not know what to do. He does not know from whence he is come, neither does he know where he is going. Man is like a leaf blown about in the wind.

Kennedy accep- accepted the responsibility in this twentieth century, in this, and faced the complex and confused world situation without succumbing to despair. He accepted the challenge, and like Jesus Christ he faced it resolutely. For he accepted the office truly, in a critical time. There was race tension throughout the universe and there are many other problems at which he faced that time will not permit me to mention tonight, that really deserves notation, but I want to confine my argument to his stand on civil rights. For truly he was a friend to the Negro.

Abraham Lincoln, the great emancipator, live today in the hearts of millions of people, and like Abraham Lincoln the memory of Kennedy still linger in our hearts. He was a friend to civil rights. In 1963 the Negro revo- revolution in America rose more rapidly than ever before. Kennedy did not start the revolution and nothing he could have done could have stopped it, but in 1963 he befriended it and, eh, gave it the high aspiration and helped guide it, that, eh, it might run more smoothly. He was not forced into this position by circumstances beyond his control, as many have written. On the contrary, the sympathy he displayed, the appointees he assembled, the courage he demonstrated in placing himself at the head of the revolution all encouraged a climate for reform and reason for hope within the southern Negro leadership. And really and truly the new efforts, eh, and, eh, pressures would probably not have been risked had there been a different attitude in the White House and in the Department of Justice, but Kennedy was there. He came on scene at such a time as this. He was the man of the hour. He seemed to have long realized that the Negro was not just a black man, the Negro was not just a brown man, but he was a man with *the same potentialities as any man in any other racial group. And all he needed was a chance. And time and time again he repeated that, eh, the Negro need a chance. He need a chance to elevate his own standard. He was a friend to civil rights. He was a blessing to the movement. Not only was he a blessing to the movement, but he was a blessing to America and he went about doing the best that he could, for he had his country, he had the people at heart, for in accepting the office he stated that he challenged America not to ask what the country could do for them, but what they could do for the country. And Jesus, when he came on the scene, stated that: "I came not into the world to be served, but I came to serve."[96] And there is a likeness between the two individuals. Jesus came on scene at a time when our world was in chaos, men were confused on every hand, they walked in gross darkness. Every man seemed to have been a law within himself and it remained that way until Jesus finally made his arrival. Jesus tabernacled here for thirty-two and a half long years. The Bible said that he went about doing good all of his days.[97] And so it was with our late president. Went about doing all of the good that he could, but, eh, in November of 1963, November the 22nd to be exact, about twelve-thirty, as he rode through the streets of Dallas, he was struck by an assassin's bullet. Possibly hadn't done anything too far wrong, but, eh, he was a friend to humanity. He believed that every man, regardless to his race, regardless to creed or color, should have a right to the tree of life. And I don't know why, nobody else really know why, that Kennedy had to die. Why did he have to die so young? Why did he have to die in the prime of his administration?*

PART TWO

Why did such a young man, such a brilliant man, a man loved by so many young people, would have to die such a horrible death? That question is on the mind and the heart of so many today: "Why did he have to die?" And so many times I have asked the question: "Why did Jesus have to die?" Why did the righteous, the innocent, miraculous Son of God have to be lifted up on that cruel cross of torture? Why did he have to die such a horrible death? Well, there are some things in God's permissive will, God permit these things to happen. And I believe that

Kennedy was in God's plan of liberation. And I believe that God permitted this thing to happen, he permitted it to happen for a purpose. You see, Medgar Evers had died, many others had died for the cause, but it didn't have the effect on America and on the world as when Kennedy died. And so I believe the Lord permitted it to be so.

If Kennedy had not died many of the civ- civil rights bills would have still been in Congress. If Kennedy had not died, ah-ha, many of our Americans would not have been able to see the sin of segregation. They would not have been able to see themselves, but when Kennedy was struck down that morning, ah-ha, America was able to see her own sins. She was able to see the blackness of her own heart. She was able to see that within her own walls there were mean men who had no regard for human life. If Kennedy had not died, oh Lord, I'm afraid that the civil rights movement may have been hindered in some way. Well, Jesus died that we might have the right to the tree of life. If he had not died, the dying thief would have been still hanging on the cross. If he had not died, we would still been living in our sin. If Jesus had not died, oh Lord, I would not have had a right to the tree of life.

On that morning, that Kennedy died, one commentator said that the Earth seemed to have stood still. Within the thirty minutes of his passing, between the crack of the first bullet and the finally determina- termination of his life, the tragedy, the tragedy had been told all over America. The news struck the East Coast about mid lunch time. The Pacific Coast in mid-morning. It stopped all of the presses in their run, it inter- rupted all television series. It stabbed with its pain men and women in the street. It knotted them about TV sets and paralyzed them in postures. First unbelieving and then stricken not until he was dead. Then all men knew that he would never again, ah-ha, point his forefinger, down from the platform, in speaking to them. Never pause before laughing, ah-ha, with his wit, ah-ha, but he was a great American. It was, eh, for Americans an episode to remember. Ah-ha, it was a clap of alarm as sharp and startling as the memory of Pearl Harbor. Oh, it was a great tragedy. Men every- where stopped in their tracks. Women screamed and cried. Men stood on the corner, shedding tears and didn't have to give any explanation as to why they were crying. Taxi drivers got tied up at the red light. Ah-ha, men everywhere was falling in their tracks. What's wrong now? Kennedy is dead! He's dead now, oh Lord. The Earth seem to have stood still for a little while.

But I wanna tell you something, ah-ha, a long time ago. Ah-ha, up on Golgotha's hill, way up on Calvary, oh yes, where the man was slain, ah-ha, the Earth stood still for a little while. And they tell me that the Earth quaked because the Son of God was dying.[98] Oh yes, on Calvary, where the dearest and the best of the Lord's work was really slain. Calvary, where justice and mercy touch one another! Calvary! Calvary! Where the Son of God died on the cross. Calvary! Lord, God. Calvary! Where I met the Lord. Calvary! On Calvary! On Calvary Jesus died. Didn't he die? Yes, he died. He died, yes, he did. He died, yes, he died. He died until the Earth would reel and rock, like a drunken man. He died until the moon took a hemorrhage and dripped away in blood. He died, when the sun refused to shine. He died until the veil of the temple rent wide open. He died, yes, he did. I said: "He died." He died for my sins. He died for your sins. He died on Calvary, a long time ago. Lord, God!

When Kennedy died, the last I heard, they buried him in the grave. But I didn't hear that he got power of the grave. But they tell me that they put Jesus in a tomb. He stayed there, in that grave. All night, Friday night. He stayed there in the grave. All night, all day. Saturday, he stayed there, all night, Saturday night. But early, early, early one Sunday morning, got tired of the grave, tore off his graveyard clothes. Yes, he did. Looked back at the old grave, said: "O death, where is thy sting? O grave, where is your victory?"[99] "All power, all power, all power is in my hand." Yes, yes, yes! I know he died. Yes, he did. Good God Almighty. I know he died for my sins and for your sins. As he hung on the cross, a trench was dug. They tell me, that the trench became a running stream of water. And one day a poet came along, looked at this fountain, he said: "There is a fountain filled with blood, drawn from Emmanuel's veins, and sinners plunged beneath this flood lose all their guilty stains."[100] Here's what it means to me: "Though there may I, though vile, vile as he, wash all, wash all, wash all my sins away."[101] Great God Almighty, I've been a-washed in the blood of the lamb. Yes, I have.

He's all right. Do you know Him? He's all right. He's my savior. Yes, he is. He's my friend, when I'm friendless. He's my lawyer in a courtroom.

My doctor in a sick room. Yea, my mother, when I'm motherless. My high tower, my walking cane when I'm old. Yea, my heart fixer, my mind regulator, my dying bed maker, my comforter in the time of sadness. Yea, yeah. Yeah, yeah. He's my all and all. The fountain of His blood. Let me overcome...

    (unintelligible)

    He watches me. He's watching me. I'm glad He died. He's all right. He died, I know He did. He died on Calvary. He died, but He got up soon one morning. Isn't that wonderful? Lord, God. I'm so glad. So glad today. He died. Oh yeah. Yes, Lord. Lord, God. So wonderful.

Give me the old ship of Zion,
Give me the old ship of Zion,
Give me the old ship of Zion.[102]

The Rev. C. L. Franklin sermon presented at the beginning of this book is the only recording analyzed here in which the artist speculates on the possibility of there being more than one sniper. Although the latest research has it that Lee Harvey Oswald worked alone, many people remain unconvinced. Even as late as 1998 blues singer Mighty Mo Rodgers (b. 1942) tried to probe the ultimate mystery in "The Kennedy Song." This is a song about the inescapability of death and the pointlessness of conspiracy theories in the face of that.

    I know what was on the eighteen minutes of the Nixon tapes,[103]
    In the movie "True Romance" Dennis Hopper said the words and they
                                      blew him away.[104]

    I know the secret of Mona Lisa's smile,
    It was a self portrait, you know the man had style.[105]

    But everybody wanna know, all they ever wanna know, how Kennedy
                                      died,
    He was a victim of the ultimate drive-by.

    I know if there's life in space, or if we're all alone,
    The answer is simple as black and white from the "Twilight Zone."[106]

On eleven twenty-two, Nineteen Sixty-three,
JFK met with destiny,
And it goes the same for you and me,
We have a rendezvous,[107]
But we just don't know with who,
'Cause everybody dies,
That's the ultimate drive-by.[108]

"The man had style," Rodgers sang about Leonardo da Vinci. The same conclusion was drawn about John Kennedy by *Chicago Defender* writer Chuck Stone in the days following the assassination:

> The one word which characterized the Kennedy administration was "style." Starting from this uncommonly brilliant young President himself and filtering down to the stenographers and messengers in government buildings, style shaped the way people did and said things during an exhilarating three years in Washington. Any leader can have a style, a gestalt, as it were. President Kennedy was one of the very few who had style and it became his charisma, displaying itself in his speeches, poetical and eloquent—his handling of people, persuasive and determined—his confrontation with domestic and world tensions, cautious, but Machiavellian when necessary. Style became almost a mystique of the "New Frontier," the concept which shaped the kinetics and velocity of the Kennedy administration.[109]

In the first two years of his presidency Kennedy was still finding his way. The extension of American involvement in Vietnam may have been his greatest failure, but the disaster of the Bay of Pigs and the lack of substantial action on civil rights also contributed to the image of a weak, inexperienced president. The days following the Cuban Missile Crisis saw an improvement, but the real change came after the Birmingham riots in April 1963. Kennedy was forced to take drastic measures, and the new presidency was born. The promise of Kennedy's new, more dynamic leadership seemed on the threshold of fulfillment, but when he was assassinated the ideas had not yet materialized into law, and a period of more violent confrontation and civil disobedience was ushered in.

From the surprising number of politically based blues and gospel lyrics of the period, the deceased president emerges as a near-saint. He constantly traveled in quest for peace, provided new jobs, inspired with his style, and charmed with his good looks, his gracious wife, and his lovely children. His death was seen as a national catastrophe, and the funeral was conducted with elaborate ceremony. The images of the white horses, the salute by his three-year-old son, and the young widow lighting an eternal flame created a lasting impression. The blues and gospel singers' president was in heaven now. Like Christ he had died for our sins.

In later years John F. Kennedy's image has been subject to deeper scrutiny. Had the sparkling rhetoric contained any meaning? Why had he held back on a given commitment to racial change until he had been forced to act? Had he given up real leadership to his "brain trust?" Had he taken the world to the brink of total atomic destruction by forcing the Cuban affair to a crisis? Was he the real cause of the horror of Vietnam? Why and how was he really killed? Were the rumors about extramarital liaisons (e.g., with film star Marilyn Monroe and Mafia-linked Judith Campbell Exner) true? Had he had an affair with Nazi-affiliated photographer Inga Arvad in World War II? Did he get daily injections against Addison's disease? Had he used cocaine at parties?

Even as early as June 1963 comedian Slappy White had joked about John Kennedy's womanizing. His satirical comment on the subject was quite atypical at the time. The reference to the Mona Lisa is topical; it was loaned to the U.S. in early 1963.[110] "Boy, that's President Kennedy: smart! He got a smart head on him, boy. Course it's tough being President, everybody is mad with President Kennedy: Russia is mad with him, Red China is mad with him, Cuba is mad with him. Now France is mad with him: they claim the Mona Lisa is pregnant. And that man's got a bad back!"[111]

On the twentieth anniversary of his death *Newsweek* published the results of a Gallup poll.[112] Asked who their favorite president was, 30 percent of those questioned answered "Kennedy," as against only 10 percent for Roosevelt. Asked what Kennedy was associated with, the answers were: "care for the poor, civil rights, activism, youth, a hard line toward the Soviets, glamour and style." For the general public the rumors and scandals clearly had had little effect on the Kennedy image. Kennedy's youthful promise had remained a symbol of all that it was thought America should stand for. In these blues and gospel songs Kennedy's death virtually eradicated any criticism of his international or political policies and left him an unadulterated hero.

When blues harp player Junior Wells (1934–1998) visited my hometown in 1992 I interviewed him on American politics. When I asked his opinion about President Kennedy he replied that he admired John and Robert Kennedy's civil rights record:

> *Young people, old people, people of all crazy colors liked Kennedy. Because he was a young president and he is the man, he is the man that pushed the issue for the whole thing that Martin Luther King was trying to do. This particular man, him and his brother, they stood behind it and they pushed it. And Mr. King was not trying to be a political person. He was only doing one thing. He just asked one thing: "How can we have our equal right thing?" This is not a discrimination thing on his behalf, or whatever, it's just a thing that anybody would like. And I was proud that his brother, the attorney general, stood up for everything and he did, in honesty.*[113]

One final example of a song recorded immediately after the murder is "JFK's Good Works Will Never Die" by the Original Soul Revivers with Ivory Lee as lead singer. It is possible that the gospel singer Ivory Lee is the same artist as the Houston-based blues singer, TV repairman, and record label operator Ivory Lee Semiens (1931–2002). The song was recorded on the obscure Faith label from Houston, Texas, and it is a summation of how African Americans viewed Kennedy in the aftermath of his assassination: strong in foreign policy, a family man, and a fighter for civil rights and justice.

> *Well, President Kennedy's good works won't ever die, oh no, it won't,*
> *He was the nation's best friend,*
> *Lord, he stood up until the end,*

President Kennedy's good works won't ever die, oh Lord.
The president had a wonderful wife, little daughter and son, oh yes, he did,
I never saw a lady so brave,
How she put the world in amaze,
President Kennedy's good works won't ever die, oh Lord.
For President Kennedy, he was a Christian man, oh yes, he was,
He believed in justice for all mankind,
Nobody could change the President's mind,
President Kennedy's good works won't ever die, oh Lord.

There's a time for everything under the heaven, oh yes, there is,
There's a time we have to laugh,
There's a time we have to cry,
President Kennedy's good works won't ever die, oh Lord.

William Do-Boy Diamond, Canton, Mississippi, August 1967. Photo: George Mitchell.

President Kennedy, he was courageous and bold, oh yes, he was,
He fought so hard for civil rights,
Lord, gonna bring it out to the light,
President Kennedy's good works won't ever die, won't die.[114]

Although it was Johnson, a Southerner, rather than Kennedy who saw the Civil Rights Act through Congress, for many years it was John F. Kennedy's portrait, along with Martin Luther King's and Robert Kennedy's, that was found on the walls of black homes all over the United States. In the late 1960s blues singer William "Do-Boy" Diamond,[115] seated before the wall of his living room in Canton, Mississippi, which held pictures of Christ, Martin Luther King, and John F. Kennedy, had not forgotten his president:

I don't know how the younger generation going be. I don't know. I think they going make things better if they keep a-going like they is. Just look like they more for the right things. Like President Kennedy was. Now he was a fine man. Look like he was a better President than any of the others been in there in wanting to help the poor people. That's the reason I liked him. Look like he was just dead for the poor people, and look like he didn't pick his color. He looked like he'd help the poor colored people just as well as he did the white.[116]

CONCLUSION

In undertaking this study my primary objective has been to shed new light on the question of how the presidency of John F. Kennedy was perceived and experienced by African Americans. With this aim in mind, I have carried out a thorough analysis of the African-American blues and gospel lyrics and comedy sketches recorded during and about his presidency that contain explicit social and political comment. I believe that these lyrics, which no one has previously attempted to collate and transcribe in a systematic way, represent an important and hitherto untapped source of African-American opinion.

In contrast to the Roosevelt era, when any such comment was for the most part restricted to describing the effects presidential decisions and policies may have had on individual singers and everyday life,[1] the aftermath of World War II saw a gradual shift toward expression of abstractions, generalizations, and proposals for reform. One particularly noticeable innovation is the growth of interest in the political process itself.

The 1960s saw the independence of many African and Caribbean countries. During Kennedy's presidency Sierra Leone, Tanzania, Burundi, Rwanda, Algeria, and Uganda became independent in Africa, Jamaica and Trinidad and Tobago in the Caribbean. However, no blues and gospel songs were recorded on these subjects during the Kennedy years.

Record sales showed a steady rise in the immediate postwar years as the shortage of raw materials was alleviated. Sales then remained relatively static until 1954, when they began to rise steadily. This trend continued in the Kennedy years, with annual record sales rising from 600 million in 1960 to 757 million in 1964.[2]

In the preceding chapters we have studied eighty-nine complete blues and gospel lyrics that contain explicit references to President Kennedy or identifiable aspects of his policies in the period from November 1960, when Kennedy successfully ran for president, to 1964, when many songs were recorded about his assassination. Of the remaining forty-two recordings, which are mentioned in the notes but have not been fully analyzed in this book, some are unissued and unavailable (14 percent), some are alternative versions of the songs under discussion (62 percent), some are entirely instrumental (7 percent), while the lyric content of others was either duplicated elsewhere or did not seem relevant to the present study (17 percent).

Only 5 percent of all the songs mentioned in this book remained unissued following the time of recording. This is a far lower number than political blues and gospel songs in the period before 1960 (22 percent of the songs in *Roosevelt's Blues* and 20 percent of the songs in *The Truman and Eisenhower Blues*). It would appear that the sometimes controversial nature of this type of lyrics presented less of a problem by the 1960s.

The recording locations of the political blues, gospel, and comedy lyrics about the Kennedy era referred to in this study are mostly known. Thirty-eight recordings took place in Chicago, IL; fifteen in Los Angeles, Hollywood, and Culver City, CA; eight in New York, NY; eight in Philadelphia, PA; five in Scotlandville and Baton Rouge, LA; three in Cincinnati, OH; three in Houston, TX; three in Copenhagen, Denmark; two in Atlanta, GA; two in Boston, MA; two in Crowley, LA; two in Detroit, MI; two in Memphis, TN; and one each in Albany, GA; Brownsville, TN; Collierville, TN; Columbus, OH; Como, MS; Elba, AL;

Jackson, MS; New Orleans, LA; Otey, TX; Pittsburgh, PA; Richmond, VA; Selma, AL; St. Louis, MO; Washington, DC; Woodstock, NY; Berlin, Germany; Stockholm, Sweden; Tokyo, Japan; and Toronto, Canada.

As a recording center California rose in importance in comparison with the period before 1960 (14 percent of the known recording locations during this period), reflecting its growth in prosperity and the wartime and postwar African-American migration to the West.

The origins of most of the blues and gospel artists discussed are known. Most of the seventy-nine solo artists were born in the southern states. Twenty-one came from Mississippi, eight from Louisiana, seven from Texas, five from Georgia, four from Tennessee, four from Arkansas, three from South Carolina, two from Alabama, two from Illinois, and one each from Indiana, Maryland, Michigan, Missouri, North Carolina, and Pennsylvania. In 1963 their average age was forty.

Some artists recorded two different songs with political comment about the Kennedy era. If we count different versions of the same song only once, they are: Avery Brady,[3] James Brewer, Fannie Brewer, Sleepy John Estes, Arvella Gray, John Lee Hooker, Lightnin' Hopkins, Mahalia Jackson, Louisiana Red, Memphis Slim, the Sensational Six of Birmingham, the Sons of David, Bob Starr, Rosie Wallace, Big Joe Williams, and Johnny Young. Of these, John Lee Hooker and Lightnin' Hopkins had also recorded a number of "political" songs in the Truman and Eisenhower eras and Sleepy John Estes and Big Joe Williams had even done so in the FDR era. Seven of these seventeen artists devoted both sides of a single record to the Kennedy presidency.

Of the ninety-four different artists or groups represented here, ten took part in Peter J. Welding and Norman Dayron's initiative to record topical blues on the death of President Kennedy. The thirteen songs from late 1963 and early 1964 by these ten artists, which were eventually released on Testament TCD 5007, constitute 10 percent of the total of 131 songs, and no less than 22 percent of the total of fifty-nine about JFK's death. Here is the list:

Avery Brady	Poor Kennedy; Poor Kennedy #2
James and Fannie Brewer	I Want to Know Why; Why Did He Have to Go? When We Got the Message

Jimmy Brown	He Was Loved by All the People
John Lee Granderson	A Man for the Nation
Bill Jackson	The 22nd Day of November
Mary Ross	President Kennedy Gave His Life
Otis Spann	Sad Day in Texas
Big Joe Williams	A Man Amongst Men
Johnny Young	I Tried Not to Cry; Tribute to J.F.K.

A concentrated effort to record gospel songs inspired by the assassination was made by Savoy Records on 29 November 1963. Rev. Lawrence C. Roberts (b. 1935), who was a gospel producer for Savoy Records for thirty years, remembers that various gospel artists called him after the assassination to let him know that they had written memorial songs. Roberts brought them together in evangelist Rosie Wallace's First Church of Love, Faith, and Deliverance in Philadelphia: "All of the songs mentioned were recorded to pay tribute to John F. Kennedy. I produced all of them. As I can recall, each session was touching and moving. I felt this was the artists' feelings regarding our President's death, being put in song. Out of the nine songs you named, the two that sold were Thermon Ruth and Rosie Wallace."[4] Here are the complete session details:

396	Thermon Ruth	That Awful Day in Dallas	Savoy 4208
397	Thermon Ruth	He'll Understand	Savoy 4208
398	Birds of Harmony	Tribute to a Great President	Gospel 1085
399	Birds of Harmony	Meet Me on the Other Side	Gospel 1085
400	Jewel Gospel Singers	The Modern Joshua	Savoy 4210
401	Sensational Six	Let Freedom Ring	Gospel 1084
402	Sensational Six	The Day the World Stood Still	Gospel 1084
403	Rosie Wallace	A Light That Shines	Savoy 4209
404	Rosie Wallace	Take Courage	Savoy 4209

Of these nine songs, only "He'll Understand" and "Meet Me on the Other Side" are not about JFK, although they are fitting flip sides of memorial records. The seven Kennedy songs from this session constitute

5 percent of the total of 131 songs, and 12 percent of the fifty-nine recordings about JFK's death.

Mrs. Rosie Wallace (b. 1935) remembers that she had already started writing a song about the assassination by the time Savoy Records called to ask her to prepare some songs for the session. She does not know how many copies of her records were sold, and did not get paid anything. There was no session fee and no royalties. For her Savoy albums she only received some minimal monthly amounts from BMI.[5]

Taken together the twenty songs of these two memorial projects are almost half of the total number of fifty-nine songs about the assassination. The Savoy gospel project was aimed at the black market, but the Testament blues project was intended for both black and white record buyers. Beginning in the early 1960s, producers of blues records increasingly shifted their attention to the white market. More and more white people began to buy black gospel records as well, although this trend started later. Although black blues recordings are mainly aimed at the white market nowadays, black gospel recordings are still predominantly bought by African Americans. Whatever market the producers of some of these songs may have had in mind, the overwhelming majority of these songs show sincere emotion and as such represent the opinions of important segments of the African-American community of the period.

Some blues and gospel lyrics of the JFK era show a dearth of poetic inspiration. This may be reflective of the first traces of an art form in decline. The many in memoriam songs were sometimes hastily composed to get the record on the market in the immediate aftermath of the assassination. Some of the songs on the draft (Sonny Martin) or the space race (Hank Ballard) are rather trivial. The latter were a continuation of the flying saucer novelty theme. The fear of an alien attack was at least in part a reflection of Cold War anxiety. To many it must have seemed that the Russians had command of space, and the songs tried to channel fear into humor. Yet the musical accompaniment often overcomes the shortcoming of the lyrics or complements them. Overall, the poetry of the blues (Otis Spann) and the magnetism of the gospel songs and sermons (Rev. C. L. Franklin) are still in evidence.

For the first time, records of African-American comedy show that the artists felt free to comment on politics. Dick Gregory and Slappy White are prime early examples of African-American comedians who dared to speak out. Here, too, the Kennedy era was a revolutionary period.

Of the 131 political songs from this period, only seventeen (13 percent) were sung by women, most of whom were gospel singers. Although the women's songs are few in number, they are certainly no less direct than the men's.

The sermon, with its spontaneous exchanges between pew and pulpit, affords a unique view of political developments as they affected everyday life, and it is fortunate that, in contrast to the Truman/Eisenhower era, topical sermons were recorded in this period. As has been noted, the development of magnetic tape and the long-play album were ideally suited to the recording of half-hour or longer sermons, and the number of them rose steadily during the mid-1960s.

Of the 131 songs selected for detailed analysis, ninety-two (70 percent) were sung by blues artists and forty-four (30 percent) by gospel artists or groups. The percentage of gospel artists recording songs and sermons on political themes is far higher than in either the period before 1945 (6 percent) or the period from 1945 to 1960 (19 percent). No gospel songs were sung about the draft, the space race, or economic conditions in the JFK years, but 38 percent of the songs about the civil rights movement were recorded by gospel artists, and gospel songs constitute 48 percent of the songs about the assassination. Thus the gospel singers, like the blues singers, had become increasingly more politically involved. The relative scarcity of blues and gospel songs directly mentioning Truman (only six) and Eisenhower (only four) is evidence that both presidents failed to inspire the African-American community. This stands in sharp contrast to the many songs making direct references to Presidents Franklin D. Roosevelt (forty-four) and John F. Kennedy (sixty-three). However, the fact that these two presidents died in office and that there are a great many in memoriam songs as a result must be taken into account.

The recording of songs devoted to the assassination in the immediate aftermath of the crime was regarded by some as being unethical. In particular it may have seemed inappropriate to profit from the sale and marketing of such records. As a result, in the case of "In the Summer of His Years" royalties were donated to good causes such as the J. D. Tippit Fund.

"Most topical songs," Bruce Jackson observes in the music magazine *Listen*, "do not last long enough to become folk songs simply because the topic that prompted them is itself too ephemeral to withstand the careless ravages of simple forgetting. If a topical song turns out to be more generally applicable to the human situation, it does survive and it does go into tradition."[6] Although virtually all of these songs have now long been forgotten by the audience for which they were intended (the African-American community and the then emergent audience of white fans of blues and gospel music), the assassination of President Kennedy is still remembered as one of the most shocking events in recent American history. As such, this poetic heritage of African-American culture deserves to be remembered. Popular topical songs of the white community[7] and Mexican-American ballads[8] have received some scholarly attention, but these African-American blues and gospel songs about John F. Kennedy have been ignored too long.

To the blues and gospel singers, John F. Kennedy was a mythical hero. He married a beautiful princess and for a brief moment the presidential couple turned the Republic into a shining monarchy. After a slow start the president appeared to lose favor in the Cuban crisis. He initiated the Civil Rights Act but was thwarted from pushing it through Congress because of a seemingly mysterious death. The gospel singers are certain that their hero is not dead, but lives on in Heaven. John F. Kennedy was only forty-six years old when he was shot. He will never grow old, but will remain in our minds as a promise unfulfilled.

THE RECORDINGS

Twenty-eight digitally remastered blues and gospel songs from the 1960s on President John F. Kennedy are available from the author at: rijn8194@planet.nl

More information on the CD, *Kennedy's Blues: African-American Blues and Gospel Songs on JFK* (Agram Blues ABCD 2019), is to be found on the Agram website at: http://home.tiscali.nl/guido/

Information on the CDs accompanying the first two books in the series, *Roosevelt's Blues* (Agram Blues ABCD 2017) and *The Truman and Eisenhower Blues* (Agram Blues ABCD 2018), will also be found on the Agram website.

The thirteen songs on the assassination of President Kennedy recorded for Testament Records are available on Testament TCD 5007, *Can't Keep from Crying: Topical Blues on the Death of President Kennedy*. See: www.hightone.com

NOTES

INTRODUCTION

1. Gates (1987): xxxi.
2. Bell (1987): 26.
3. Gates (1988): xii.
4. Levine (1993): 36.
5. Evans (1982): 27–30.
6. An excellent study of soul music and race relations is Brian Ward's 1998 *Just My Soul Responding*.

1. JOHN F. KENNEDY, THE MAN AND THE MYTH

1. *Michigan Chronicle*, 30 November 1963 as quoted in Salvatore (2005): 264.
2. Kennedy (1940).
3. Kennedy (1955).
4.
   "And when he fell in whirlwind, he went down,
   As when a lordly cedar, green with boughs,
   Goes down with a great shout upon the hills,
   And leaves a lonesome place against the sky."

   Edwin Markham (1852–1940), "Lincoln, the Man of the People." From: Louis Untermeyer, ed. *Modern American Poetry*. New York: Harcourt, Brace and Howe, 1919.
5. Cf. 2 Samuel 1.
6. Franklin here quotes from Charles Albert Tindley's 1905 hymn "We'll Understand It Better By and By." Cf. Heilbut (1985), 24–25.
7. Rev. C. L. Franklin, "Why Have the Mighty Fallen (Tribute to the Kennedys)" (= Chess Sermon 67), Detroit, prob. November 1968; issued on Chess 2ACH LP 87.

8. The Gallup Poll, Presidential Job Approval Ratings of 6–8 February 2004 at: http://www.gallup.com/poll/content/default.aspx?ci=10534
9. Rose Kennedy (1974): 112.
10. Schlesinger (1965): 73.
11. Theodore H. White, "For President Kennedy: An Epilogue," *Life* (6 December 1963): 159.
12. W. Nicholas Knight, "Lancer: Myth-Making and the Kennedy Camelot," *Avalon to Camelot*, vol. II, no. 1 (1988): 26–31.
13. Cf. Bailyn (1967).
14. Thomas Brown (1988): 42–43.
15. *Newsweek* (25 March 1968): 21.
16. *Newsweek* (28 November 1983): 65.
17. *Newsweek* (29 December 1979): 14–16.
18. Cf. Bruce A. Rosenberg, "Kennedy in Camelot: The Arthurian Legend in America," *Western Folklore* 35 (January 1976): 52–59.
19. *Newsweek* (3 October 1966): 65.
20. Raglan (1956): 174–75.
21. Ibid., 184–85.
22. Collier and Horowitz (1985): 87.
23. Ibid., 155.
24. Adler (1964): 53.
25. Manchester (1967): 681.
26. *Newsweek* (25 March 1968): 27.
27. Cf. Bruce A. Rosenberg, "Kennedy in Camelot: The Arthurian Legend in America," *Western Folklore* 35 (January 1976): 52–59.
28. Thomas Brown (1988): 120, note 132.
29. *Time* (13 December 1963): 27.
30. Robert Frost, "For John F. Kennedy His Inauguration: Gift Outright of 'The Gift Outright,'" Washington, DC (20 January 1961): 70–77, in: Connery Lathem (1974): 424.
31. Campbell (1949): 353.
32. Chafe (1991): 219.
33. Alfred, Lord Tennyson, *Idylls of the King*: "Gareth and Lynette," lines 270–73.

2. JFK SAYS I'VE GOT TO GO

1. John F. Kennedy's Voting Record and Stands On Issues, page 5, at: www.jfklibrary.org
2. Guido van Rijn, report of the "Martin Luther King Memorial Conference," *Blues & Rhythm* 131 (August 1998): 14. The story was told by Harry Belafonte during a conference interview by Brian Ward and Tony Badger.
3. Carl Rowan, "Who Will Get the Negro Vote?" *Ebony* (November 1960): 40–49.
4. "Men on the Street: Viewers Give Their Opinions on Kennedy–Nixon TV Debate," *Chicago Defender* (1 October 1960): 1.
5. Ibid., 8.

6. "The Hope of Tomorrow and Today," *Chicago Defender* (Week of 8–14 October 1960).
7. "Kennedy Is Our Choice," editorial in the *Chicago Defender* (Week of 22–28 October 1960): 1-2.
8. Ibid., 7.
9. "Mahalia Jackson Believes in Kennedy," *Chicago Defender* (Week of 29 October–4 November 1960): 12.
10. See: www.stanford.edu/~tommyz/1960s/NAACP.htm
11. Watkins (1999): 495–503.
12. Catholic churches in America are associated with bingo nights as fundraising events.
13. Dick Gregory, "Commentary on Affairs Political," Chicago Playboy Club, 1961; issued on Colpix LP 417.
14. Wolf von Eckhardt, "Oral History Interview with August Heckscher," New York: Kennedy Papers (10 December 1965): 14–15.
15. Murray (1987): 419–20.
16. Memphis Slim, "The Big Race," Chicago, November 1960; issued on Folkways LP (5)3536. (The standard discography gives October 1960, but election day was on 8 November 1960.)
17. Chafe (1991): 197.
18. Wills (1981): 223.
19. Champion Jack Dupree, "President Kennedy Blues" (composer credit: Champion Jack Dupree), Copenhagen, Denmark, 4 October 1961; issued on Sonet LP 614.
20. In 1965 a freedom song recorded in Selma, Alabama, used the Berlin Wall as a metaphor: "We're gonna break this Berlin Wall, Berlin Wall, Berlin Wall, We're gonna break this Berlin Wall in Selma, Alabama." "Berlin Wall," 15 March 1965; issued on *Freedom Songs: Selma, Alabama*, Folkways FHLP 5594.
    The Sons of Blues, with vocalist Billy Branch, sang another song entitled "Berlin Wall" in public at a Berlin Festival and recorded it for Alligator Records in 1978. The Sons of the Blues (vocalist: Billy Branch), "Berlin Wall" (composer credit: B. Branch–L. Barner), Chicago, 1978; issued on Alligator LP 7703; reissued on Sonet SNTF LP 786.
21. Sorensen (1965): 627.
22. Dick Gregory, "At the Blue Angel," New York City, 15 September 1961; issued on Colpix LP 420.
23. Norbert Hess, "Wilbert Harrison: Sein 'Kansas City' wurde zum Welt-Hit," *Blues Forum* 10 (Second quarter of 1983): 6.
24. Wilbert Harrison, "Drafted" (composer credit: Wilbert Harrison), New York City, 1961; issued on Fury 1055; reissued on Agram ABCD 2019.
25. Lightning Hopkins and His Guitar, "War Is Starting Again" (composer credit: Hopkins-Semiens), Houston, 10 March 1961, Ivory 91272; reissued on Vee-Jay LP 1044 and Joy LP 115.
26. Sonny Martin, "Air Force–U.S. Navy" (composer credit: S. Martin–J. West), Crowley, LA, 1961; issued on Excello 2207; reissued on Flyright FLYLP 608.
27. For transcription and analysis see *Roosevelt's Blues* (1997): 142–43.

28. For transcription and analysis see *Roosevelt's Blues* (1997): 73–74.
29. "Big" Joe Williams, "Army Man Blues," New York City, 7 October 1961; issued on Bluesville LP 1056; reissued on Agram ABCD 2019.
30. Snooky Pryor, "Uncle Sam Don't Take My Man" (composer credit: James Pryor), Chicago, 1963; issued on JOB 1126; reissued on Flyright FLYLP 100. There are two alternative takes of this song: "Big Guns," and "Uncle Sam Don't Take My Man," 1963; both JOB unissued; issued on Flyright FLYLP 565.
31. Norman Darwen, "I'm the One Gave This Big Sound to the Harmonica," Snooky Pryor interview, Colne, Germany, 31 May 1993, *Blues & Rhythm* 152 (September 2000): 11. See also my letter to the editor of *Blues & Rhythm* 153 (October 2000): 7.
32. Teddy Reynolds, "I Thought the War Was Over," Los Angeles, 1962; issued on Agram ABCD 2019.
33. See: www.sss.gov/fslocal.htm
34. Jimmy Anderson, "Draft Board Blues," Crowley, LA, 1962–63; issued on Flyright LP 607; reissued on Agram ABCD 2019.
35. George R. White, "Interview with Bo Diddley," 1982–85. In George R. White (1995): 125.
36. Ibid., 124.
37. Bo Diddley, "Mr. Khrushchev" (composer credit: E. McDaniel), Chicago, 24 January 1962; issued on Agram ABCD 2019. A later version is: Bo Diddley, "Mr. Kruschev" (composer credit: Ellas McDaniel), Joyous Lake, Woodstock, NY, 21 October 1977; issued on M.F. LP 77-1002.
38. For a transcription and an analysis see *Roosevelt's Blues* (1997): 179–80.
39. This is a reference to guitarist Willie Chambers (b. 1938).
40. This is a reference to guitarist Brownie McGhee (1915–1996).
41. Luke "Long Gone" Miles, "War Time Blues" (composer credit: Luke Miles), Los Angeles, 5 February 1962; issued on Smash 1755; reissued on Sundown LP 709-05. Miles later recorded this song with virtually the same lyrics as: "I Don't Need No Army," Los Angeles, 1969; Kent unissued; issued on P-Vine CD 3058.
42. Sonny Boy Williamson, "I Have Got to Go" (composer credit: Sonny Boy Williamson), Chicago, 11 December 1941; issued on Bluebird B 8992; reissued on Document DOCD 5058.
43. Billy Boy Arnold, "We All Got to Go" (composer credit: S.B. Williamson), Chicago, 15 April, 1962; issued on Testament TCD 6011. A later version of this song is Johnny Jones, "I Have Got to Go" (composer credit: Williamson), Chicago, 25 July 1963; issued on Alligator LP 4717; reissued on Alligator CD 4717.
44. Charters (1977): 31–32.
45. J. D. Short, "Fighting for Dear Old Uncle Sam" (composer credit: Short), St. Louis, 3 July 1962; issued on Folkways LP 2467; reissued on Verve FV LP 9035.
46. Ray Charles, "The Danger Zone" (composer credit: Percy Mayfield), Los Angeles, 5 July 1961; issued on ABC-Paramount 10244; reissued on ABC LP 415. A later version is Ray Charles, "The Danger Zone" (composer credit: Percy Mayfield), West Berlin, Germany, 6 March 1962; issued on Pablo CD 5301. The composer was later to record the song himself: Percy Mayfield, "Danger Zone" (composer credit: Percy Mayfield), Chicago, 1969; issued on Brunswick LP 75415.

47. See: www.geocities.com/americanpresidencynet/1962.htm
48. Big Bill, "Just a Dream (On My Mind)," Chicago, 6 February 1939; issued on Vocalion 04706; reissued on Document DOCD 5130.
49. Sleepy John Estes, "It Was a Dream" (composer credit: W.L. Broonzy), 19 April 1962; issued on Testament TCD 6008.
50. Dallek (2003): 570.
51. Ray Charles, piano (1930–2004), Sam "Lightnin'" Hopkins, guitar (1912–1982), Jimmy Reed, guitar/harmonica (1925–1976), Bo Diddley, guitar (b. 1928) and "Big" Maybelle Smith, vocals (1924–1972).
52. Louisiana Red, "Red's Dream" (composer credit: Glover–Levy–Reig), New York City, October 1962; issued on Roulette 4469; reissued on Agram ABCD 2019.
53. Slappy White, "At the Club Harlem," Atlantic City, New Jersey, 29 June 1963; issued on Chess LP 1481.
54. Eddie (Big Blues) Carson, "The Bloody Bloody Bombs" (composer credit: E. Carson–C. Anderson) or "The Bombs of Destruction" or "The Devastating Bombs," Detroit, 1962; issued on M.R.C. 1203.
55. Schlesinger (1965): 291.
56. Chafe (1991): 268.
57. Schlesinger (1965): 848.
58. Chafe (1991): 271.
59. Peter Goldman, "Kennedy Remembered," *Newsweek* (28 November 1983): 64.
60. Schlesinger (1965): 848.

3. TWISTIN' OUT IN SPACE

1. Hank Ballard and The Midnighters, "The Twist" (composer credit: Hank Ballard), Cincinnati, 11 November 1958; issued on King 5171. Chubby Checker, "The Twist," February 1960; issued on Parkway 811.
2. Betty Beale, "Dancing at the White House: Adlai Stevenson Honored," *Washington Evening Star* (13 November 1961).
3. Dawson (1995): 59–60.
4. Lulu Reed & Freddy King with Sonny Thompson and His Orchestra, "Do the President Twist" (composer credit: Thompson-Bridge), Cincinnati, 7 February 1962; issued on Federal 12457; reissued on Agram ABCD 2019.
5. The Mann Act makes it a federal offense to transport a woman across a state line for immoral purposes.
6. Stage name of jazz trumpet player Louis Armstrong (1901–1971).
7. Stage name of jazz trumpet player John Birks Gillespie (1917–1993).
8. Dick Gregory, "At the Hungry I," San Francisco, ca. 11 July 1961; issued on Colpix LP 420.
9. Chess 1827, January 1962.
10. Delmark CD 608, 3 March 1964.
11. Some of the titles are quite telling: Bo Diddley, "Mama Don't Allow No Twistin'" (composer credit: E. McDaniel), Chicago, July 1962; issued on Checker LP 2984. Roy

Brown, "Stop the Twist," Los Angeles, 1962; issued on D.R.A. 321. John Lee Hooker, "(Twist Ain't Nothin') But the Old Time Shimmy," New York City, 14 October 1968; issued on BluesWay LP 6023. Henry Strogin, "Old Folks Boogie While the Young Ones Twist," Los Angeles, 1960; issued on Ball 1012.

12. Hank Ballard and the Midnighters, "The Float" (composer credit: Cowan-Ballard), Cincinnati, 26 May 1961; issued on King 5510; reissued on Rare Bird BID LP 8003.
13. Possibly "space-jockey," slang for astronaut.
14. Robert Parker, "Twistin' Out in Space" (composer credit: R. Parker), New Orleans, 4 April 1962; issued on Imperial 5842; reissued on Agram ABCD 2019.
15. Mack McCormick, "Walkin' This Road by Myself," sleeve notes to Bluesville LP 1057, ca. 1963. See also Charters (2004): 226–27.
16. Lightnin' Hopkins, "Happy Blues for John Glenn," (composer credit: Hopkins), Houston, 20 February 1962; issued on Bluesville LP 1057; reissued in two parts on Bluesville 45-820.
17. Valerie Prilop, "John Glenn as Astronaut," *Houston Chronicle*, at: www.chron.com/content/interactive/space/johnglenn/astronaut.html
18. For a transcript of John Glenn's official communication with the Command Center, see: www.classbrain.com/artteenst/publish/article_120.shtml
19. Little Willie John, "Mister Glenn" (composer credit: Toombs–King); Cincinnati, 7 March 1962; issued on King 5628; reissued on Agram ABCD 2019.
20. Johnny Acey, "I Go into Orbit" (composer credit: LaCharles Harper); New York City, 1962; issued on Fling 728; reissued on Agram ABCD 2019.
21. See: www.homeofheroes.com/presidents/speeches/kennedy_space.html
22. In 1974 blues guitarist Lee Jackson (1921–1979), accompanied by an unknown bassist and drummer, recorded a rough-hewn instrumental entitled "Apallo 17" [sic] commemorating the final mission of the project that started on 7 December 1972.

    Apollo 17, with Eugene Cernan, Ronald Evans, and Harrison Schmidt on board, left on 7 December 1972 for a twelve-day flight that took men to the moon for the last time. Although the inadvertent misspelling of the title hints at a lack of resources in the production of the record, the musicians launched into the theme with gusto. A terse spoken introduction linked three iconic figures with one of the most remarkable technical achievements of the era. The two Kennedys and Martin Luther King were often depicted in portraits as the three martyrs of the civil rights movement. "President Kennedy had a dream about the Apollo 17; all goes the same (for) Robert Kennedy and Martin Luther King. Now count down!" Lee Jackson, "Apallo 17" (composer credit: Lee Jackson–Carl O'Jones), Chicago, 1974; issued on C.J. 668. Note: Jackson had recorded "Apallo 15" for Bea & Baby 132 in 1971, but that record was never released.
23. Watkins (1999): 491.
24. A fashionable holiday resort in Miami Beach.
25. This is an onomatopoeic representation of a fart.
26. Slappy White, "At the Club Harlem," Atlantic City, NJ, 29 June 1963; issued on Chess LP 1481.
27. Cleaver (1968): 173–83.

A recording not used in this chapter because its lyrics are not relevant in spite of its title is: Big John, "Astronote Blues" (composer credit: Charles D. Scott), ca. 1963; issued on Astrol unnumbered.

4. THE WELFARE TURNS ITS BACK ON YOU

1. Letters from Chicago sent by St. Louis Jimmy Oden to Jacques Demêtre in Paris, 2 June 1961 and 14 December 1961. *Blues World* 8 (May 1966): 6-7.
2. Herman E. Johnson, "Depression Blues" (composer credit: Herman E. Johnson), Baton Rouge, LA, 5 April 1961; issued on Arhoolie LP 1060; reissued on Arhoolie CD 440. A later recording of this song is: Herman E. Johnson, "Depression in '61," Baton Rouge, LA, 12 May 1961; Arhoolie unissued.
3. The civilian unemployment rates were: 6.7 percent (1961), 5.5 percent (1962), and 5.7 percent (1963). (Source: U.S. Bureau of the Census.)
4. Smoky Babe, "Hard Time Blues," Scotlandville, LA, 10 March 1961; unissued. I have not heard this song. However, a transcription was presented by Harry Oster on page 205 of his *Living Country Blues* (1969).
5. Jimmy Lee Robinson, "Times Is Hard" (composer credit: J. L. Robinson), Chicago, 1962; issued on Bandera 2510; reissued on Ace CD 808.
6. Schlesinger (1965): 548.
7. Telephone conversation between Bernard Jolivette (= King Karl) and the author, 8 August 2005.
8. "Chuck" Brown, "Hard Times at My Door" (composer credit: B. Jolivette), Nashville, 1962; issued on Excello 2210.
9. Inflation rates were: 1.0 percent (1961), 1.0 percent (1962), and 1.3 percent (1963).
10. Cf. Van Rijn, "The Dollar Has the Blues: Deflation and Inflation in African-American Blues Songs," in Springer, ed. (2001): 86–87.
11. King Solomon, "Inflation Blues" (composer credit: King Solomon), Los Angeles, 1962; issued on Don-J 303 (as "I Got to Move" by "King Solomon"); reissued on Fay 105 (as by Howlin Wolf Jr.); reissued on Agram ABCD 2019.
12. Muddy Waters, "Tough Times" (composer credit: Brown–Morganfield), Chicago, January 1962; issued on Chess 1819; reissued on Charly CD Red Box 3.
13. Schlesinger (1965): 814.
14. Freddie King, "(The Welfare) Turns Its Back on You" (composer credit: S. Thompson–L. Weaver), Cincinnati, 28 November 1962; issued on Federal 12499; reissued on Agram ABCD 2019. Later versions are: Nyles Jones (pseudonym for Robert Jones, later Guitar Gabriel), "The Welfare Blues" (composer credit: R. Jones), Pittsburgh, 1970; issued on Gemini 101; reissued on Gemini LP 7101. Albert Collins, "When the Welfare Turns Its Back on You," Chicago, May 1978; issued on Alligator AL LP 4713; reissued on Sonet SNTF LP 707. Robert Cray, "When The Welfare Turns Its Back on You" (composer credit: S. Thompson–L. Weaver), Los Angeles, July 1978; issued on Tomato TOM LP 7041; reissued on Charly CRB LP 1140.
15. Stump Connolly, "Politics, The Rev. Al," accessed 6 February 2004 at: www.theweekbehind.com/articles/sharpton.html

16. Emanuel Laskey, "Welfare Cheese" (composer credit: T. Gordy–J. Laskey–R. Street), 1963; issued on Thelma 100; reissued on Agram ABCD 2019.

5. MARCH ON, DR. MARTIN LUTHER KING

1. Memphis Slim ("Leroy"), Big Bill Broonzy ("Natchez"), and Sonny Boy Williamson ("Sib"), *Blues in the Mississippi Night*, New York City, 1–2 March 1947; issued on Nixa NJLLP 8; reissued on Rounder CD 1860. See van Rijn (2004): 56.
2. For a blues song on Bilbo, see van Rijn (2004): 49–51, 70.
3. For Crump and the blues see van Rijn, "Mr. Crump and the Memphis Jug Band," *Blues & Rhythm* 62 (July 1991): 4–6.
4. This is not correct. Blues singer Arbee Stidham was born in Arkansas in 1917 and settled in Chicago ca. 1954. He died in Chicago in 1988.
5. Memphis Slim, "Down South," Chicago, November 1960; issued on Folkways LP (5)3536.
6. Stefan Solding, "Living Blues Interview: Champion Jack Dupree," *Living Blues* 32 (May/June 1977): 13.
7. Champion Jack Dupree, "Free and Equal" (composer credit: Dupree), Copenhagen, Denmark, 4 October 1961; issued on Storyville SLP 145; reissued on Storyville STCD 8013.
8. Williams (1988): 135.
9. Haskins (1986): 151–52.
10. The original four were Ezell Blair Jr. (Jibreel Khazan), David Richmond, Joseph McNeil, and Franklin McCain.
11. "Jail for Martin Luther King," *Chicago Defender* (Week of 22–28 October 1960): 1.
12. Although the term is here used for sexual freedom, see van Rijn (2004): 51–52 for the background of the original freedom train.
13. B.B. King, "I'm Gonna Sit In Till You Give In" (composer credit: Dave Clark–B.B. King), Los Angeles, 1 March 1962; issued on ABC-Paramount 10316; reissued on Agram ABCD 2019.
14. Arvella Gray (Blind Street Singer), "Freedom Bus," Chicago, 1965; issued on Gray 100.
15. Cary Baker, sleeve notes for *The Singing Drifter*, Birch LP 60091, recorded on 22 September 1972.
16. Arvella Gray (Blind Street Singer), "Freedom Riders," Chicago, 1965; issued on Gray 100.
17. For Louisiana Red and the events at Little Rock Central High School, see van Rijn (2004): 147–48.
18. Louisiana Red, "Ride on Red, Ride on" (composer credit: Glover–Levy–Reig), New York City, October 1962; issued on Roulette 4469; reissued on Agram ABCD 2019. Two alternative takes were recorded at that session, both also entitled "Ride On Red, Ride On." These second (slow with harmonica) and third (fast with guitar) versions are on Sequel CD 213.
19. Chuck Berry, "Promised Land" (composer credit: Chuck Berry Music Inc), Chicago, 20 February 1964; issued on Chess LP 1488; reissued on Chess 1916.

20. Berry (1987): 216–17.
21. Virginia Historical Society. "The Civil Rights Movement in Virginia." www.vahistorical.org/civilrights/massiveresistance.htm
22. Ward (1998): 213.
23. Quintard Taylor, "African Americans in the Enchanted State: Black History in New Mexico, 1529–1990," Historical introduction to "A History of Hope: The African-American Experience in New Mexico," exhibit, The Albuquerque Museum, Albuquerque, New Mexico, February 4 to April 7, 1996, 13–14.
24. "Mystery Donor Pays Jail Fines of Dr. King, Rev. Abernathy," *Chicago Defender* (Week of 14–20 July 1962): 3.
25. Williams (1988): 164–72.
26. Kennedy News Conference #40, 1 August 1962: www.jfklibrary.org/jfk_press_conference_620801.html
27. "Racial and Religious Prejudices Bring Threats on Kennedy's Life," *Chicago Defender* (Week of 21–27 July 1962): 3.
28. "Rockin' Jerusalem" was recorded postwar by the Fisk Jubilee Singers, Howard University Choir, and Tuskegee Institute Choir.
29. SNCC Freedom Singers, led by Bertha Gober, "Oh Pritchett, Oh Kelly" (composer credit: Traditional, arranged by Gober–Culbreth), Los Angeles, August 1963; issued on Smithsonian LP R023.
30. Williams (1988): 173.
31. A pun on "peat moss."
32. Slappy White, *At the Club Harlem*, Atlantic City, NJ, 29 June 1963; issued on Chess LP 1481.
33. Deuteronomy 32: 11–12. The same text was also used for the most popular sermon by Rev. C. L. Franklin, recorded circa 1953 for JVB/Chess 61-3.
34. Patrick Henry (1736–1799) was Governor of Virginia. He protested British tyranny and fought for American liberty. His famous "Give me liberty or give me death" speech was delivered in 1775.
35. "Greater love hath no man than this, that a man lay down his life for his friends" (John 15:13).
36. Rev. Ben Gay, "As the Eagle Stirreth Her Nest," sermon delivered for the people of Albany, from *Freedom in the Air: Albany, Georgia 19612*, a documentary by Guy Carawan and Alan Lomax, Albany, GA, 1962; issued on SNCC LP 101.
37. "Miss. Governor Faces Jail for Barring Negro Student," *Chicago Defender* (Week of 22–28 September 1962): 1–2.
38. On 18 August 1963 James Meredith graduated from the University of Mississippi with a B.A. in political science. Three years later he was shot while leading a civil rights march through Mississippi, but survived. Blues singer J. B. Lenoir sang a song about the assassination attempt which will be studied in a sequel: "Shot On Meredith," Chicago, 2 September 1966; issued on Polydor LP 2482014; reissued on Evidence CD 26068.
39. Theodore Bilbo (1877–1947), governor of Mississippi, and Strom Thurmond (1902–2003), in 1962 governor of South Carolina.
40. "Ross Barnett: One of a Fading Breed," *Chicago Defender* (Week of 29 September–5 October 1962): 3.

41. "Ray Charles Denies He'll Join Birmingham Fight," *Chicago Defender* (Week of 13–19 April 1963): 1.
42. Charles (1979): 273.
43. "King Defies Injunction to Halt Alabama Protests," *Chicago Defender* (Week of 13–19 April 1963): 1.
44. Williams (1988): 188–99.
45. Bob Starr, "The Jail House King" (composer credit: Ruby M. Cash), Hollywood, CA, 1963; issued on Fable 800.
46. "Telegram from Martin Luther King to President Kennedy," in Carson (1998): 185.
47. Branch (1989): 784–86.
48. John Lee Hooker, "Birmingham Blues" (composer credit: John Lee Hooker), Chicago, May 1963; issued on Vee-Jay 538; reissued on Agram ABCD 2019.
49. Jackie Robinson, "Birmingham Poses Moment of Truth for JFK on Rights," *Chicago Defender* (Week of 18–24 May 1963): 2.
50. Haskins and Benson (1991): 155–57.
51. Williams (1988): 221.
52. Radio and Television Report to the American People on Civil Rights, 11 June 1963, Public Papers of the Presidents: 468.
53. "Too Little, Too Late Policy Killed Evers, NAACP Aide Tells Solons," *Chicago Defender* (Week of 15–21 June 1963): 1.
54. ". . . That He Shall Not Have Died in Vain," *Chicago Defender* (Week of 15–21 June 1963): 1.
55. "New Miss. Violence! Club-Swinging Jackson Cops Attack Evers Murder Protest March," *Chicago Defender* (Week of 15–21 June 1963): 1.
56. "Remember Evers Children, Donate to School Fund," *Chicago Defender* (Week of 22–28 June 1963): 1.
57. Robert Laughton, e-mail to the author, 24 January 2005.
58. SNCC Freedom Singers, led by Matthew Jones, "Ballad of Medgar Evers" (composer credit: Jones), SNCC Conference in Atlanta, spring 1964 or 1965 (the sleeve notes are at odds); issued on Smithsonian LP R023.
59. "Predicts 50 Co-Sponsors to Push Kennedy's Rights Bills," *Chicago Defender* (Week of 22–28 June 1963): 1.
60. Salvatore (2005): 230.
61. Ibid., 251.
62. Speech at the Great March on Detroit, 23 June 1963, in Clayborne Carson and Kris Shepard, eds., *A Call to Conscience: The Landmark Speeches of Dr. Martin Luther King, Jr.* New York: Warner (2002): 57–74.
63. Salvatore (2005): 256.
64. McNeil (2005): 86.
65. Heilbut (1985): 167.
66. The Gospel Harmonettes, "The Hymn," 1964; issued on Vee-Jay LP 5064; reissued on Collectables CD 7203.
67. Van Rijn (1997): 143.
68. Williams (1988): 197.
69. Bob Starr, "The Freedom March" (composer credit: Ruby M. Cash), Hollywood, CA, 1963; issued on Fable 800.

70. Williams (1988): 199.
71. Wald (2000): 277.
72. See: www.fpp.co.uk/docs/ADL/Leo_Frank/
73. SNCC Freedom Singers, led by Rutha Harris, "We Shall Not Be Moved" (composer credit: Traditional, arranged by the Freedom Singers), Los Angeles, August 1963; issued on Smithsonian LP R023.
74. This is one of perhaps six different gospel groups listed as Sons of David in the standard gospel discography: The Mighty Sons of David with Ernest Frazier lead, "March On Dr. Martin Luther King," Boston, 1963; issued on Freedom Songs unnumbered; reissued on Wolf WNJCD 022.
75. The Mighty Sons of David with Ernest Frazier lead, "We Want Freedom in This Land," Boston, 1963; issued on Freedom Songs unnumbered; reissued on Wolf WNJCD 022.
76. "Rev. Martin Luther King's Speech Was History Talking." *Chicago Defender* (Week of 31 August–6 September 1963): 4.
77. "Our Leadership," editorial in *New York Amsterdam News* (7 September 1963): 10.
78. Roy Wilkins, "The Greatest Day!" *New York Amsterdam News* (7 September 1963): 10.
    Recordings not used in this chapter because they are instrumental, unissued, or not relevant are: The World Famous "Upsetters," "Freedom Ride" (instrumental), 1961; issued on Little Star 128. Smoky Babe, "Ain't It Hard to Be a Nigger," and "Segregation Blues," Scotlandville, LA, 11 August 1961; unissued. Voices of Jordan, "Black Race," 8 January 1962; Gospel unissued. Church of God and Saints of Christ Singers, "Democracy," Columbus, OH, 3 October 1963; issued on King LP 898.

6. THE DAY THE WORLD STOOD STILL

1. One remarkable tribute to Abraham Lincoln by an African-American artist is Leadbelly, "Abraham Lincoln," recording location and date unknown; unissued Smithsonian acetate 282; issued on Smithsonian Folkways SF CD 40045.
2. In reality it was a deadly tornado that hit Tupelo on 5 April 1936. The final death toll was set at 233 (not necessarily including African Americans, who were frequently excluded from death tolls until the 1950s).
3. See Luigi Monge, "Death by Fire: African-American Popular Music on the Natchez Rhythm Club Fire," in Springer (2006). The Natchez fire occurred on 23 April 1940.
4. John Lee Hooker, "Ballad to Abraham Lincoln" (composer credit: Hooker–Besman), Culver City, CA, 9 March 1961; issued on Lauren 361; reissued on America AMLP 6074.
5. "Good-bye, Dear Friend," cartoon by "Eugene" in the *Chicago Defender* (Week of 7–13 December 1963): 11.
6. Simeon Booker, "How JFK Surpassed Abraham Lincoln," *Ebony* (February 1964): 25–34.
7. Champion Jack Dupree, "Schoolday Blues" (composer credit: Dupree), Copenhagen, Denmark, 3 October 1961; issued on Storyville LP 145; reissued on Storyville CD 8013.

8. Champion Jack Dupree, "School Day" (composer credit: Jack Dupree), Frankfurt, Germany, 16 November 1970; issued on Scout LP 7; reissued on L+R CD 42021.
9. Bro. Sidney Harris and the Sunset Jubilee, "My Friend Kennedy" (composer credit: S. Harris), possibly Richmond, VA, 1964; issued on Turn Tage 1608.
10. The Dixie Hummingbirds, "Our Prayer for Peace" (composer credit: Walker), 1964; issued on Peacock 3012, reissued on Peacock LP 115 and 128.
11. Southern Sons Quartette, "A Prayer for Tomorrow" (composer credit: James Walker), Jackson, MS, March 1953; issued on Trumpet 206; reissued on Alligator CD 2802. See Ryan (2004): 117–18.
12. Ashley James and Ray Allen, *We Love You Like a Rock*, Searchlight Films, 1994, as quoted in Zolten (2003): 272.
13. The Dixie Hummingbirds, "Our Prayer for Peace," *TV Gospel Time* broadcast #53, unissued, Washington, DC, 1964.
14. "But they that wait upon the Lord shall renew their strength; they shall mount up with wings as eagles; they shall run, and not be weary; and they shall walk, and not faint." Isaiah 40: 31.
15. See "Restoration and Beyond," at: www.cuaa.org/reb.htm
16. Rosie Wallace, "Take Courage" (composer credit: R. Wallace), Philadelphia, 29 November 1963; issued on Savoy 4209.
17. Telephone conversation between the author and Mrs. Rosie Wallace, 26 September 2005.
18. Brauer (1977): 312–13.
19. The Sensational Six of Birmingham, Ala, "The Day the World Stood Still" (composer credit: Jenkins Holman), Philadelphia, 29 November 1963; issued on Gospel 1084; reissued on Agram ABCD 2019.
20. James Brewer, "Why Did He Have To Go?" Chicago, July 1964; issued on Testament LP 01; reissued on Testament TCD 5007.
21. Schlesinger (1965): 124.
22. Chafe (1991): 216.
23. Bill Jackson, "The 22nd Day of November," possibly Philadelphia, PA, December 1963; issued on Testament LP 01; reissued on Testament TCD 5007.
24. Abraham Zapruder made the only film of the entire assassination. It is an 8 mm silent color film of the Kennedy motorcade, just before, during, and immediately after the assassination.
25. Dixie Nightingales, "Assassination" (composer credit: Hoskins), 1965; issued on Chalice 102; reissued on Agram ABCD 2019.
26. This is probably a reference to the Pershing Hotel and Ballroom at 64th and Cottage Grove Avenue.
27. Dana Calvo, "The President's Been Shot," *Smithsonian Magazine* (November 2003): 2. www.smithsonianmag.com/smithsonian/issues03/nov03/pdf/jfk.pdf
28. Perry Tillis interview by Kevin Nutt, Samson, AL, 18 July 2004. In Guido van Rijn, "I Found a Solid Rock in Jesus: The Life and Recordings of Bishop Perry Tillis," *Blues & Rhythm* 199 (May 2005): 16–18.
29. Perry Tillis, "Kennedy Moan" (composer credit: Perry Tillis), Elba, AL, 15 September 1971; issued on Flyright LP 501; reissued on Agram ABCD 2019.

30. Goreau (1984): 282–86.
31. Salvatore (2005): 368.
32. Mahalia Jackson, "In the Summer of His Years (Tribute to President J. F. Kennedy)" (composer credit: H. Kretzmer–D. Lee), Chicago, 29 November 1963; issued on Columbia 42946; reissued on Agram ABCD 2019.
33. "BBC Kennedy Broadcast Is Hot Item," *Billboard* (14 December 1963): 3.
34. Mahalia Jackson, "Abraham, Martin and John" (composer credit: D. Holler), Los Angeles, 28 August 1969; issued on Columbia 4-45068; reissued on Columbia LP 9950. Other gospel artists who recorded the song were the Angelic Choir, Robert Patterson, Rev. Cleophus Robinson, Clara Ward, and Billy Watkins. Secular singers such as Dion, Moms Mabley, Smokey Robinson, and Marvin Gaye scored hits with it and blues singer Charles Brown recorded it as well.
35. Part two of Avery Brady's song is discussed before part one because they fit better in the narrative this way.
36. Avery Brady, "Poor Kennedy #2," Chicago, early 1964; issued on Testament TCD 5007.
37. Thermon Ruth had previously recorded topical songs as a member of the Selah Jubilee Singers. These are analyzed in my books about Roosevelt and Truman. For Ruth's obituary see Todd Baptista. *Blues & Rhythm* 173 (October 2002): 21.
38. For the song's history see van Rijn (1997): 155–60.
39. Bro. Therman Ruth and the Harmoneers, "That Awful Day in Dallas" (composer credit: Therman Ruth), Philadelphia, 29 November 1963; issued on Savoy 4208; reissued on Agram ABCD 2019.
40. Posner (2003). *The Kennedy Assassination: Beyond Conspiracy,* a TV documentary written and directed by Mark Obenhaus for P.J. Productions & Springs Media Inc., in coproduction with the BBC.
41. Otis Spann, "Sad Day in Texas," Chicago, early 1964; issued on Testament LP 01; reissued on Agram ABCD 2019.
42. The Echoes of Zion, "Atlanta's Tragic Monday," Atlanta, GA, 1952; issued on Gerald 103; reissued on Krazy Kat KKLP 7417.
43. For a transcription and an analysis see Guido van Rijn (1997): 197–203.
44. Southern Bell Singers, "The Tragedy of Kennedy" (composer credit: Southern Bell Singers), November/December 1963; issued on Vee-Jay 934; reissued on Agram ABCD 2019.
45. The Birds of Harmony, "Tribute to a Great President" (composer credit: Edward Lightner), Philadelphia, PA, 29 November 1963; issued on Gospel 1085; reissued on Agram ABCD 2019.
46. Rita Griffin, "Will Hairston Limits Performances to Church," *Michigan Chronicle* (25 May 1968).
47. Taken from Guido van Rijn, "The Hurricane of the Motor City: The Life Story of Brother Will Hairston," *Blues & Rhythm* 167 (March 2002): 14–17.
48. Many blues and jazz artists were employed by Ruby in his nightclub. Blues guitarist A. D. "ZuZu" Bollin (1922–1990) told how Ruby had to pay him $40 to $70 more after his first record had appeared ca. 1951–52 (Torch 6910, recorded in Dallas). When Bollin's booking agency heard about this, they told Ruby he could

get cheaper groups. Ruby became angry and reacted by using his influence to ban Bollin's record off the air. See Tim Schuller, "The Return of ZuZu Bollin: Lone Star Bluesmaster," *Living Blues* 89 (December 1989): 18. Other musicians who have recalled working for Jack Ruby include alto saxophonist Buster Smith (1904–1991), bandleader Red Calhoun, and tenor saxophonist David "Fathead" Newman (b. 1933). With a chuckle, Newman remembered how Ruby ordered the black band to turn around when the white strippers performed. Only the drummer was able to watch the bumps and grinds. See Josh Alan Friedman, "Jack Ruby: Dallas' Original J.R." (1997): 1–8, at: www.wfmu.org/LCD/20/ruby.html.

49. Brother Will Hairston—The Hurricane of the Motor City, "Story of President Kennedy," Detroit, ca. 1964; issued on Knowles 3946; reissued on Knowles LP 1,000,000.
50. Deacon L. J. Bates (= Blind Lemon Jefferson), "See That My Grave's Kept Clean," Chicago, ca. October 1927; issued on Paramount 12585; reissued on Document DOCD 5018. A later version is "See That My Grave Is Kept Clean," Chicago, c. February 1928; issued on Paramount 12608; reissued on Document DOCD 5019.
51. Fred McDowell, "Six White Horses," Como, MS, 24 November 1963; issued on Testament CD 5019; reissued on Testament CD 5021.
52. Avery Brady, "Poor Kennedy," Chicago, early 1964; issued on Testament LP 01; reissued on Testament TCD 5007.
53. Van Rijn (1997): 195–97.
54. James Darey, "Tribute to a Great Leader," *Chicago Defender* (Week of 30 November–6 December 1963).
55. Big Joe Williams, "A Man Amongst Men," Chicago, ca. December 1963; issued on Testament LP 01; reissued on Testament TCD 5007.
56. Big Joe Williams, "A Man Amongst Men" (composer credit: Big Joe Williams), Chicago, 1965; issued on Testament TCD 6010.
57. Ronda Mitchell & Mrs. Lovell, "J.F. Kennedy's Reservation" (composer credit: Crumbley), Chicago, ca. 1964; issued on Decca LKLP 4748; reissued on Agram ABCD 2019.
58. Fannie Brewer, "When We Got the Message," Chicago, July 1964; issued on Testament LP 01; reissued on Testament TCD 5007.
59. Goreau (1984): 282.
60. Ibid., 286.
61. Son House, "American Defense," Robinsonville, MS, 17 July 1942; Library of Congress unissued, matrix 6607-B-1(a); issued as "This War Will Last You for Years" (composer credit: House), on Verve-Folkways LP 9035. Cf. *Roosevelt's Blues* (1997): 164–65.
62. Son House, "President Kennedy" (composer credit: Son House), New York City, 14 April 1965; issued on Columbia CD 471662; reissued on Agram ABCD 2019.
63. John F. Kennedy, "Inaugural Address," Washington, DC, 20 January 1961.
64. Johnny Young, "I Tried Not to Cry," Chicago, early 1964; issued on Testament LP 01; reissued on Testament TCD 5007.
65. Johnny Young, "Tribute to J.F.K.," Chicago, early 1964; issued on Testament TCD 5007.

66. Harold Bowen Singers, "Dear President," demo from Sam Phillips's Sun Studio, Memphis, 1964; unissued. (The name "Rosinberg" written on the label probably refers to Memphis lawyer Seymour Rosenberg, who was involved in music in the 1960s and was co-owner of the Memphis label, according to David Evans, owner of the demo 45.)
67. The literal spelling on the president's pronunciation card is "Ish bin ein Bearleener." Facsimile in Dherbier & Verlhac (2003): 270.
68. James and Fannie Brewer, "I Want to Know Why," Chicago, July 1964; issued on Testament LP 01; reissued on Testament TCD 5007.
69. *Can't Keep from Crying: Topical Blues on the Death of President Kennedy*, Testament LP S 01, issued in 1964.
70. John Lee Granderson, "A Man for the Nation," Chicago, ca. December 1963; issued on Testament LP 01; reissued on Testament TCD 5007.
71. *Can't Keep from Crying: Topical Blues on the Death of President Kennedy*, Testament TCD 5007, 1994. The Testament album was released in Britain on the Elektra subsidiary Bounty for European distribution in 1967 (Bounty BY LP 6035).
72. "Sergei Khrushev Remembers 40th Anniversary of Kennedy Assassination." At: www.watsoninstitute.org/news_detail.cfm?id=153
73. Rosie Wallace, "A Light That Shines (A Tribute to John F. Kennedy)" (composer credit: R. Wallace), Philadelphia, 29 November 1963; issued on Savoy 4209.
74. The Sensational Six of Birmingham, Ala, "Let Freedom Ring" (composer credit: Marvin Bradshaw), Philadelphia, 29 November 1963; issued on Gospel 1084.
75. Little David and the Mighty Gospel Supremes, "Beloved Kennedys" (composer credit: Ligotti–Jones), ca. 1968; issued on S Star 1001. This record was probably bootlegged for the calypso market as: Lord Hummingbird and His Gospel Singers, "Beloved Kennedy," ca. 1968; issued on Hummingbird 212.
76. Jimmy Brown, "He Was Loved by All the People," Chicago, early 1964; issued on Testament LP 01; reissued on Testament TCD 5007.
77. "And ye shall compass the city, all ye men of war, and go round about the city once. Thus shalt thou do six days. And seven priests shall bear before the ark seven trumpets of rams' horns: and the seventh day ye shall compass the city seven times, and the priests shall blow with the trumpets. And it shall come to pass, that when they make a long blast with the ram's horn, and when ye hear the sound of the trumpet, all the people shall shout with a great shout; and the wall of the city shall fall down flat, and the people shall ascend up every man straight before him." Joshua 6:3–5 (Authorized Version).
78. The Jewel Gospel Singers, "The Modern Joshua" (composer credit: Doris Ann Allen), Philadelphia, PA, 29 November 1963; issued on Savoy 4210; reissued on Agram ABCD 2019.
79. Mary Ross, "President Kennedy Gave His Life," Chicago, early 1964; issued on Testament LP 01; reissued on Testament TCD 5007.
80. Johnnie H. Robinson, "Assassination of the President," Ramsey Farm, Otey, TX, ca. 1964–65; issued on Elektra LP (7)296; reissued on Bounty LP 6016.
81. Little Junior and the Butler-aires, "Jackie, Don't You Weep," ca. 1964; issued on Fuller 6438; reissued on Agram ABCD 2019.

82. Sleepy John Estes, "I Stayed Away Too Long" (composer credit: John Adam Estes), London, 24 October 1964; issued on Delmark LP 611; reissued on Delmark DDCD 611.
83. Willie Dixon (1915–1992) was the bass player at the 1964 AFBF.
84. Instead of "a seabird" Estes perhaps sang about "a Seeburg," a famous brand of jukeboxes from 1927 onwards.
85. Hammie Nixon (1908–1984) was the harmonica player who accompanied Sleepy John at the 1964 AFBF.
86. Hammie Nixon with Sleepy John Estes, "I'm Going Home" (composer credit: Estes), Copenhagen, Denmark, 8 October 1964; issued on Storyville LP 222; reissued as "Blues for JFK" on Delmark DDCD 611. Harmonica player Sonny Boy Williamson (="Rice" Miller, 1912–1965) learned the song from Sleepy John Estes during the 1964 tour of the American Folk Blues Festival, and sang his version of it in Stockholm on 9 December 1964. The concert was filmed, issued on LP and later reissued on videotape: Sonny Boy Williamson, "Going Back Home," Stockholm, Sweden, 9 December 1964; issued on Storyville LP 8012; reissued on Storyville Video SV 6032. (In William E. Donoghue's discography of Sonny Boy's recordings, both the date and the location are wrong.)
87. At: www.braille2000.com/brl2000/docs/OCRprimer.pdf
88. Heymann (1989): 437.
89. Sleepy John Estes, "Newport Blues," Chicago, 3 or 5 December 1968; issued on Delmark DECD 619.
90. Sleepy John Estes, "President Kennedy Stayed Away Too Long" (composer credit: John Estes), Memphis, 9 June 1969; issued on Blue Thumb LP 600; reissued on Arhoolie LP 1084. Later versions of this song are: Sleepy John Estes, "President Kennedy," Collierville, TN, poss. 1972; issued on Reprise MSLP 2117; reissued on Reprise KLP 44224. "Sleepy" John Adam Estes, "President Kennedy" (composer credit: John Adam Estes), Brownsville, TN, 31 December 1972; issued on Albatros VPALP 8285. Sleepy John Estes & Hammie Nixon, "The Death of President Kennedy," Toronto, Canada, 1974; issued on Wolf LP 120916. Sleepy John Estes, "President Kennedy Stayed Away Too Long," 20 March 1974; issued on Memphis Archives MACD 7008. Sleepy John Estes, "President Kennedy" (composer credit: John Adam Estes), Tokyo, Japan, 28 November 1974; issued on Delmark TD-8.
91. Haskins (1989): 143.
92. Titon (1989).
93. This is probably a mistake for "twentieth century."
94. W. H. Auden received the Pulitzer Prize for his poem "The Age of Anxiety" in 1948.
95. Vance Packard wrote a famous book about advertising called *The Hidden Persuaders* in 1957.
96. This may be a corruption of John 12:47: "And if any man hear my words, and believe not, I judge him not: for I came not to judge the world, but to save the world."
97. Acts 10:38: "How God anointed Jesus of Nazareth with the Holy Ghost and with power: who went about doing good, and healing all that were oppressed of the devil; for God was with him."
98. The Bible does not say that the Earth stood still when Jesus died, but Matthew 27:51 says: "And, behold, the veil of the temple was rent in twain from the top to

the bottom; and the Earth did quake, and the rocks rent." Perhaps the Reverend is confusing this with Revelations 8:1: "And when he had opened the seventh seal, there was silence in heaven about the space of half an hour."

99. 1 Corinthians 15:55: "O death, where is thy sting? O grave, where is thy victory?"
100. Hymn by William Cowper. "There Is A Fountain Filled With Blood" (1771).
101. Ibid.
102. Rev. O. L. Holliday, "The Assassination of President Kennedy and the Crucifixion of Christ," Greater New Pleasant Grove Baptist Church, Houston, 1966 or 1967; issued on Jewel LP 0008.
103. The Nixon tapes were played during the Watergate investigation, but a gap of eighteen minutes and thirty seconds remains, the tape going from the hiss and echoes of the long ago recorded conversations to a steady hum.
104. In the Tony Scott film *True Romance* (1993, screenplay by Quentin Tarantino) Cliff (Dennis Hopper) says to Coccotti (Christopher Walken):

> It's a fact. Sicilians have nigger blood pumping through their hearts. If you don't believe me, look it up. You see, hundreds and hundreds of years ago the Moors conquered Sicily. And Moors are niggers. Way back then, Sicilians were like the wops in northern Italy. Blond hair, blue eyes. But, once the Moors moved in there, they changed the whole country. They did so much fucking with the Sicilian women, they changed the bloodline forever, from blond hair and blue eyes to black hair and dark skin. I find it absolutely amazing to think that to this day, hundreds of years later, Sicilians still carry that nigger gene. I'm just quoting history. It's a fact. It's written. Your ancestors were niggers. Your great, great, great, great, great-grandmother was fucked by a nigger, and had a half-nigger kid. That is a fact. Now tell me, am I lying?

Next Coccotti pumps three bullets through Cliff's brains.

105. See: "Why Is the Mona Lisa Smiling?" for a computer metamorphosis by Lillian Schwartz, at: library.thinkquest.org/13681/data/link2.htm
106. *The Twilight Zone* premiered on black and white television in 1956 and aired for five seasons. Rod Serling directed, often wrote and always introduced each segment.
107. In his speech for the Democratic National Convention of 27 June 1936, President Franklin D. Roosevelt had said: "There is a mysterious cycle in human events. To some generations much is given. Of other generations much is expected. This generation of Americans has a rendezvous with destiny."
108. Mighty Mo Rodgers, "The Kennedy Song" (composer credit: M. Rodgers), Los Angeles, March–September 1998; issued on Blue Thumb CD 314547781.
109. Chuck Stone, "A Stone's Throw," editorial in the *Chicago Defender* (Week of 30 November–6 December 1963).
110. See: www.nga.gov/past/data/exh222.shtm
111. Slappy White, "At the Club Harlem," Atlantic City, NJ, 29 June 1963; issued on Chess LP 1481.
112. Peter Goldman, "Kennedy Remembered," *Newsweek* (28 November 1983): 64.

113. "Junior Wells Another Vintage Interview from the Files of Guido van Rijn," *Blues & Rhythm* 174 (November 2002): 6.
114. Original Soul Revivers (Lead: Ivory Lee), "JFK's Good Works Will Never Die" (composer credit: Ivory Lee), Houston, ca. December 1963; issued on Faith 502.
115. The artist's real name was William Du Bois Diamond, obviously bestowed in honor of radical civil rights leader W. E. B. Du Bois. This information comes from David Evans, who made an extensive study of the blues artists' nicknames.
116. Mitchell (1971): 167.

Songs not used in this chapter because the author never heard them or because there are no lyrics are: Zilla Mays, "Prayer for Jackie, Parts 1 and 2," 1961; issued on Checker 973. Byther Smith and the Lover Boys, "Thanks You Mr. Kennedy," Chicago, ca. 1962; issued on Eda 1556 (instrumental). Earlene Tucker, "Loving Memory of John F. Kennedy, Parts 1 and 2," ca. 1963; issued on Gardena 135. Leroy Cannon and His Religious Combo of Philadelphia, PA, "March on Washington" and "It Was a Sad Day" (composer credit: Ruby L. Graham), Philadelphia, Nov/Dec 1963; issued on Fine Art 237. Brother Henderson–Narrator, "Eleven-Twenty-Two Nineteen Sixty Three, Parts I and II" (composer credit: McGee-Henderson-Bufkin), Los Angeles, Nov/Dec 1963; issued on Proverb 11-22-1963.

CONCLUSION

1. Guido van Rijn, *Roosevelt's Blues: African-American Blues and Gospel Songs on FDR*, Jackson, MS: University Press of Mississippi, 1997.
2. Figures are from Rachlin (1981): 316. Source: Recording Industry Association of America, Inc.
3. The back of Testament TCD 5007, *Can't Keep from Crying: Topical Blues on the Death of President Kennedy*, says: "Brady recorded half a dozen versions of this song—every one of them different!" That would mean that Testament Records (now HighTone) still holds four unissued ones. Research by Bruce Bromberg of HighTone Records failed to produce these recordings (e-mail from Bruce Bromberg to the author, 26 November 2004).
4. Rev. Lawrence C. Roberts, e-mails to the author, 27 and 29 January 2005.
5. Telephone conversation between the author and Mrs. Rosie Wallace, 26 September 2005.
6. Bruce Jackson in *Listen*, as quoted in the sleeve notes of Bounty LP 6035, *Can't Keep from Crying: Topical Blues on the Death of President Kennedy*, by Peter J. Welding, 1967.
7. One example with notes about white songs on President Kennedy is Paul Dennis Hoffman, "Rock and Roll and JFK: A Study of Thematic Changes in Rock and Roll Lyrics since the Assassination of John F. Kennedy," *Popular Music and Society*, vol. 10, no. 2 (1985): 59–79. Folk singer Art Thieme's attempt to find a publisher for a book entitled "Songs of the Life, Times and Assassination of President John Fitzgerald Kennedy" failed. He deposited h
is notes at the Library of Congress. Archive of Folk Culture #1980/014, American Folklife Center #19979.
8. Dickey (1978).

BIBLIOGRAPHY

Adler, Bill. *The Kennedy Wit*. New York: Bantam, 1964.
———. *More Kennedy Wit*. New York: Bantam, 1965.
Allen, Ray. *Singing in the Spirit: African-American Sacred Quartets in New York City*. Philadelphia: University of Pennsylvania Press, 1991.
Bailyn, Bernard. *The Ideological Origins of the American Revolution*. Cambridge, MA: Harvard University, 1967.
Baker, Cary. Sleeve notes for *The Singing Drifter*, Birch LP 60091, recorded on 22 September 1972.
Baptista, Todd. "Thermon Ruth Obituary." *Blues & Rhythm* 173 (October 2002): 21.
Barlow, William. *Looking up at Down: the Emergence of Blues Culture*. Philadelphia: Temple University, 1989.
Beale, Betty. "Dancing at the White House: Adlai Stevenson Honored." *Washington Evening Star* (13 November 1961).
Bell, Bernard W. *The Afro-American Novel and Its Tradition*. Amherst: University of Massachusetts Press, 1987.
Berry, Chuck. *The Autobiography*. London and Boston: Faber and Faber, 1987.
Beyer, Jimmy. *Baton Rouge Blues: A Guide to the Baton Rouge Bluesmen and Their Music*. Baton Rouge, LA: Arts and Humanities Council, 1982.
Booker, Simeon. "How JFK Surpassed Abraham Lincoln." *Ebony* (February 1964): 25–34.
Branch, Taylor. *Parting the Waters: America in the King Years, 1954–63*. New York: Simon & Schuster, 1988; reprint, New York: Touchstone, 1989.
———. *Pillar of Fire: America in the King Years, 1963–65*. New York: Simon & Schuster, 1998.
Brauer, Carl M. *John F. Kennedy and the Second Reconstruction*. New York: Columbia University Press, 1977.
Broonzy, William, and Yannick Bruynoghe. *Big Bill Blues: Big Bill Broonzy's Story*. London: Cassell, 1955.
Brown, Thomas. *JFK: History of an Image*. London: I.B. Tauris, 1988.
Calvo, Dana. "The President's Been Shot." *Smithsonian Magazine* (November 2003): 2. www.smithsonianmag.com/smithsonian/issueso3/novo3/pdf/jfk.pdf

Campbell, Joseph. *The Hero with a Thousand Faces*. New York: Pantheon, 1949.
Carawan, Guy and Candie. *Sing for Freedom: The Story of the Civil Rights Movement Through its Songs*. Bethlehem, PA: Sing Out, 1990.
Chafe, William H. *The Unfinished Journey: America since World War II*. Oxford: Oxford University Press, 1986; reprint, New York, 1991.
Charles, Ray, and David Ritz. *Brother Ray: Ray Charles' Own Story*. London: MacDonald & Jane's, 1979.
Charters, Samuel B. *The Legacy of the Blues: A Glimpse into the Art and the Lives of Twelve Great Bluesmen*. New York: Da Capo, 1977.
Cleaver, Eldridge. *Soul on Ice*. New York: Dell, 1968.
Collier, Peter, and David Horowitz. *The Kennedys: An American Drama*. London and Sydney: Collier, 1985.
Connery Lathem, Edward, ed. *The Poetry of Robert Frost*. New York: Holt, Rinehart and Winston, 1969; reprint 1974.
Connolly, Stump. "Politics, The Rev. Al." (6 February 2004). www.theweekbehind.com/articles/sharpton.html
Cozzens, Lisa. "Freedom Rides." (1997): 1–2. www.watson.org/~lisa/blackhistory/civilrights-55-65/freeride.html
Dallek, Robert. *An Unfinished Life: John F. Kennedy 1917–1963*. Boston, New York and London: Little, Brown, 2003.
Danchin, Sebastian. *Blues Boy: The Life and Music of B.B. King*. Jackson, MS: University Press of Mississippi, 1998.
Darey, James. "Tribute to a Great Leader." *Chicago Defender* (Week of 30 November–6 December 1963).
Darwen, Norman. "I'm the One Gave This Big Sound to the Harmonica," interview of Snooky Pryor, Colne, Germany, 31 May 1993. Published in *Blues & Rhythm* 152 (September 2000): 11.
Dawson, Jim. *The Twist: The Story of the Song and Dance That Changed the World*. Boston and London: Faber & Faber, 1995.
Dherbier, Yann-Brice, and Pierre-Henri Verlhac. *John Fitzgerald Kennedy: A Life in Pictures*. New York: Phaidon, 2003.
Dickey, Dan William. *The Kennedy Corridos: A Study of the Ballads of a Mexican American Hero*. Austin: University of Texas Press, 1978.
Donoghue, William E. *'Fessor Mojo's "Don't Start Me to Talkin'."* Seattle, WA: Mojo Visions, 1997.
Eckhardt, Wolf von. "Oral History Interview with August Heckscher." New York: Kennedy Papers (10 December 1965): 14–15.
Evans, David. *Big Road Blues: Tradition and Creativity in the Folk Blues*. Berkeley: University of California Press, 1982.
Fairlie, Henry. *The Kennedy Promise: The Politics of Expectation*. New York: Doubleday, 1973.
Fishwick, Marshall. *The Hero: American Style*. New York: David McKay, 1969.
Ford, Robert. *A Blues Bibliography: The International Literature of an Afro-American Music Genre*. Bromley, UK: Paul Pelletier, 1999.
Franklin, Reverend C. L. *Give Me This Mountain: Life History and Selected Sermons*. Edited by Jeff Todd Titon. Urbana and Chicago: University of Illinois Press, 1989.

Friedman, Josh Alan. "Jack Ruby: Dallas' Original J.R." (1997): 1–8. www.wfmu.org/LCD/20/ruby.html
Gallup, George, H. *The Gallup Poll: Public Opinion 1935–1971.* New York: Random House, 1972.
Gates, Henry Louis, Jr.. *Black Literature and Literary Theory.* New York: Methuen, 1984.
———. *Figures in Black: Words, Signs, and the "Racial" Self.* New York: Oxford University Press, 1987.
———. *The Signifying Monkey: A Theory of Afro-American Literary Criticism.* New York: Oxford University Press, 1988.
Golden, Harry. *Mr. Kennedy and the Negroes.* Cleveland and New York: World Publishing, 1964.
Goldman, Peter. "Kennedy Remembered." *Newsweek* (28 November 1983): 64.
Goldman, Roger, with David Gallen. *Thurgood Marshall: Justice for All.* New York: Carroll & Graf, 1992.
Goreau, Laurraine. *Just Mahalia, Baby: The Mahalia Jackson Story.* Waco, TX, 1975; reprint, Gretna, LA: Pelican, 1984.
Grauberger, Steve. "The Bishop Perry Tillis." *Alabama Folklife Association* (February 1995): 1–2. www.arts.state.al.us/actc/articles/frmfldtl.htm
Griffin, Rita. "Will Hairston Limits Performances to Church." *Michigan Chronicle* (25 May 1968).
Groden, Robert J. *The Killing of a President.* New York: Viking, 1993.
Hacker, Andrew. *Two Nations: Black and White, Separate, Hostile, Unequal.* New York: Charles Scribner's, 1992.
Harris, Sheldon. *Blues Who's Who: A Biographical Dictionary of Blues Singers.* New Rochelle, NY: Arlington House, 1979; reprint, New York: Da Capo, 1989.
Harvey, Roy. "Denomination Blues: Meeting Bishop Tillis." *BN* 5 (2003): 10–12.
Haskins, James. *Nat King Cole: The Man and His Music.* London: Robson Books, 1986.
———. *Hamp: An Autobiography of Lionel Hampton.* New York: Warner, 1989.
Haskins, James, and Kathleen Benson. *Lena: A Biography of Lena Horne.* Chelsea, MI: Scarborough, 1991.
Heilbut, Anthony. *The Gospel Sound: Good News and Bad Times.* New York: Garden City, 1971; reprint, New York: Limelight, 1985.
Hess, Norbert. "Wilbert Harrison: Sein 'Kansas City' Wurde Zum Welt-Hit," article in *Blues Forum* 10 (second quarter 1983): 6.
Heymann, C. David. *A Woman Named Jackie.* New York: Signet, 1989.
Hoffman, Paul Dennis. "Rock and Roll and JFK: A Study of Thematic Changes in Rock and Roll Lyrics since the Assassination of John F. Kennedy." *Popular Music and Society,* vol. 10, no. 2 (1985): 59–79.
Kennedy, John Fitzgerald. *Why England Slept.* 1940. Reprint, New York: Greenwood Press, 1961.
———. *Profiles in Courage.* New York: Harper & Row, 1955.
Kennedy, Rose Fitzgerald. *Times to Remember.* New York: Collins, 1974.
Khrushev, Sergei. "Remembers 40th Anniversary of Kennedy Assassination." The Watson Institute for International Studies (21 November 2003). www.watsoninstitute.org/news_detail.cfm?id=153

King, B.B., and David Ritz. *B.B. King: The Autobiography*. London: Hodder & Stoughton, 1997.

King, Martin Luther. *Why We Can't Wait*. 1964. London: Signet, 2000.

Kirk, Elise K. *Music at the White House: A History of the American Spirit*. Urbana: University of Illinois Press, 1986.

Knight, W. Nicholas. "Lancer: Myth-Making and the Kennedy Camelot." *Avalon to Camelot*, vol. II, no. 1 (1988): 26–31.

Komara, Edward, ed. *Encyclopedia of the Blues*, vols. 1 (A–J) and 2 (K–Z). New York and London: Routledge, 2006.

Laughton, Robert, and Cedric J. Hayes. *Gospel Records, 1943 to 1969: A Black Music Discography*. London: Record Information Services, 1992.

Lawson, Steven F. *Running for Freedom: Civil Rights and Black Politics in America since 1941*. New York: McGraw Hill, 1991; 2nd ed. 1997.

Leadbitter, Mike, and Neil Slaven. *Blues Records 1943–1970, Volume One: A to K*. London: Hannover Books, 1987.

Leadbitter, Mike, Neil Slaven, and Leslie Fancourt. *Blues Records 1943–1970, Volume Two: L to Z*. London: Record Information Services, 1994.

"Legacy JFK Leaves to Negroes, The." *Jet*, vol. XXV, no. 8 (12 December 1963): 1–67.

Lemann, Nicholas. *The Promised Land: The Great Black Migration and How It Changed America*. New York: Alfred A. Knopf, 1991.

Leuchtenberg, William E. *In the Shadow of FDR: From Harry Truman to Ronald Reagan*. Ithaca, NY: Cornell University Press, 1983.

Levine, Lawrence W. *Black Culture and Black Consciousness: Afro-American Folk Thought from Slavery to Freedom*. Oxford, UK: Oxford University Press, 1977 reprint, New York, 1980.

———. *The Unpredictable Past: Explorations in American Cultural History*. New York: Oxford University Press, 1993.

Manchester, William. *The Death of a President: November 20–November 25, 1963*. London: Michael Joseph, 1967.

McCormick, Mack. "Walkin' This Road by Myself." Sleeve notes to Bluesville LP 1057 (ca. 1963).

McGrath, Bob. *The R&B Indies, Volume One: A–L*. West Vancouver, Canada: Eyeball, 2000.

———. *The R&B Indies, Volume Two: K–Z*. West Vancouver, Canada: Eyeball, 2000.

Mitchell, George. *Blow My Blues Away*. Baton Rouge: Louisiana State University Press, 1971.

Monge, Luigi. "Death By Fire: African-American Popular Music on the Natchez Rhythm Club Fire." In Robert Springer, ed. *Nobody Knows Where the Blues Come From: Lyrics and History*. Jackson: University Press of Mississippi (2006): 151–63.

Moore, Allan, ed. *Cambridge Companion to Blues and Gospel Music*. Cambridge, UK: Cambridge University Press, 2002.

Murray, Albert. *Good Morning Blues: The Autobiography of Count Basie*. London: William Heinemann, 1986; reprint, London: Paladin, 1987.

O'Reilly, Kenneth. *Nixon's Piano: Presidents and Racial Politics from Washington to Clinton*. New York: Free Press, 1995.

Oster, Harry. *Living Country Blues.* Detroit: Folklore Associates, 1969.
Parmet, Herbert S. *JFK: The Presidency of John F. Kennedy.* New York: Dial, 1983.
Posner, Gerald. *Case Closed: Lee Harvey Oswald and the Assassination of JFK.* New York: Random House, 1993; reprint, New York: Anchor, 2003.
Pratt, Ray. *Rhythm and Resistance: Explorations in the Political Uses of Popular Music.* New York: Praeger, 1990.
Prilop, Valerie. "John Glenn as Astronaut." *Houston Chronicle.* www.chron.com/content/interactive/space/johnglenn/astronaut.html
Rachlin, Harvey. *The Encyclopedia of the Music Business.* New York: Harper & Row, 1981.
Raglan, Lord. *The Hero: A Study in Tradition, Myth and Drama.* New York: Vintage, 1936; reprint 1956.
Reagon, Bernice Johnson. *Songs of the Civil Rights Movement, 1955–1965: A Study in Culture History.* Ph.D. thesis, Howard University, 1975.
Rijn, Guido van. *Roosevelt's Blues: African-American Blues and Gospel Songs on FDR.* Jackson, MS: University Press of Mississippi, 1997.
———. Review of the "Martin Luther King Memorial Conference." *Blues & Rhythm* 131 (August 1998): 14.
———. "The Dollar Has the Blues: Deflation and Inflation in African-American Blues Songs." In Robert Springer, ed. *The Lyrics in African-American Popular Music/Le Texte dans la Musique Populaire Afro-Américaine.* Bern and New York: Peter Lang (2001): 77–90.
———. "Climbing the Mountain Top: African-American Blues and Gospel Songs from the Civil Rights Years." In Brian Ward, ed. *Media, Culture, and the Modern African-American Freedom Struggle.* Gainesville: University Press of Florida (2001): 122–44.
———. "The Hurricane of the Motor City: The Life Story of Brother Will Hairston." *Blues & Rhythm* 167 (March 2002): 14–17.
———. "Imagery in the Lyrics." In Allan Moore, ed. *The Cambridge Companion to Blues and Gospel Music.* Cambridge, UK: Cambridge University Press (2002): 141–57.
———. *The Truman and Eisenhower Blues: African-American Blues and Gospel Songs, 1945–1960.* London and New York: Continuum, 2004.
———. "Happy Am I: The Life of Elder Lightfoot Solomon Michaux." *Blues & Rhythm* 190 (June 2004): 14–17.
———. "I Found a Solid Rock in Jesus: The Life and Recordings of Bishop Perry Tillis." *Blues & Rhythm* 199 (May 2005): 14–16.
———. "Coolidge's Blues: African-American Blues Songs on Prohibition, Migration, Unemployment, and Jim Crow." In Robert Springer, ed. *Nobody Knows Where the Blues Come From: Lyrics and History.* Jackson: University Press of Mississippi (2006): 151–63.
Robinson, Jackie. "Birmingham Poses Moment of Truth for JFK on Rights." *Chicago Defender* (Week of 18–24 May 1963): 2.
Rosenberg, Bruce A. "Kennedy in Camelot: The Arthurian Legend in America." *Western Folklore* 35 (January 1976): 52–59.
Rowan, Carl. "Who Will Get the Negro Vote?" *Ebony* (November 1960): 40–49.

Rowe, Mike. *Chicago Breakdown*. London: Eddison Bluesbooks, 1973.
Ryan, Marc. *Trumpet Records: Diamonds on Farish Street*. Jackson: University Press of Mississippi, 2004.
Salvatore, Nick. *Singing in a Strange Land: C. L. Franklin, the Black Church, and the Transformation of America*. New York and Boston: Little, Brown, 2005.
Scheiber, Harry N., Harold G. Vatter, and Harold Underwood Faulkner. *American Economic History*. New York: Harper & Row, 1976.
Scherman, Tony. *Backbeat: Earl Palmer's Story*. Washington: Smithsonian Institution, 1999.
Schlesinger, Arthur M., Jr. *A Thousand Days: John F. Kennedy in the White House*. London: Andre Deutsch, 1965.
———. *History of American Presidential Elections, 1789–1968*, vol. IV. New York: Chelsea House, 1971.
Schuller, Tim. "The Return of Zuzu Bollin: Lone Star Bluesmaster." *Living Blues* 89 (December 1989): 18.
Seeger, Pete, and Bob Reiser. *Everybody Says Freedom: A History of the Civil Rights Movement in Songs and Pictures*. New York: W.W. Norton, 1989.
Shaar Murray, Charles. *Boogie Man: The Adventures of John Lee Hooker in the American Twentieth Century*. London: Viking, 1999.
Solding, Stefan. "Living Blues Interview: Champion Jack Dupree." *Living Blues* 32 (May/June 1977): 13.
Sorensen, Theodore C. *Kennedy*. New York: Harper & Row, 1965.
———. *The Kennedy Legacy*. London: Weidenfeld and Nicholson, 1969.
Spragens, William C. *Popular Images of American Presidents*. New York: Greenwood, 1988.
Springer, Robert, ed. *The Lyrics in African-American Popular Music/Le Texte dans la Musique Populaire Afro-Américaine*. Bern and New York: Peter Lang, 2001.
———, ed. *Nobody Knows Where the Blues Come From: Lyrics and History*. Jackson: University Press of Mississippi, 2006.
Stewart, Maria W. "The Miseries We Tasted." www.pbs.org/wgbh/amex/lincolns/filmmore/ps_stewart.html
Stone, Chuck. "A Stone's Throw." Editorial in the *Chicago Defender* (Week of 30 November–6 December 1963): 1.
Taylor, Quintard, Jr. "An Early Civil Rights Victory in New Mexico." www.faculty.washington.edu/qtaylor/Courses/313_AAW/313_manual_cp_09.htm
Tooze, Sandra B. *Muddy Waters: The Mojo Man*. Toronto, ON, Canada: ECW Press, 1997.
Toscano, Vincent L. *Since Dallas: Images of John F. Kennedy in Popular and Scholarly Literature 1963–1973*. Ph.D. dissertation. Albany: State University of New York, 1975.
Wald, Elijah. *Josh White: Society Blues*. Amherst: University of Massachusetts Press, 2000.
———. *Escaping the Delta: Robert Johnson and the Invention of the Blues*. New York: Harper Collins, 2004.
Ward, Brian. *Just My Soul Responding: Rhythm and Blues, Black Consciousness and Race Relations*. London: UCL, 1998.

———, ed. *Media, Culture, and the Modern African-American Freedom Struggle.* Gainesville: University Press of Florida, 2001.
Ward, Brian, and Tony Badger, eds. *The Making of Martin Luther King and the Civil Rights Movement.* New York: New York University Press, 1996.
Watkins, Mel. *On the Real Side: A History of American Comedy.* Chicago: Lawrence Hill, 1994; reprint, 1999.
White, George R. *Bo Diddley: Living Legend.* Chessington, UK: Castle Communications, 1995.
White, Theodore H. "For President Kennedy: An Epilogue." *Life* (6 December 1963): 159.
———. *The Making of the President 1964.* New York: Atheneum, 1965.
Wilkins, Roy. "The Greatest Day!" *New York Amsterdam News* (7 September 1963): 10.
Williams, Juan. *Eyes on the Prize: America's Civil Right Years, 1954–1965.* New York: Viking Penguin, 1987; reprint, Harmondsworth, UK: Penguin, 1988.
Wills, Garry. *The Kennedy Imprisonment: A Meditation on Power.* Boston: Little, Brown, 1981.
Wolfe, Charles. "Where the Blues Is At: A Survey of Recent Research." *Popular Music and Society* 1 (1971–72): 153.
Zolten, Jerry. *Great God A'Mighty! The Dixie Hummingbirds.* New York: Oxford University Press, 2003.

SONG INDEX

"Abraham, Martin and John," 124–25, 187n34
"Abraham Lincoln," 185n1
"Ain't It Hard to Be a Nigger," 185n78
"Air Force—U.S. Navy," 31, 177n26
"American Defense," 138, 188n61
"Apallo 17" [sic], 180n22
"Apollo 15," 180n22
"Army Man Blues," 31–32, 178n29
"As the Eagle Stirreth Her Nest," xiii, 89, 183n36
"Assassination," 119–20, 186n25
"Assassination of President Kennedy and the Crucifixion of Jesus, The," Parts 1 & 2, 155–61, 191n102
"Assassination of the President," 148–50, 189n80
"Astronote Blues" [sic], 58, 181n27
"Atlanta's Tragic Monday," 127, 187n42

"Ballad of Medgar Evers, The," x, 101, 184n58
"Ballad to Abraham Lincoln," 109–10, 185n4
"Barefootin'," 51

"Beloved Kennedy," 145, 189n75
"Beloved Kennedys," 145, 189n75
"Berlin Wall," 177n20
"Big Guns," 178n30
"Big Race, The," 25–26, 177n16
"Birmingham Blues," 96–97, 184n48
"Black Race," 185n78
"Bloody Bloody Bombs, The," 43, 179n54
"Blues for JFK" ("I'm Going Home"), 151–52, 190n86
"Blues in the Mississippi Night," 182n1
"Bombs of Destruction, The," 43, 179n54

"Check Up on My Baby," 36

"Danger Zone," 178n46
"Danger Zone, The," 39–40, 178n46
"Day Is Past and Gone, The," 115
"Day the World Stood Still, The," 109, 115–16, 170, 186n19
"Dear President," 141, 189n66
"Death of President Kennedy, The," 190n90

"Democracy," 185n78
"Depression Blues," 60, 181n2
"Depression in '61," 181n2
"Devastating Bombs, The," 43, 179n54
"Do the President Twist," xiii, 48–49, 179n4
"Down South," xvi, 69–72, 182n5
"Draft Board Blues," 34, 178n34
"Drafted," 29–30, 177n24

"Eleven-Twenty Two Nineteen Sixty Three, Parts I and II," 192n116

"Fighting for Dear Old Uncle Sam," 38–39, 178n45
"Float, The," 50–51, 180n12
"Free and Equal," 73–74, 182n7
"Freedom Bus," 77–78, 182n14
"Freedom March, The," 104, 184n69
"Freedom Ride" (instrumental), 185n78
"Freedom Riders," 77–79, 182n16

"Going Back Home," 190n86
"Going Down Slow," 59

"Happy Blues for John Glenn," Parts 1 & 2, 52–54, 180n16
"Hard Time Blues," 61, 181n4
"Hard Times at My Door," 63, 181n8
"He Was Loved by All the People," 146, 170, 189n76
"He'll Understand," 170
"His Spirit Lives On," 134
"Hit the Road, Jack," 39
"Hymn, The," 103–4, 184n66

"I Don't Need No Army," 178n41
"I Go into Orbit," 56, 180n20

"I Got to Move," 181n11
"I Have Got to Go," 37, 178n42–43
"I Shall Not Be Moved," 105
"I Stayed Away Too Long," 151, 190n82
"I Thought the War Was Over," 33–34, 178n32
"I Tried Not to Cry," 139–40, 170, 188n64
"I Want to Know Why," 142, 169, 189n68
"I'm Going Home" ("Blues for JFK"), 151–52, 190n86
"I'm Gonna Sit in Till You Give In," x, 76, 182n13
"In the Summer of His Years (Tribute to President J. F. Kennedy)," 122–24, 172, 187n32
"Inflation Blues" ("I Got To Move"), 64, 181n11
"It Was a Dream," 40–41, 179n49

"J. F. Kennedy's Reservation," 136–37, 188n57
"J. F. K.'s Good Works Will Never Die," 164–65, 192n114
"Jackie Don't You Weep," 150, 189n81
"Jail House King, The," xvii, 95, 184n45
"Jesse James," 101
"Just a Dream (On My Mind)," 40–41, 179n48

"Kennedy Moan," 121–22, 186n29
"Kennedy Song, The," 161–62, 191n108

"Let Freedom Ring," 145, 170, 189n74
"Light That Shines (A Tribute to John F. Kennedy), A," 143–45, 170, 189n73
"Loving Memory of John F. Kennedy, Parts 1 & 2," 192n116

"Mama Don't Allow No Twistin'," 179n11
"Man Amongst Men, A," 134–36, 170, 188n55–56
"Man for the Nation, A," 142–43, 170, 189n70
"March on Dr. Martin Luther King," 69, 106, 185n74
"Meet Me on the Other Side," 170
"Mister Glenn," 54–55, 180n19
"Modern Joshua, The," 146–47, 170, 189n78
"Mr. Khruschev," 34–36, 178n37
"My Friend Kennedy," 111–12, 186n9

"Newport Blues," 152–53, 190n89

"Oh Pritchett, Oh Kelley," 86–87, 183n29
"Old Folks Boogie While the Young Ones Twist," 180n11
"Our Prayer for Peace," 113–14, 186n10, 186n13

"Pinetop's Boogie Woogie," xix
"Poor Kennedy," 134, 169, 188n52
"Poor Kennedy #2," 125, 169, 187n36
"Prayer for Jackie, Parts 1 & 2," 192n116
"Prayer for Tomorrow, A," 113, 186n11
"President Kennedy," xv, 138–39, 188n62, 190n90
"President Kennedy Blues," 27, 177n19
"President Kennedy Gave His Life," 147–48, 170, 189n79
"President Kennedy Stayed Away Too Long," 151, 153–54, 190n90
"Promised Land," 82–84, 182n19
"Providence Help the Poor People," 31

"Red's Dream," 41–42, 80, 179n52
"Ride On Red, Ride On," x, 81–82, 182n18
"Rockin' Jerusalem," 87, 183n28

"Sad Day in Texas," 127, 170, 187n41
"School Day," 111–12, 186n8
"School Day Blues," 111, 185n7
"See That My Grave Is Kept Clean," 133, 188n50
"Segregation Blues," 185n78
"Shot on Meredith," 183n38
"Six White Horses," 133, 188n51
"Star Spangled Banner," 122
"Stop the Twist," 180n11
"Story of President Kennedy," 131–33, 188n49

"Take Courage," 114–15, 170, 186n16
"Tell Me Why You Like Roosevelt," 128
"Thanks You Mr. Kennedy" (instrumental), 166, 192n116
"That Awful Day in Dallas," 126–27, 170, 187n39
"This War Will Last You for Years," 188n61
"Times Is Hard," 62, 181n5
"Too Poor to Die," 80
"Tough Times," xii, 66, 181n12
"Tragedy of Kennedy, The," 127–28, 187n44
"Tribute to a Great President," 128–29, 170, 187n45
"Tribute to J. F. K.," 140, 170, 188n65
"22nd Day of November, The," 118–19, 170, 186n23
"(Twist Ain't Nothin') But the Old Time Shimmy," 180n11
"Twist, The," 47, 179n1

"Twistin' Out in Space," 51–52, 180n14
"Two White Horses," 133

"Uncle Sam Don't Take My Man," 19, 32–33, 178n30

"War Is Starting Again," xii, 30, 177n25
"War Time Blues," 31–32, 36–37, 178n41
"We All Got to Go," 37–38, 178n43
"We Shall Not Be Moved," 105, 185n73
"We Want Freedom in This Land," 106–7, 185n75
"(The Welfare) Turns Its Back on You," 59, 66, 181n14

"Welfare Blues, The," 181n14
"Welfare Cheese," 67, 182n16
"We'll Understand It Better By and By," 175n6
"What a Time," 126
"When the Welfare Turns Its Back on You," 181n14
"When We Got the Message," 137–38, 169, 188n58
"Why Did He Have to Go?," 117–18, 169, 186n20
"Why Have the Mighty Fallen (Tribute to the Kennedys)," Parts 1 & 2, 3, 175n7

ARTIST INDEX

Acey, Johnny, 56, 180n20
Allen, Doris Ann, 146–47, 189n78
Anderson, Jimmy, 34, 178n34
Angelic Choir, 187n34
Arden, Toni, 123–24
Armstrong, Louis, 50, 179n6
Arnold, Billy Boy, 37, 178n43

Ballard, Hank, xv, 47, 50, 171, 179n1, 180n12
Barnes, Walter, 109
Basie, William "Count," 25
Berry, Charles "Chuck," 82–84, 182n19–20
Big John, 58, 181n27
Big Maybelle (Mabel Louise Smith), 42, 179n51
Birds of Harmony, 128–29, 170, 187n45
Bo Diddley (Ellas McDaniel/Ellas Bates), xv, 34–35, 42, 178n35, 178n37, 179n11, 179n51
Bollin, A. D. "ZuZu," 187n48
Bowen, Harold, 141, 189n66
Brady, Avery, 125, 134, 169, 187n35–36, 188n52, 192n3

Branch, Billy, 177n20
Brewer, "Blind" James, xv, 117–18, 137–38, 142, 169, 186n20, 189n68
Brewer, Fannie, 137–38, 142, 169, 188n58, 189n68
Broonzy, "Big" Bill, 40–41, 69, 179n48–49, 182n1
Brown, Charles, 187n34
Brown, "Chuck"/"King Karl" (Bernard Jolivette), 63, 181n7
Brown, Jimmy, 146, 170, 189n76
Brown, Roy, 180n11

Calhoun, Red, 188n48
Cannon, Leroy, 192n116
Caravan, Guy and Candy, 101
Carolina Freedom Fighters, 101
Carson, Eddie "Big Blues," 43, 179n54
Chambers, Willie, 37, 178n39
Charles, Ray, xv, 39, 42, 93, 178n46, 179n51, 184n41–42
Checker, Chubby, 47, 179n1
Church of God and Saints of Christ Singers, 185n78
Coates, Dorothy Love, 103

[205]

Cole, Nat "King," 21, 25, 74
Collins, Albert, 181n14
Cooke, Sam, xv
CORE Freedom Singers, 101
Cray, Robert, 181n14
Culbreth, Janie Lee, 86, 183n29

Davis, "Blind" John, 37
Davis, Sammy, Jr., 154
Diamond, William "Do-Boy/Du Bois," 165–66, 192n115
Dion, 187n34
Dixie Humming Birds, 113, 186n10, 186n13
Dixie Nightingales, xi, 119–20, 186n25
Dixon, Willie, 151, 190n83
Dupree, "Champion" Jack, 27, 72–74, 111, 177n19, 182n6–7, 185n7, 186n8

Echoes of Zion, 127, 187n42
Eckstine, Billy, 25
Estes, "Sleepy" John Adam, 40, 50, 151–54, 169, 179n49, 190n82, 190n84–86, 190n89–90

Fetchit, Stepin, 23
Fisk Jubilee Singers, 183n28
Fitzgerald, Ella, 25
Four Tops, 103
Francis, Connie, 123–24
Franklin, Aretha, 3
Franklin, Rev. C. L., 3, 102–3, 155, 161, 171, 175n6–7, 183n33
Franklin, Erma, 103
Frazier, Ernest, 106, 185n74

Gay, Rev. Ben, xiii, 89–91, 183n36
Gaye, Marvin, 187n34
Gillespie, John Birks "Dizzy," 50, 179n7

Gober, Bertha, 86–87, 183n29
Gospel Harmonettes, 103, 184n66
Granderson, John Lee, 142–43, 170, 189n70
Gray, Arvella (Walter Dixon), 77–79, 169, 182n14, 182n16
Gregory, Dick, 23, 28, 49, 171, 177n13, 177n22, 179n8

Hairston, "Brother" Will, "The Hurricane of the Motor City," 129–33, 187n46–47, 188n49
Hampton, Lionel, 154
Harmoneers (Harmonizing Five), 126–27
Harris, Brother Sidney, 112, 186n9
Harris, Rutha, 105, 185n73
Harrison, Wilbert, xv, 28–29, 177n23–24
Henderson, Brother, 192n116
Hibbler, Al, 93
Holliday, Rev. Omie L., 155–61, 191n102
Hooker, John Lee, xi, 96–97, 109–10, 169, 180n11, 184n48, 185n4
Hopkins, Sam "Lightnin'," xii, 30, 42, 52–54, 169, 177n25, 179n51, 180n16
Horne, Lena, 98
Hoskins, Ollie, 119–20, 186n25
House, Son, xv, 138, 188n61–62
Howard University Choir, 183n28

Ivory Lee, 164–65

Jackson, Bill, 118–19, 170, 186n23
Jackson, Lee, 180n22
Jackson, Mahalia, xi, 22, 25, 105, 108, 122–25, 138, 169, 177n9, 187n32, 187n34
Jackson, Otis, 128

Jefferson, "Blind" Lemon, 133, 188n50
Jewel Gospel Singers, 146–47, 170, 189n78
John, "Little" Willie, xv, 54–55, 180n19
Johnson, Herman E., 60, 181n2
Jones, Nyles "Guitar Gabriel" (Robert Jones), 181n14
Jones, Rev. Matthew A., 101, 184n58

King, B.B. (Riley B. King), x, 76, 120, 182n13
King, Freddy/Freddie, 48–49, 59, 66, 179n4, 181n14

Lanin, Lester, 48
Laskey, Emanuel, 67, 182n16
Leadbelly (Huddie Ledbetter), 185n1
Lenoir, J. B., 183n38
Lewis, Ramsey, 103
Little David, 145, 189n75
Little Junior, 150–51, 189n81
Lord Hummingbird (Alberto Riberio), 145, 189n75
Louisiana Red (Iverson Minter), 10, 21, 80–82, 169, 179n52, 182n17–18

Mabley, Moms, 187n34
Martin, Millicent, 124
Martin, Sonny, 31, 171, 177n26
Mayfield, Percy, 39, 178n46
Mays, Zilla, 192n116
McDowell, "Mississippi" Fred, 133, 188n51
McGhee, Brownie, 37, 178n40
McGriff, Jimmy, 103
Memphis Jug Band, 182n3
Memphis Slim (Peter Chatman), xv, 25, 69–70, 169, 177n16, 182n1, 182n5
Mighty Gospel Supremes, 145, 189n75

Mighty Sons of David, 69, 106–7, 169, 185n74–75
Miles, Luke "Long Gone," 36, 178n41
Mitchell, Ronda and Mrs. Lovell, 136–37, 188n57
Muddy Waters (McKinley Morganfield), xii, 50, 65–66, 181n12

Newman, David "Fathead," 188n48
Nixon, Hammie, 152, 190n85–86, 190n90

Oden, "St. Louis" Jimmy, 59, 181n1
Original Soul Revivers, 164–65, 192n114

Parker, Robert, xv, 51, 180n14
Patterson, Robert, 187n34
Pryor, James "Snooky," 19, 32–33, 45, 178n30–31

Reagon, Bernice Johnson, x
Reed, Jimmy, 42, 179n51
Reed, Lula, xiii, 48, 179n4
Reynolds, Teddy, 33, 45, 178n32
Roberts, Rev. Lawrence C., 170, 192n4
Robinson, Jimmy Lee, 62, 181n5
Robinson, Johnnie H., 148–50, 189n80
Robinson, Smokey, 187n34
Rodgers, "Mighty" Mo, 106–7, 191n108
Ross, Mary, 147–48, 170, 189n79
Ruth, "Brother" Thermon, 126–27, 170, 187n37, 187n39

Selah Jubilee Singers, 187n37
Semiens, "Ivory" Lee, 164, 177n25, 192n114
Sensational Six of Birmingham, Ala., 115, 126, 145, 169–70, 186n19, 189n74

Short, J. D., 38, 178n45
Sissle, Noble, 155
Smith, Buster, 188n48
Smith, Byther, 166, 192n116
Smith, Kate, 124
Smoky Babe (Robert Brown), 61, 181n4, 185n78
SNCC Freedom Singers, x, 87–88, 101–2, 105, 183n29, 184n58, 185n73
Solomon, King "Howlin Wolf Jr.," 64, 181n11
Sons of Blues, 177n20
Southern Bell Singers, 127–28, 133, 187n44
Southern Sons Quartette, 113, 186n11
Spann, Otis, xi, 127, 139, 170–71, 187n41
Starr, Bob (Carl Tate), xv, 95–96, 104–5, 169, 184n45, 184n69
Stidham, Arbee, 71–72, 182n4
Strogin, Henry, 180n11

Thompson, Sonny, 48, 179n4, 181n14
Tillis, Perry, 120–22, 186n28–29
Tucker, Earlene, 192n116
Tuskegee Institute Choir, 183n28

Upsetters, 185n78

Voices of Jordan, 185n78

Walker, James Emerdia, 113, 186n10–11
Wallace, Rosie, 114–15, 143–45, 169–71, 186n16–17, 189n73, 192n5
Ward, Clara, 187n34
Washington, Dinah, 103
Watkins, Billy, 187n34
Wells, Junior, 164, 192n113
White, Josh, 105
White, Melvin "Slappy," 42, 57–58, 87–89, 163, 171, 179n53, 180n26, 183n32, 191n111
Williams, "Big" Joe, 31, 134–36, 143, 169, 170, 178n29, 188n55–56
Williams, Bert, 23
Williamson, Sonny Boy, I, 31–33, 36–37, 69, 178n42–43, 181n1
Williamson, Sonny Boy, II, 190n86
Willis, Charles "Slim," 139

Young, Johnny, 139–41, 169–70, 188n64–65

GENERAL INDEX

ABC (American Broadcasting Corporation), 20
ABC-Paramount, record company, 76, 124
Abernathy, Rev. Ralph, civil rights leader, 86, 93–94, 96
Abraham, patriarch, 91
Acheson, Secretary of State Dean, 27–28
Addison's disease, 163
Africa, 26, 94, 167
African Americans: army, xxiii; comedians, xxv, 23, 171, 172
Agram, record company, xix, xxvi, 174
Air Force, 28, 30, 134
Air Force One, 134
Alabama, 50, 57, 82, 90, 93–94, 169
Albany, Georgia, xii–xiii, xxiv, 84–91, 101, 168
Albany Movement, 85, 87, 91
Albuquerque, New Mexico, 83–84
Algeria, 167
Allotment pay, 38

Amalekites, 7
American, The, 12
American Bandstand, television show, 47
American Dream, The, 107
American Folk Blues Festival, 111, 139, 151, 190n86
Anniston, Alabama, 79
Apollo, space program, 56
Apollo 15, 180n22
Apollo 17, 180n22
Arizona, 82, 153
Arkansas, 97, 169
Arlington National Cemetery, Virginia, 15–16, 99, 136
Armory District, Providence, Rhode Island, 25
Armstrong, Neil, American astronaut, 57
Arthur, legendary king of Britain, 9–12, 16–17
Arvad, Inga, photographer, 163
As We Remember Joe, 5
Asia, 26, 94

Atlanta, Georgia, 82–83, 86, 101, 168
Atlantic City police department, 88
Atlantic Ocean, 54
Atomic bomb, ix, 40–42, 44, 50
Auchincloss, Hugh D., III, Jacqueline Kennedy's stepbrother, 152
Auden, W. H., poet, 156
Australia, 25
Austria, 142

Bahamas, 142
Baker, Cary, blues writer, 78
Barnett, Governor Ross, 3, 92
Basie, Kate, Count Basie's wife, 25
Baton Rouge, Louisiana, 60, 168
Bay of Pigs, Cuba, 14, 26, 41, 162
BBC (British Broadcasting Corporation), 123–24
Beckwith, Byron de la, Medgar Evers's murderer, 101–2
Belafonte, Harry, entertainer and civil rights activist, 19–20, 22, 25, 96, 176n2
Berlin, Germany, 27–28, 31, 99, 142, 169, 189n67
Berlin Wall, 14, 41, 177n20
Bermuda, 142
Bible, The, 130, 148, 158
Bigelow, Albert S., pacifist, 84
Bihari brothers, record producers, 76
Bilbo, Senator Theodore, 69, 70, 92
Bill of Rights (1791), 105
Billboard, 47
Birmingham, Alabama, xxiv, 79, 82–83, 93–94, 98, 102, 162
Birmingham News, 94
Bissell, Captain Richard, 26–27
Black Jack, the riderless horse, 133

Blackett Strait, Solomon Islands, 13
Blues and gospel recordings, xv, xxv
Blues & Rhythm, xix
Blues Unlimited, xix
BMI (Broadcast Music Incorporated), 171
B'nai Brith, 105
Bomber planes, 37–38
Bond, James, 27
Boston, Massachusetts, 4, 12–13, 106, 168
Boutwell, Mayor Albert, 93
Bouvier, John V., III, Jacqueline Kennedy's father, 14
Bouvier, Lee, Jacqueline Kennedy's sister, 14
Bracken, Vivian and James, record producers, 97
Bronze Star, 99
Brookline, Massachusetts, 4–5
Brotherhood of Sleeping Car Porters (BSCP), 107
Brown, Thomas, historian, 10, 16
Brown v. Board of Education, 81
Brownsville, Tennessee, 67, 151, 168
Burden, Andrew, dancer, 48
Burundi, 167
Byrd, Senator Harry, 84

Cabot Lodge, Henry, Jr., Republican politician, 6, 13
California, "The Golden State," 54, 73, 81, 83, 169
Calypso music, 145
Camelot, 9–11, 15–18
Campbell, Joseph, author, 17
Canaan, 146
Canada, 142

Can't Keep from Crying, Testament LP and CD dedicated to JFK, 143, 168–69, 174, 189n71
Canton, Mississippi, 165–66
Cape Canaveral, Florida, 16, 57
Caribbean, The, 167
Carousel strip club, Dallas, Texas, 131, 187n48
Castro, Fidel, President of Cuba, 26, 41–42, 98
Chafe, William, historian, 17
Chappaquiddick, Massachusetts, 16
Charlotte, North Carolina, 82
Chenet-Hairston, Sandranette, Brother Will Hairston's daughter, 130
Chicago, Illinois, 20, 23–24, 33, 57, 62, 73, 97, 117, 125, 136, 139–40, 142–43, 168
Chicago Defender, 21–22, 81, 85–86, 92, 107, 109, 135, 162
China, 24, 163
Chrysler factory, Eight Mile Road, Detroit, Michigan, 129–30
Churchill, Sir Winston, British prime minister, 9
CIA (Central Intelligence Agency), 26, 41
Cincinnati, Ohio, 168
Civil rights, ix–x, xvii, xxiii, 22, 35, 69–108, 155–56; Big Six, 107; demonstrations, xiii, 77, 96, 103–6; legislation, xiv–xv, xxiv, 14, 20, 93, 98, 102; recordings, xxv, 131, 172
Civil Rights Act (1964), 102, 154–55, 166, 173
Civil Rights Bill (1963), 108

Clarksdale, Mississippi, 125
Cleaver, Eldridge, writer, 58
CNN (Cable News Network), 9
Cobo Hall, Detroit, Michigan, 103
Cold War, ix–x, xvi–xvii, xxiv, 26, 138, 171
Cole, Carol, Nat "King" Cole's daughter, 74
Collier, Peter, author, 13
Collierville, Tennessee, 168
Colombia, 142
Columbia Broadcasting System (CBS), 20, 123, 125, 155
Columbus, Ohio, 168
Communism, xii, 24, 28, 35, 44
Como, Mississippi, 168
Congress, xxiv, 4, 6, 13–14, 40–42, 56–57, 68, 74, 99, 102, 159, 166
Congress of Racial Equality (CORE), xi, 77, 84
Connally, Governor John, 118–19, 135–36
Connally, Nellie, Governor Connally's wife, 118
Conner, Theophilus Eugene "Bull," public safety commissioner of Birmingham, 79, 93, 96
Contract on America, 15
Coolidge, President Calvin, xxiii
Cooper, James Fenimore, writer, 9
Copenhagen, Denmark, 73, 151, 168
Copyright, 123–24
Costa Rica, 142
Cottage Grove, Chicago, Illinois, 24
Cox, Judge William Harold, xi
Crowley, Louisiana, 168
Crump, Mayor Edward, 69–70
Cuba, 26, 41–42, 163

Cuban missile crisis, xii, 14, 41, 43, 162–63, 173
Culver City, California, 168
Cushing, Richard Cardinal, 134
CWA (Civil Works Administration), 136

da Vinci, Leonardo, painter, 162
Dallas, Texas, 3, 15, 108, 110, 114, 116, 118, 121, 123–24, 126, 128, 132, 135, 145, 158
Darey, James, poet, 135
Darwen, Norman, blues writer, 33
David, King of Israel, 7–8
Dawson, William L., Congressman, 22
Dayron, Norman, record producer, 169
Dealey Plaza, Dallas, Texas, 118
Decca, record company, 123
Demêtre, Jacques (Dimitri Vicheney), blues writer, 59
Democratic Party, xii, xxiv, 19–22, 25, 44, 47, 67, 74, 102, 116
Detroit, Michigan, "The Motor City," 73, 102–3, 129, 168
Detroit News, 103
Dewey, Governor Thomas E., 20
Diem, Ngo Dinh, President of South Vietnam, 44
Dillon, Douglas, Secretary of the Treasury, 61
Dinner with the President, television program, 105
Double V, xxiii
Draft, xii–xiii, xxiv, 28–31, 34, 36, 44, 172
Dutch Blues and Boogie Organization (NBBO), xix

Ebony, 20, 110
Economy, x, 172

Education, 34, 99
Eisenhower, President Dwight David, ix, xxiii–xxiv, 24–26, 44, 47, 169, 172
Elba, Alabama, 121, 168
Ellendale, Tennessee, 143
Elliot, Judge J. Robert, 87
Elm Street, Dallas, Texas, 16, 118
Esso Refinery, Baton Rouge, Louisiana, 60
Evans, David, blues historian, xxii, 192n115
Evers, Charles, Medgar's brother, 100–1
Evers, Darryl, Medgar's son, 100–1
Evers, Medgar, field secretary of NAACP, x, xxiv, 3, 91–92, 98–105, 159
Evers, Myrlie, Medgar's wife, 99–101
Evers, Reena, Medgar's daughter, 100–1
Executive Order 8802 (1941), 104
Exner/Campbell, Judith, JFK's mistress, 163

Fable, record company, 104
Fair Employment Practices Committee (FEPC), 22
Faith, record label, 164
Farmer, James, national director of CORE, 107–8
FBI (Federal Bureau of Investigation), 77
First Church of Love, Faith and Deliverance, Philadelphia, Pennsylvania, 114, 170
Fitzgerald, John F., JFK's grandfather, 4
Folk music, xxv, 173
Fontainebleau, Florida, 57

Fort Lauderdale, Florida, 48
Fort Worth, Texas, 116–17
France, 142, 163
Frankfurt, Germany, 111
Freedom in the Air, documentary, 89
Freedom rides, x, xii, 35, 57, 77–79, 81, 83–84, 87
Freedom songs, 86, 101
Freedom train, 182n12
Friendship VII, American space craft, 50–51, 55
Frost, Robert, poet, 17
Fury, record company, 28–29

Gagarin, Yuri, Russian astronaut, 50
Gallup poll, 9, 20, 115, 163
Gandhi, Mahatma, political activist, 8
Gates, Henry Louis, Jr., cultural critic, xxi–xxii
Geneva, Switzerland, 27, 86
Georgetown, Washington, DC, 152
Georgia, 50, 75, 81–82, 87, 89–90, 97, 169
Germany, 28, 31, 142
Gift Outright, The, 17
Glenn, John, astronaut, 50–55
Goldwater, Senator Barry, 153–55
Golgotha Hill/Calvary Hill, 91, 148–49, 160–61
Goreau, Laurraine, Mahalia Jackson's biographer, 123, 138
Gospel, record label, 170
Gray, record label, 77
Great Britain, 10, 12–13, 142
Great Depression, The, ix
Greater New Pleasant Grove Baptist Church, Houston, Texas, 155
Greensboro, North Carolina, 75, 77
Greenwood, Mississippi, 81, 102

Greyhound bus, 79, 82–83
Griffin, Rita, journalist, 130
Grissom, Virgil I., astronaut, 50
Guinevere, King Arthur's queen, 10

Halsted Street, Chicago, 77
Hammersmith Farm, Newport, Rhode Island, 152–53
Hampton, Gladys, Lionel's wife, 154
Harding, President Warren, xxiii
Harlem Club, New York, 87–88
Harrington, Michael, writer, 118
Harvard University, 5, 10
Heckscher, August, JFK's special consultant on the arts, 24
Heller, Walter, JFK's chairman of the Council of Economic Advisors, 61, 118
Henry, Governor Patrick, 91, 183n34
Hero: A Study in Tradition, Myth and Drama, The, 11
Hero with a Thousand Faces, The, 17
Highlander Research and Education Center, Tennessee, 101
Hilton Hotel, Los Angeles, 74
Holiday House, Pittsburgh, Pennsylvania, 87–88
Holler, Dick, song writer, 125
Hollywood, California, 168
Hollywood Palladium, Los Angeles, 74
Hood, James, student at the University of Alabama, 99
Hoover, President Herbert, xxiii
Hopper, Dennis, film star, 161
Horowitz, David, author, 13
Housing, xi
Houston, Texas, 52, 83, 155, 164, 168
Houston Street, Dallas, Texas, 118
Human rights, 21

Hummingbird, record label, 145
Humphrey, Senator Hubert, 15, 19
Hyannis Port, Massachusetts, 9, 57

"I Have a Dream," MLK speech, 103, 107–8, 145
Idylls of the King, 18
Illinois, 169
"In Living Black + White," 23
Indiana, 169
Industrial Boulevard, Dallas, Texas, 118
Inflation, 60, 64, 181n9
Interstate Commerce Commission, 80
Interstate travel, 80
Ireland, 142
Irish guard, 141
Isaiah, prophet, 114, 186n14
Italy, 142

Jackson, Bruce, blues writer, 173
Jackson, Mississippi, 3, 98, 100–1, 146, 169
Jackson State University, 91
Jamaica, 167
Jamaica, New York, 113
Japan, 5, 13
Jazz Wereld, xix
Jericho, Palestine, 146
Jesus Christ, 128, 133, 147–48, 150, 155–61, 163, 166
Jet, 19
Jim Crow, 73
Jody Man, The, 30
Johnson, Lyndon Baines, Vice President under JFK, xv, 9, 14, 16, 19, 21–23, 41, 44–45, 136, 153–56, 165
Jonah, prophet, 90–91
Jonathan, son of King Saul, 4, 6
Jones, Charles, SNCC activist, 85

Jordan River, 146
Joshua, prophet, 146–47, 189n77
Juke Blues, xix
Jupiter rockets, 41

Kelley, Mayor Asa, 86–87
Kennedy, Caroline Bouvier, JFK's daughter, 15, 48, 137, 139, 165
Kennedy, Senator Edward Moore, JFK's brother, 15–16
Kennedy, Jacqueline, first lady, 9–10, 13, 15, 17, 21, 48–49, 118–19, 126–29, 132, 134, 136–37, 142, 150–51, 153–54, 163, 165, 173
Kennedy, Joe, Jr., JFK's brother, 5–6, 12
Kennedy, John Fitzgerald "John-John," Jr., JFK's son, 15, 48–49, 134, 139, 163, 165
Kennedy, Joseph Patrick, JFK's father, 4–5, 12
Kennedy, Patrick Bouvier, JFK's son, 15
Kennedy, Patrick J., JFK's grandfather, 4
Kennedy, President John Fitzgerald (JFK): African Americans, xi, xxiv, 17, 19, 25, 74–75, 115, 120; assassination, x–xi, xiii–xiv, xxiv, 3–4, 6, 15–16, 41, 63, 103–4, 108–66, 168–73; autopsy, 133; civil rights, xi–xiv, xxv, 25, 35, 69–110, 140, 163–66; Cuba, 41–42; draft, 28–31; economy, 59–68; election (1956), 6; election (1960), xi–xii, 19–27, 74, 154, 168; eternal flame, 136–37; foreign affairs, xii, 26; France, 59; funeral, 133, 136–37, 141, 163; illness, 12, 163; inauguration, 17, 25, 112–14, 138–39; legacy, xxiv–xxv; life, 3–18, 132; march on Washington, 104; music,

[214]   General Index

24, 147; poetry, 24–25; Roman Catholicism, 23–24, 49, 86, 125, 165; space travel, 56; State of the Union, 40; television, xiv, 98–99, 105, 113, 119, 123, 131, 133–34, 136–38, 142, 159; travels, 135, 137, 140, 142; Vietnam, 44–45; welfare, xii
Kennedy, Robert Francis, Attorney General, xii, xiv–xv, 15, 44, 50, 59, 77, 79–80, 86, 89–90, 94, 125, 146, 164, 166
Kennedy, Rose Fitzgerald, JFK's mother, 4
Kennedy Imprisonment, The, 26
Kennedy's Blues, accompanying CD, 174
Kentucky, 97
Keynes, John Maynard, British economist, 61
Khrushchev, President Nikita, 14, 26–28, 33–37, 41–42, 79, 144
Khrushchev, Sergei, Nikita's son, 144
King, Coretta, wife of Martin Luther King, xi, 20
King, Rev. Martin Luther, Jr., civil rights leader, xv, xxiv, 19, 69–108, 125, 130, 145, 164, 166, 176n2; articles, xi, xiii; in jail, xi, 20, 75, 85–86, 94–96
King Arthur and the Round Table, 9
Knight, W. Nicholas, author, 10
Korea, xiii, xxiii, 26, 44
Kremlin, 41
Kretzmer, Herbert, song writer, 123
Ku Klux Klan, 72, 79–80, 96

Laughton, Robert, gospel discographer, 101
Lee, David, composer, 123

Leeds Music, 123
Lerner, Alan Jay, Broadway lyricist, 9
Letter from a Birmingham Jail, 94
Levine, Lawrence, historian, xxii
Levy, Lou, president of Leeds Music, 123–24
Lewis, John, president of the SNCC, 84, 107–8
Life, 10
Lightner, Edward, composer, 128
Limited Test Ban Treaty (5 August 1963), 41
Lincoln, President Abraham, "The Great Emancipator," 3, 6, 8, 24, 43, 104–5, 107, 109–12, 154, 156
Lincoln Convertible (1961), 118, 128, 149
Lincoln Memorial, Washington, DC, 107
Listen, 173
Little Rock, Arkansas, 81–82
Living Blues, xix
Lloyd, Morgan, police officer, 21
Local draft board, 28, 34
Loewe, Frederick, Austrian-American composer, 9
London, Great Britain, 5, 123–24
London School of Economics, 5
Long Play Album (LP), 155, 172
Los Angeles, California, 64, 83, 168
Louisiana, 31, 34, 50, 82–83, 169
Love Field Airport, Dallas, Texas, 118
Love Tabernacle Church, Detroit, Michigan, 129

Mafia, 15, 163
Magnetic tape recordings, 172
Main Street, Dallas, Texas, 118
Malcolm X, civil rights leader, xiv

Malone, Vivian, student at the University of Alabama, 99
Malory, Sir Thomas, author, 10
Manchester, William, historian, 10
Mann Act, The, 50, 179n5
Mannlicher Carcano, rifle, 122
March for Jobs and Freedom in Washington, xiv, xxiv, 102, 104–8
Marines, 5, 29–30, 40, 122, 133
Markham, Edwin, poet, 6, 175n4
Marlborough: His Life and Times, 9
Marshall, Judge Thurgood, 92
Maryland, 169
Mason-Dixon Line, 69–70, 81
Maxwell Street, Chicago, 77
McCormick, Mack, blues writer, 52
McKinley, President William, 138
Media, xiv, xvi, 20–21, 24, 28, 32, 39, 54, 93–94, 102, 105, 118–19, 128, 131–34, 136–38, 142, 159
Medicaid, 68
Medicare, 68
Memphis, Tennessee, 168
Meredith, James, civil rights leader, 91–92, 98, 183n38
Merlin, King Arthur's Druid magician, 10
Mexican-American ballads, 173
Mexico, 142
MGM (Metro-Goldwyn-Mayer), record company, 123
Michigan, 169
Michigan Chronicle, 3
Midnight Flyer, train, 82–83
Million-Air certificate, 125
Minimum wage, 68
Minnesota, 108
Mississippi, 50, 79, 82–83, 90, 92, 97, 99, 108, 117, 134, 139, 169

Missouri, 169
Mockingbird Lane, Dallas, Texas, 118
Mona Lisa, 161, 163, 191n105
Monroe, Marilyn, film star, 163
Montgomery, Alabama, bus boycott (1955–56), 75, 79
Moon, The, 27, 50, 52, 56, 57
Moonshine, bootleg whiskey, 127
Moorhead, Mississippi, 71
Mordred, King Arthur's incestuous son, 10
Morgana, King Arthur's half sister, 10
Morte D'Arthur, Le, 10
Moses, prophet, 146, 156
Motown, record company, xv

NASA (National Aeronautics and Space Administration), 52
Nashville, Tennessee, 63, 79
Natchez, Mississippi, 109, 185n3
Nation, The, xi, xiii
National Association for the Advancement of Colored People (NAACP), x, 23, 84, 92, 98–100
National Guard, 28, 40, 96
National Urban League (NUL), 84, 87
Navy, 5, 13, 28, 30, 36, 134
NBC (National Broadcasting Company), 20
Negro American Labor Council (NALC), 84
New Frontier, The, xi, 11, 68, 162
New Mexico, 82
New Orleans, Louisiana, 27, 73, 77, 79, 81–83, 87–88, 169
New York, 13, 57, 67, 73, 82, 126, 152, 168
New York Amsterdam News, 84, 100, 107

New York Times, 13
Newark, New Jersey, 70
Newark riots (1967), 103
Newport, Rhode Island, 153
Newport Folk Festival, 153
Newsweek, 44, 163
92nd Division, 38
Nineveh, Assyria, 90
Nixon, President Richard Milhous, 14, 20–21, 23, 44, 47, 57, 97–98, 154, 161, 191n103
Norfolk, Virginia, 82–83
Normandy, France, 99
North Carolina, 50, 82, 169

Obenhaus, Mark, film director, 127, 187n40
O'Donnell, Kenneth, JFK's special assistant, 116
Oliver, Paul, blues historian, ix
Once and Future King, The, 10
Oral history, xxiv
Oster, Harry, blues writer, 60–61
Oswald, Lee Harvey, JFK's assassin, 6, 10, 15, 114, 119, 122–23, 127, 129, 131–35, 150–51, 161
Oswald, Robert, Lee Harvey's brother, 127
Otey, Texas, 169
Other America, The, 118
Our Savior Jesus Holiness Pentecostal Church, Samson, Alabama, 121

Pacific Ocean, 27, 33, 38
Paris, France, 59, 69, 142
Paris Blues, film, 25
Parkland Memorial Hospital, Dallas, Texas, 16, 118, 128
Peace and Freedom Party, 49

Pearl Harbor, 159
Pennsylvania, 169
Perry, Malcolm, physician, 16
Pershing Hotel and Ballroom, Chicago, Illinois, 120, 186n26
Philadelphia, Pennsylvania, 118, 168
Pittsburgh, Pennsylvania, 87, 169
Playboy Club, Chicago, Illinois, 23
Poitier, Sidney, actor, 25
Poland, 14
Pop music, xxv, 173, 192n7
Posner, Gerald, author, 127
Post, The, 12
Powell, Adam Clayton, civil rights hero, 22
Powers, Gary, U-2 pilot, 26
Pritchett, Laurie, Albany police chief, xii, 85–87
Project C (Confrontation), 93
Protestantism, 24
PT 109 (Patrol Torpedo Motor Boat), 13, 100

Racism, 69
Radziwill, Prince Stanislaus, Lee Bouvier's husband, 14
Raglan, Lord, author, 11–12, 16
Raleigh, North Carolina, 82–84
Ramsey Farm, Texas State Prison, 148
Randolph, A. Philip, president of the BSCP, 19, 104, 107–8
Rap music, 131
RCA Victor, record company, xxvi
Reagon, Cordell, SNCC activist, 85
Reconstruction, 42
Record sales, 167–68
Recording industry, xxvi, 80, 171
Rent, 64
Republican Party, xxiv, 19, 21, 24, 155

Rhythm & Blues, xv
Richmond, Virginia, 169
Riverdale, New York, 5, 9
Robinson, Bobby, record label owner, 28
Robinson, Jackie, baseball player, 19, 97
Rock & Roll, xv–xvi, 70
Rock Hill, South Carolina, 82, 84
Roosevelt, Eleanor, first lady, 21
Roosevelt, President Franklin Delano (FDR), ix, xiii, xix, xxiii–xxiv, 20–22, 104, 118, 133–34, 136, 163, 167, 169, 172, 191n107
Roosevelt, President Theodore, xxiii
Rowan, Carl, journalist, 20
Ruby, Earl, Jack's brother, 131
Ruby, Jack, Oswald's murderer, 131, 133, 187n48
Rwanda, 167

S Star, record label, 145
Salinger, Pierre, JFK's press secretary, 48
San Francisco, California, 50
Santa Claus, 32
Saul, King of Judah and Israel, 3–7
Savoy, record label, 146, 170–71
Scheim, David E., author, 15
Schlesinger, Arthur M., Jr., historian, 9–10, 44
Scotlandville, Louisiana, 60, 168
Secret Service, 86
Segregation, 70, 75, 77, 80–81, 86, 88–89, 93, 98–99, 103, 156
Selma, Alabama, 169
Sermons, xxv–xxvi, 155, 161, 171–72
78 Quarterly, xix
78 Records, 155

Sharpton, Rev. Al, civil rights activist, 67
Shaw University, Raleigh, North Carolina, 77
Shepard, Alan B., astronaut, 50
Sherrod, Charles, SNCC activist, 85
Shreveport, Louisiana, 81–82
Shuttlesworth, Rev. Fred, civil rights leader, 93
Sierra Leone, 167
Sit-ins, 75–77, 79, 182n10
Sixteenth Street Baptist Church, Birmingham, Alabama, 103–4
Slavery, xxv
Smith and Wesson .38, revolver, 131
SNCC (Student Nonviolent Coordinating Committee), 77, 79, 84–86, 89, 101
Social Security, 63
Socrates, Greek philosopher, 3, 8
Solomon, King of Israel, 7
Solomon Islands, 5
Soul music, xv
South Carolina, 82, 126, 169
Southern Christian Leadership Conference (SCLC), 84, 102, 107
Southern University, Baton Rouge, Louisiana, 60
Soviet Union, 14–15, 24, 26–28, 41–42, 50, 86, 150, 163
Space race, x, 27, 33, 50–57, 156, 171–72
St. Louis, Missouri, 83, 117, 146, 169
St. Matthew's Roman Catholic Cathedral, Washington, DC, 134
Stars and Stripes, The, 133
Stax, record company, xv
Stevenson, Governor Adlai, 19, 116
Stockholm, Sweden, 169

Stone, Chuck, journalist, 161
Strikes, 76
Supreme Court, 58, 80, 92
Sverdlovsk, Soviet Union, 26

Taft, President William Howard, xxiii
Talmadge, Governor Herman Eugene, 87–88
Tanzania, 167
Tax, 68
Tennessee, 97, 142, 169
Tennyson, Alfred, Lord, poet, 18
Testament, record label, 143, 169, 171, 174, 192n3
Texas, 30, 33, 82, 116, 123, 127, 137, 169
Texas School Book Depository, Dallas, Texas, 119, 128, 131
Texas Theater, Jefferson Boulevard, Dallas, Texas, 131
Thirteenth Amendment (abolition of slavery), 109
Thompson, Mayor Allan C., 98
Thurmond, Governor Strom, 92
Tidewater, Virginia, 83
Till, Emmett, civil rights hero, 130
Time, 16
Tin Pan Alley, 123
Tippit, J. D., police officer, 123–24, 131, 172
Titon, Jeff Todd, blues historian, 155
Tobago, 167
Tokyo, Japan, 169
Toledo, Ohio, 43
Toombs, Rudy, song writer, 54
Topical songs, 173
Toronto, Canada, 169
Trade Mart, Dallas, Texas, 119
Trenton, Georgia, 88

Trinidad, 167
True Romance, film, 161, 191n104
Truman, President Harry S., ix, xxiii–xxiv, 20, 24, 120, 169, 172
Tupelo, Mississippi, 109, 185n2
Turkey, 41
TV Gospel Time, television program, 113
Twilight Zone, television program, 161, 191n106
Twist, The, dance, 47–48, 50, 58

U-2 (Utility reconnaissance plane known as "Dragon Lady"), 26
Uganda, 167
Uncle Sam, 31, 37–38
Unemployment, 61–62, 64, 66
United Nations (UN), 41–42
University of Alabama, xiv, 99
University of Mississippi, "Ole Miss," 92, 98
University of New Mexico, 84
UPI (United Press International), 100

Vatican City, 142
Vee-Jay, record company, 97
Venezuela, 142
Vicksburg, Mississippi, 80
Vienna, Austria, 28, 79
Vietnam, xiii, 44–45, 99, 130, 162–63
Virginia, 82
Voter Education Project (VEP), xii
Voter registration drives, 103
Voting Rights Act (1965), 102

Wallace, Governor George, xiv, 3, 93, 96, 99, 121
Wallingford, Connecticut, 5

Warren Commission, 15
Washington, DC, 24, 42, 48, 103–8, 133, 152, 154, 161, 169
Watkins, Mel, journalist, 23
Watts, Isaac, father of English hymnody, 115
Welding, Peter J., record producer, 142, 143
Welfare, 59–68
White, George R., blues writer, 34
White, Terence Hanbury, English writer, 9
White, Theodore H., political journalist, historian and novelist, 9–10
White Citizens' Council, 81, 92, 102
White Company, The, 9
White House, The, xiii, xxiv, 21, 24, 27, 40, 48–49, 66, 98–100, 107, 133, 154, 156
Why England Slept, 5
Wilkins, Roy, executive secretary of the NAACP, 107–8
Wills, Garry, historian, 26

Wilson, President Woodrow, xxiii
WJLB, John Lord Booth's Detroit radio station, 131
Wofford, Harris, one of JFK's speech writers, 74
Woodstock, New York, 169
Woolworth's lunch counters, Jackson, Mississippi, 98
Woolworth's store, Greensboro, North Carolina, 75
World War One, 44
World War Two, ix, xiii, xxiii, 22, 31, 33, 35, 38, 42, 44, 163, 167
WPA (Works Progress Administration), 32

Young, Ernie, record producer, 63
Young, Whitney, executive director of the NUL, 107–8

Zapruder, Abraham, film maker, 119, 186n24
Ziklag, Judah, 7

www.ingramcontent.com/pod-product-compliance
Lightning Source LLC
Chambersburg PA
CBHW030341240426
43661CB00052B/1707